THE CHRISTIAN STORY

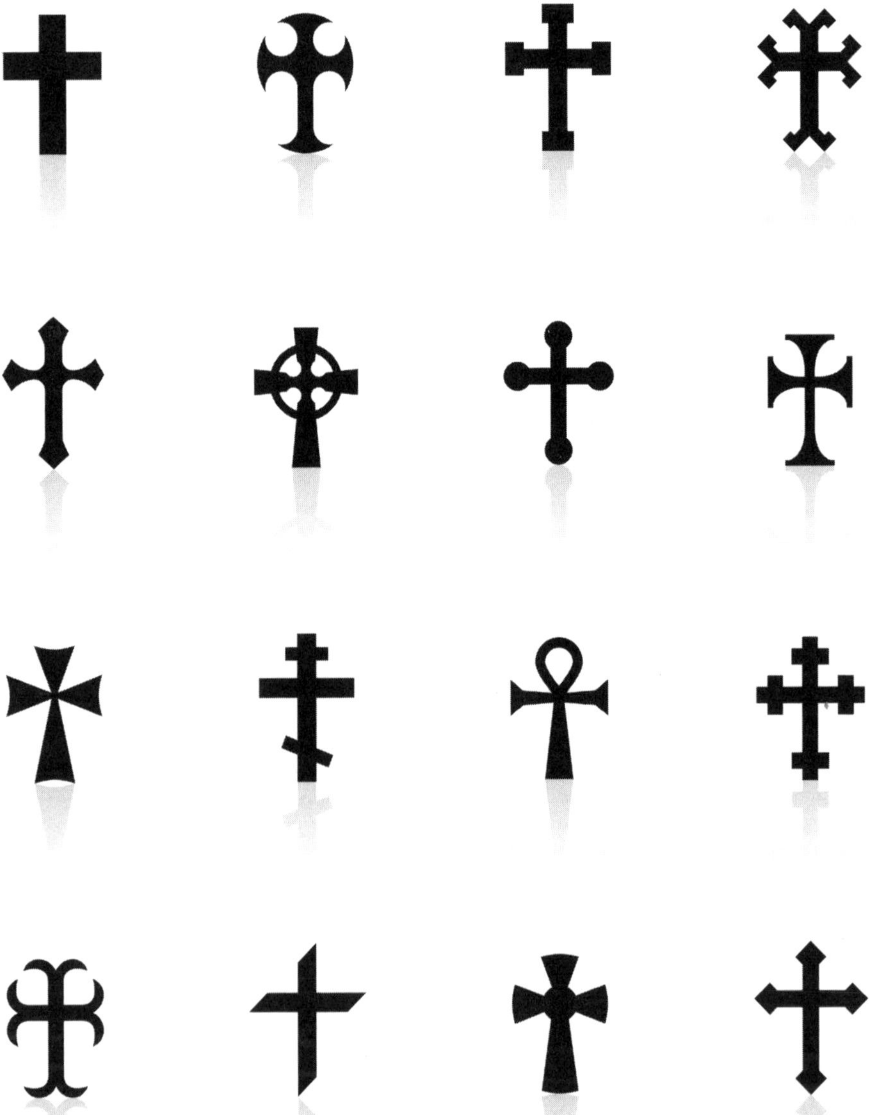

Dr. John M. Oakes

THE CHRISTIAN STORY

*Finding the Church
in Church History*

Volume I

ILLUMINATION PUBLISHERS

THE CHRISTIAN STORY: FINDING THE CHURCH IN CHURCH HISTORY

Printed in the United States of America.

ISBN: 978-0-9849087-4-5

Cover and book interior design: Toney Mulhollan.

A special thanks to Paul Ramsey for proofing and to Amy Morgan for her editorial contributions.

John Oakes is a professor of chemistry at Grossmont College. John became a Christian while attending graduate school in 1978. He earned a Ph.D. in chemical physics in 1984 from the University of Colorado. That same year he married his wife, Jan. They have three children and reside in San Diego, California. John also serves as president of the Apologetics Research Society. Some of his other books include: *Is There A God?*, *From Shadow to Reality*, *Reasons for Belief*, *Daniel: Prophet to the Nations*, *That You May Believe* and *Field Manual for Christian Apologetics*. For more about John's work, go to www.EvidenceForChristianity.org.

www.ipibooks.com

Illumination Publishers International
www.ipibooks.com
6010 Pinecreek Ridge Court
Spring, Texas 77379-2513

TABLE OF COΠTEΠTS

ACKNOWLEDGMENTS

I would like to acknowledge a few who helped me with this book. First of all, thank you to Dr. Everett Ferguson, who helped with advice on a number of key questions on the story of early Christianity. He is perhaps the greatest living expert on the early Church. I found his book *Church History, Volume I* to be particularly helpful. Although the great majority of sources in this book are the primary literature, anyone reading both his book and mine will realize that I borrow from Dr. Ferguson liberally.

I would also like to thank my friend John Madden (the philosopher; not the football coach) for helpful comments on the manuscript.

Thanks to my publisher, Toney Mulhollan. His attention to detail and commitment to this project made a big difference.

I would also like to express my gratitude to my friend Foster Stanback, whose support, intellectually and otherwise, allowed me to pursue this lengthy project.

Lastly, I would like to thank my dear wife, Jan, without whose support none of my far-flung projects would ever come to fruition.

INTRODUCTION

Aquinas and Augustine, Baptists and Anabaptists, Wyclyffe and Wesley, *homoiousios* versus *homoousios*, Councils and Creeds, Reformation and Counter-Reformation—a lot of information—probably too much for most believers to sort through. Why would anyone want to take on the overwhelming subject of church history? After all, none of this is Scripture. There is no such thing as inspired church history, is there?[1] God does not speak to us directly through events that occurred after the New Testament canon was complete. And besides, church history is a series of mistakes, heresies and false starts at reform. Isn't it preferable to simply start with Scripture and let it be our sole guide to determine how best to do church? Again, why should I wade into this morass of confusing and often not very inspiring material?

One good response is to remind ourselves of the famous motto: "Those who do not learn from history are doomed to repeat it."[2] If church history is a litany of mistakes and false starts then it offers an unlimited number of opportunities to learn; it is a great source of practical advice on what not to do. No sect of Christianity is without fault. All of us need significant midcourse corrections to the path our own particular local congregation, denomination or church movement is following. At the risk of offending the reader right from the beginning, all of us teach at least some false doctrines, no matter what religious group we associate with. Church history tells us this has to be true. How are we to determine which changes are most needful right now? What practical steps do we need to take to pursue these changes? Of course, the divinely inspired word of God is the first rule for determining our steps. The personal example of Jesus Christ—God in the flesh—is our most useful example. Having said that, we have at our disposal in the study of the history of Christianity an almost unlimited number of practical examples of Christian groups who have gone down the same errant path we are walking right now. We can see responses that did not help at all and we can see individuals and groups of people who took practical steps that brought much glory to God. With the wisdom thus acquired, combined with determination and hard work on our part, working with the providence of God, we too can bring abundant glory to God.

After all, as Solomon said, "There is nothing new under the sun," and "What has been will be again, what has been done will be done again" (Ecclesiastes 1:9). The annals of Christianity are a good example of this principle. Your church is struggling with finding a biblical balance between the doctrine of grace and works? Many have struggled with this same issue and some have found a practical path to navigate this difficult question. We can learn from them. Solomon was a very wise person. He told us that "Wise men store up knowledge" (Proverbs 10:14). The systematic study of the annals of Christianity is perhaps the most efficient means at our disposal to store up knowledge as it relates to how to "do" church. It certainly is more effective (and less painful) a means of gaining practical knowledge than trial and error.

If we want to direct our steps as God would have us do, as individuals or as a group of believers, the first principle is to obey the commandments of God. If God has spoken on a particular topic, that settles the question. Should the church tolerate divorce among its members? God has said, "I hate divorce" (Malachi 2:16) and Jesus has come down squarely on this issue (Matthew 19:1–9). The second principle by which a body of believers can determine the will of God is through the application of biblical principles. If we are trying to decide what kind of leadership structure will best help the church to grow and bring glory to God, we can apply the principle that "whoever wants to become great among you must be your servant" (Matthew 20:26). Any structure that does not foster servant leadership is going astray.

There is a third principle for determining the best path for our church to pursue—for achieving "knowledge of his will through all spiritual wisdom" (Colossians 1:9). This is the principle of experience. "Wise men store up knowledge," and godly wisdom is acquired by humble people who have a wealth of experience about what works and what does not. Of course we always must remember that our personal experiences do not trump biblical principles or commandment. If our experience tells us that lying has some good things to recommend its practice—that it works—we reject the conclusion reached from this experience. However, our Creator expects us to use our God-given minds to learn from experience. This is how we become wise. It is in large measure how we come to know what God's will is. When we study church history, even the young and relatively inexperienced among us have available to us a vast storehouse of such knowledge. We can learn from the mistakes of others! We do not have to try dozens of different approaches by trial and error to find God's "good, pleasing and perfect will" (Romans 12:2). When you ask yourself, "Is this particular incorrect teaching important enough for me to take a stand and possibly divide the church over it?" you are not the first one to face this question. You have a wealth of wisdom at your disposal.

But of course the history of Christianity is much more than a series of embarrassing slipups caused by sinful men and women who thwarted God's plan to bring salvation to the world through the church. It is also a story of how communities of believers, subject to all the passions and temptations common to mankind, have tried to worship God in spirit and truth—to discover correct theology and to live out that theology. What works at one time and in one culture may not work exactly the same for another. Mixed in among the negative stories there are plenty of inspiring stories of men and women who won many to Christ, restored biblical Christianity in a significant way and brought much glory to God. Not all these positive examples are found in the Bible. In fact, the great majority happened after 100 AD. Let us see what these great men and women of faith did and follow their example.

In the end, simply making it to heaven is sufficient. Despite all Lot's mistakes, God calls him a righteous man (2 Peter 2:7). Lot made it. Just making it to spend eternity with God is enough. Hopefully, I can be content with that, but to be honest, I want more. For myself, I want my life to count. I want to play a significant role in God's will being done on the earth. Studying church history has helped me to do this and it can do the same for you.

The history of Christianity is messy. But then, the Christian life is messy. Just when we think we have proved to ourselves that a particular group is wrong on some doctrine or aspect of Christian living, we find out that we are about as far off—except in the other direction—as they. When I was a young Christian I thought that nearly all questions had simple answers. I thought that if we had the right mind and heart and the Scripture in our hands we could march from one victory to another. Any momentary defeat would be a prelude to God doing something even greater through us (us being the group of Christians I was part of). Things were black and white, not grey. I could quote numerous scriptures to back up this thinking. After all, the word of God can divide between soul and spirit, and God will always lead us in triumphal procession. But then I found out that some of the teachings I had learned were not necessarily biblical at all. The family of churches I am part of went through a time of discouraging defeat. A study of church history will do much to lessen the shock of these discoveries. We can learn from numerous examples that any Christian movement, no matter how marvelously it is doing God's will, is just a generation away from losing most or all of what it has gained. Perhaps even more discouraging, ALL definable Christian groups lose their way, more or less, eventually. We have to assume that this includes the group you and I are part of, unless Jesus comes back to interrupt the process.

But God does not leave us in this depressing mire, and neither does church history. The overall lesson as I see it is that "doing" Christianity is a never-ending story. Every group of disciples of Jesus and every individual follower needs to be part of a never-ending quest to pursue correct doctrine and a God-honoring lifestyle. We will never arrive. Church history tells us that if we think we have arrived, then we are doomed to eventual defeat. As Paul said, "Let him who thinks he stands take heed that he does not fall" (1 Corinthians 10:12, NASB). The seemingly discouraging news that we will never find the perfect balance has a silver lining. We are part of something important. By obeying biblical commands, applying biblical principles and learning the lessons of church history, we can have a hand individually in moving the plot of this endless story in the right direction. Some of us play a bigger role and some of us a smaller one, but all are important. By reading this book, by studying the story of Christianity and applying the lessons contained therein, we are made into more useful vessels to do this work.

There are a number of other reasons it is worth the investment of our time and mental energy to study church history. It is an exciting story. The story is far too big for Hollywood to be able to distill it into a 120-minute movie. There is intrigue. There are heroes and villains. There is human drama. Unfortunately, there is also corruption and warfare. Church history is fun. It is reality TV on a grand scale.

Why Do We Do What We Do?

A study of church history can give us self-knowledge. This is especially true if we study the history of our particular branch of the Christian tree. Why do we do what we do as a local church, a denomination or a movement of churches? Why do we do what we do in our individual lives? Those of us who are committed to using the Bible as our standard for Christian behavior like to think we do what we do because it is biblical. We organize the church in a particular way (role of elders, pastors, deacons, ministers and teachers, for example) because we are applying biblical commands or principles. We have certain stands on moral issues and hold to recognizable traditions or doctrines because they are apostolic in origin. The problem with this belief is that it simply is not always true. Even a simple glance at church history tells us that this is in large measure self-deception.

Of course, much of what we do is governed by biblical teaching, but a large proportion of our doctrines and practices come from our historical roots and are not biblical per se. To give a relatively minor example, some call the one who leads the local congregation a minister, others call him a pastor, some label him an elder, others call their leader a priest, and still others an evangelist. Which is the correct biblical label? The "correct" answer is not important here. The point is that the label you use is determined (hopefully) in part by a careful study of the correct biblical name for a church leader. However, the name you use for your church leader is probably determined at least as much by the tradition handed to you by common descent through the evolutionary chain that produced the branch of Christianity you are grafted into. How should the Lord's Supper be done, what should we call it and how often should we observe it? Many of us think our answer comes from the Bible, but more likely it comes from the tradition that precedes us. Not long ago I was on a run in an unfamiliar area. As I ran up a hill, I saw a coyote on the side of the road. Then, as I approached, I realized it was a deer. Then as I got even closer, I realized it was a mailbox. The point is that when we see only a few details, our mind can create an optical illusion, filling in the lacking details, but we are unaware we are doing this. The Bible is often less specific about church practice than we think. Our personal church history/tradition is how we fill in the blank areas, but by analogy to the optical illusion, we can be unaware of how we fill in the blank areas.

In some cases, which is the correct way of doing things is very important; in other cases it is insignificant. The point being raised here is that often when we think we are acting biblically, we are in fact acting in a way determined by our history. This knowledge can do a couple of things. It can help us to be less judgmental of those who practice Christianity differently from the way we do. It can produce greater Christian unity. This is a very good thing! It can also free us up to take a less biased view of what the Bible teaches and what we ourselves do or ought to do. By understanding our own particular history we can be freed from slavery to this history. Perhaps the word slavery is too negative. Tradition can be very problematic if we teach it as if it were biblical doctrine (Matthew 15:8–9) or if we practice it when in doing so we disobey what God has commanded us to do (Matthew 15:3–6). But clearly not all tradition is evil. Without tradition we have chaos. Our tradition creates a place within which we feel safe. In using particular words in a traditional sense it facilitates our communication. Having said this, all of us who call ourselves Christians have traditions and common practices that are not right. They are not God's will. They violate God's will because they are unbiblical. Either that or they are not necessarily wrong, but they make us ineffective in accomplishing our God-given mission. Knowing our history and taking a clear-minded look at this history can free us up to do God's will.

Pendulum Swinging

As a corollary to this, one of the chief lessons we will learn from church history is that to an extent none of us would like to admit, much of what we do and believe is not the result of convictions we have gained from reading the Bible. Church history will tell us that the impulse for many if not most church movements has been a response to what was perceived by a particular leader as heretical, that is, a false doctrine or an incorrect practice in another group. When we see the pendulum swung too far toward the ascetic, we swing it right back to the "don't worry, be happy" style of Christianity, where grace is being taught to the exclusion of "works." Our solution to this problem is to make the mark of our particular Christian group obedience to God's commands. But then what happens to the grace of God? We see a stale, intellectual Christianity. As a response to this, others find solace in religious emotional experience that loses track of rational biblical exegesis. We will see that Augustine allowed his doctrine to be shaped by a response to Pelagius and the Donatists as much as it was formed by biblical thinking. The Protestants allowed their theology to be formed as a reaction to the perceived faults of the Roman Catholic Church as much as it was shaped by biblical theology. Medieval groups reacting to the arid scholasticism of their day turned their backs on some good traditions and tended toward heretical beliefs.

Perhaps what you or I believe and practice is shaped in part by our desire to turn away from what we rightly perceive to be the excesses of another. Not perhaps—definitely. This is human nature. Studying church history will not bring pendulum-swinging to an end. Only God can do that. However, it seems reasonable to propose that the study of the path of God's people through history will help us to reduce the amplitude of these swings, to the glory of God.

In the Interest of Full Disclosure

There are two kinds of history books. Some are written simply as a well-organized and structured list of the facts of history. The historical data from primary sources is presented in an unbiased manner in order to give the reader the information he or she can use to reach personal conclusions about the lessons of history. Others are written with a definite agenda in mind. The facts of history are chosen for didactic reasons in order to make a definite point. The purpose of the writer of this kind of history is to move the mind of the reader toward a particular conclusion. Historical data that is not relevant to the thesis of the author, no matter how important in the big picture, is left out. This is not necessarily an indictment of this kind of historical writing. However, this kind of history is telling a story, and good storytellers select their information in a way that leads the reader toward a particular conclusion.

There are some limitations with the first sort of history book. For one, they can be boring. In order to grab our attention sufficiently for us to learn, history must tell a story. History requires a storyteller. Although it may satisfy a certain ideal to simply list the facts in the complete absence of bias, to do so makes history lose its life. Another limitation with this kind of history is that it is an ideal that is never obtained. There is no such thing as completely unbiased history. It is like a perpetual motion machine. Through very careful engineering, one can approach making a machine that has perpetual motion. However, it is literally impossible to make one that is 100% efficient. Besides, a machine that is so efficient would not be able to do anything useful. Real machines, in order to do something we want them to do, must waste energy. Not to push the analogy too far, but the ideal unbiased history is not particularly useful.

Of course a machine with zero per cent efficiency is also not very useful. History that is too strongly biased is problematic. It can be used to manipulate and deceive the reader. In the case of church history, where is the best balance between impartiality and history that tells a definite story with a definite lesson? This depends on how the book is to be used. A church history book to be assigned in a university course must tend largely toward the unbiased and impartial end of the spectrum. Scholarly work should, in general, tend in this direction as well. The book you have in your hand is not principally intended as a scholarly work. Whether or not I am a scholar is perhaps debatable, but I definitely am not a trained historian. Neither is it intended for use in a college course on church history. This book will be used to tell a story and to teach lessons that we can learn from church history. I will try to do a reasonable job of filling in the basic outline of church history. Hopefully, no truly monumental part of the story of Christianity will be left off simply because I perceive it to be not relevant to the points I intend to make. However, I will be picking and choosing those anecdotes in the history of Christianity which best help to make the points and teach the important lessons I believe need to be gleaned from the fascinating story of the Jesus movement.

If I am going to tell a particular story, then it seems to be a good idea to inform the reader up front what my bias and what my perspective is. I was raised in the Episcopalian Church. This is a Protestant denomination that had its genesis in the 1780s. My family on my mother's side goes all the way back to Bishop Seabury, the founding bishop of this offshoot of the Anglican Church. Having said this, my perspective on church history is not principally shaped by this background. As a youth I did not take Christianity or the teaching of the church in which I was raised to heart. The event that principally shaped my thinking about Christianity and church history was my conversion to Jesus while in a PhD program at the University of Colorado in 1978. I was baptized at a Church of Christ and eventually became part of a movement of churches within the churches of Christ known as the International Churches of Christ. The Church of Christ traces its roots to what is commonly known as the Restoration Movement. The Restoration Movement was begun in the Second Great Awakening in the 1820s and 1830s by men such as Alexander Campbell and Barton Stone. The members of this group of churches stressed being "Christians only." They were attempting to step away from partisanship and denominationalism by following the Bible only and by being liberal on questions that are not matters of biblical faith. That branch of the Restoration Movement which became the Church of Christ (as opposed to the Christian Church/Disciples of Christ) particularly stressed restoring the doctrine, teaching and practice of the primitive church. Of course, there is a lot to be said for this approach. However, in stressing the importance of primitive, New Testament Christianity the tendency of the Churches of Christ has been to disown its own historical roots, as though it appeared out of nowhere. As if to illustrate this point, some churches of Christ have inscribed in the cornerstone of their building, "Church of Christ, established 33 AD." The International Churches of Christ have not completely broken with this pattern of losing track of their history.

This being my own background, I am particularly interested in writing this account of church history in order to convey that no matter what we tell ourselves, the fact is that what we think and what we do as a body of believers is very strongly shaped by our history. The Restoration Movement did not appear out of thin air. Its founders came from Presbyterian and Methodist stock, principally. Their movement contained (and continues to contain) elements both in continuity with these traditions and formed as a reaction against the beliefs and practices of Presbyterianism and Methodism. Although this history will include information on most major Christian religious groups, particular attention will be focused on Christian movements relevant to the idea of Christian restoration. These will include the primitive church, the Anabaptist movement and, naturally, the Restoration Movement.

Why Another Church History?

The main reason this book is being written is that I, as the author, feel I have something worthwhile to say about the subject that will help believers gain new and useful perspectives which can ultimately help them to be stronger Christians. Solomon has already been quoted here. "There is nothing new under the sun." There will probably not be a great number of brand new ideas in this book, although there may be many that are new for the reader. This is not principally a scholarly work. I will be using much primary source material, but some of the background is from other works of church history.

There is one perspective I bring to this work that is "new" as far as I know from other accounts of Christian church history I have read. This perspective is that the history of Israel in the Old Testament is part of "church" history. As alluded to above, one of the limitations when we study church history is that we do not have divine commentary to help us interpret the events. It would be nice to have a modern-day prophet to let us know how God feels about Calvin's theology of predestination or to provide inspired commentary on where the church should ideally fall in the spectrum between extreme asceticism and becoming like the world in order to win the world. Actually, we are not completely without such inspired interpretation of church history. Revelation 2 and 3, as well as a significant proportion of the material in the letters of Paul, serve this purpose for Christianity as it was practiced in the first two generations after the life and death of Jesus.

One thesis of this book is that the Old Testament is another source of inerrant commentary on "church" history. Are physical/political Israel and the church one and the same? No, but both the earthly kingdom established by David and the church for which Christ gave up his life are visible expressions of the invisible kingdom of God. God's relationship with Judah and Samaria is in many ways the same as his relationship with the church. The same can be said for God's relationship with patriarchs such as Abraham and Jacob. The chapters in this book are organized chronologically according to different periods of church history. Most chapters will include expositions of analogous material in the Old Testament through which the inspired writer can help us to find God's perspective on the lessons of church history. The sixteenth century was a time of reformation of Western Catholicism, both within and without. The books of Ezra and Haggai report reformation movements as well. The early Middle Ages were a time when Christianity relied largely on political power to maintain orthodoxy, and the leadership, not surprisingly, became corrupt. We will find relevant lessons from the time of the Divided Kingdoms.

Outline of This Series

1. Beginnings: The New Testament record.

2. Early church fathers: Finding unity, setting a canon, and fighting heresy.

3. Persecution, institutionalism, and the fight for theological unity.

4. Legalization, the early ecumenical councils, the influence of Augustine, the joining of church and state, and the paganization of Christianity.

5. The rise of the papacy, Eastern Orthodoxy, the medieval church, and the Muslim challenge.

6. Scholasticism and dissent; Thomas Aquinas.

7. Early attempts at reformation and the beginning of the Inquisition; Wyclyffe, Huss, Waldo.

8. The Reformation and the Counter-Reformation; Luther, Zwingli, Calvin and the Anabaptists.

9. The Holiness Movement and attempts at revival; Puritans, Baptists, Quakers and Methodists.

10. Skepticism and the Awakening on the American frontier: Unitarians, Deists, the Restoration Movement, Mormons, and Adventists.

11. The twentieth-century church: Challenge to Protestantism; ecumenicism, Pentecostalism, and the Evangelical Movement.

CHAPTER NOTES: _____

1. Actually, one of the theses of this book is that there *is* inspired church history. We will study some of this scriptural church history in this book.

2. Commonly attributed to George Santayana (1863–1952), essayist, poet, philosopher and novelist.

CHAPTER ONE
BEGINNINGS, AD 30–95

The story of the first sixty years of the church is one of amazing growth and of seeming defeats that turned into victories. It is a story of the dramatic shift from a fairly small Aramaic-speaking Jesus sect within Judaism to a principally Greek-speaking Gentile movement spread across over two thousand miles from present-day Spain to Iraq. It is the story of a Jewish movement defining itself in a Greek world and the backlash of Jewish Christians against the changes wrought by that redefinition. It is a story of a young church with a lot of the typical young-church problems striving toward maturity and a leadership to take care of the needs of its members. Can the church bring the gospel to the Hellenistic Roman Empire without losing its unique call of discipleship to Jesus? How will the church structure itself as it grows from a group of a few hundred in one location to many tens of thousands scattered across the vast Roman Empire? How tightly defined will the theology of the church be and how will those who insist on bringing in divisive elements of Jewish and Greek thought be treated? These are just a few of the issues we will see raised and answered in the first two generations of Christianity. In large measure, these are the same issues the modern Christian church faces today. We will do well to pay careful attention to the underlying causes, the good examples set, the problems encountered, the victories and the defeats of the early church.

There is a sense in which the first sixty years of the Christian church is the period we know the most about, but there is another sense in which it is the period we know the least about. We know the most about these years because this is the only period from which we have biblical material. Relatively few Christians read books on the Christian story after about AD 90, but anyone who reads the Bible on a regular basis is quite familiar with the story of the beginnings of the church in Jerusalem, its early growth under the leadership of the apostle Peter and the expansion of the church to reach the Gentiles, principally through the work of the apostle Paul. The book of Acts provides a limited but very useful summary of church history from about AD 30–60. This commentary has the added benefit of being inspired by God. No concern about historical reliability is required in this case. We know somewhat less about the second thirty years of Christianity, but the letters of Peter and John and the book of Revelation (especially chapters 2 and 3) give us something to go on.

But there is another sense in which this is the period of church history we know the least about. Beginning with the earliest writings by the church fathers[1] (the *Letter of Clement of Rome*, the *Didache* and the *Epistle of Barnabas*, for example) in the last decade of the first century, we have access to an ever-increasing flood of writings. Such written accounts of goings-on in the early church come from mainstream Christian leaders and to a lesser extent from the writings of those from heretical groups and from Jewish and Roman historians. We know a modest amount about both the lifestyle and the teaching of the church from firsthand accounts of the second-century writers. Our available material from the third, fourth and fifth centuries increases exponentially. The writings of the important orthodox church fathers through the fifth century runs to several volumes. By contrast, we have no extant materials from authors—either Christian or outside of Christianity—writing about the Christian church from the time before AD 90 except that found in the New Testament. We know almost nothing about what the apostles Thomas, Matthew and Bartholomew did. We know a fair amount about how the church spread to the West, but we know virtually nothing from the New Testament about how it spread to the East (to Mesopotamia and Armenia) and to the South (into Egypt and Ethiopia). From later material we know that the church began to spread into these regions at least by the early second century, but surely the gospel was brought to these regions in the late first century as well. The New Testament historical information is of very low quantity but very high quality. This is the primary source material for this chapter.

Our concern here is not to analyze or discuss the doctrinal teaching of the New Testament. It is not even to expose the life of Jesus Christ. We will be considering what the historical content in the New Testament tells us about how the church evolved over time, how it interacted with the pagan and Jewish cultures that surrounded it and how it responded to both external and internal forces. We will look at the development of the movement that was produced by the teachings of Jesus Christ in the first two generations after his resurrection. The cultural, organizational and theological changes that occurred in the first sixty years of the Christian church will serve as a foreshadowing of the future.

From Jerusalem to Judea and Samaria and to the Ends of the Earth

Let us first trace the geographic and numerical spread of the Jesus movement. Immediately after the crucifixion of their leader, Jesus of Nazareth, a small group of bedraggled, discouraged, fearful followers were meeting in a locked room "for fear of the Jews," when a transformative event occurred. Jesus appeared among them, apparently resurrected from the dead, saying "Peace be with you" (John 20:19). What are the implications? Does this mean that the physical kingdom of God will in fact be reestablished in Jerusalem? Later on, Jesus recommissioned Peter to lead the band of believers (John 21:15–25). After appearing a number of times to the apostles and to groups of believers numbering at least 500 (1 Corinthians 15:6), Jesus gave a group of perhaps 200 followers who stayed back in Jerusalem a vision of the future for the kingdom of God. "You will receive power when the Holy Spirit comes on you; and you will be my witnesses in Jerusalem, and in all Judea and Samaria, and to the ends of the earth" (Acts 1:8). Within sixty years, this vision of Jesus had been realized. Of course, a massive amount of work remained to be done, but by AD 90 this group of uneducated Aramaic-speaking Jews had established beachheads throughout most of the Roman Empire, even spilling into the Parthian realm to the East and possibly south to Abyssinia and even to the subcontinent of India. How did this unlikely vision of Jesus come to fruition? Let us see.

It is difficult to estimate the number of Christians in Jerusalem, or in any city of the Roman Empire for that matter, in the first few centuries. Outside of a couple of statistics mentioned early in Acts, our sources, both in the first century and even later into the second and third centuries, do not give hard numbers. One thing we can say for sure is that the church in Jerusalem became very large very quickly. Three thousand were baptized into Christ on the first day the gospel was preached (Acts 2:41). Within an unstated, but presumably short period of time, the church in Jerusalem had grown to something like ten thousand (Acts 4:4). Later, in Acts 6:1, it is stated by Luke that the number of disciples was increasing even further. It was not just common folks who were being baptized, as we know that "a large number of priests became obedient to the faith" (Acts 6:7).

Those converted to Jesus included Hellenized Jews. The number of Greek-speaking Jewish converts was magnified because the outpouring of the Spirit in Jerusalem occurred at the Feast of Pentecost, at which time Jews from all the nations where they had been scattered came to Jerusalem for the harvest festival. This explains the striking variety of nationalities and languages represented that day (Acts 2:9–11). Apparently those from outside Palestine who were converted stayed for the time being in Jerusalem. This is shown by the dispute that arose between the Aramaic- and Greek-speaking Jews as recorded in Acts 6. Here we find the first recorded potential schism in the church. The Greek-speaking disciples were presumably more needy because they had stayed behind in the city rather than return to their homes scattered across the

Mediterranean. Presumably, many of them gave up their source of income by staying behind in Jerusalem.

Despite the good deeds and the miracles done by the members of the nascent church (or perhaps because of them), a minor persecution directed by the Sadducees broke out against the sect, as recorded in Acts 4 and 5. Some wanted to put the apostles to death, but cooler heads prevailed, encouraged by the great Jewish Rabbi and statesman, Gamaliel. The interlude of peace for the church that followed this persecution allowed the church to grow and mature.

Some time later (we are not told how long, but presumably months or even a couple of years) a much more significant persecution broke out. As Luke describes, the persecution was precipitated by the preaching of Stephen. Stephen was one of the Hellenized Jewish converts. He was brought up before the Sanhedrin on charges of speaking against the Law of Moses. He gave an incredibly bold speech, charging the Jewish leaders to their face that they had, almost without exception, always rejected the men God had sent to bear witness to himself. According to Stephen, Jesus was the last in a long line of prophets rejected by the Jews. The fact that this charge came from a foreign Jew was probably particularly galling to these prideful men. Without the courtesy of a trial, they murdered Stephen and began a furious attack against the church. The threat of death was sufficient to drive nearly the entire group of followers of Jesus out of Jerusalem. Twenty thousand or so believers spread throughout Judea and Samaria preaching the good news, and thus the second stage of Jesus' prophecy was begun.

To those of us who read the Hebrew Scripture and listen to the words of Jesus, it may seem that the apostles were particularly thickheaded not to notice that Jesus had intended all along to take the gospel to the Gentiles. In the first few years, the Nazarene sect only reached out to Jews. It was not until the persecution following the murder of Stephen that the young believers came into contact with a good number of non-Jews. The church was established as far away from Jerusalem as Damascus, in present-day Syria. Damascus had a large colony of Jews, but it was principally a Greek city. Not content with stamping out the Nazarene sect in Jerusalem, the young Pharisee Saul traveled to this hotbed of Jesus' followers to arrest them and bring them back to Jerusalem for trial.

Saul (Paul) of Tarsus

At this point we must briefly stop our narrative of the early growth of the Christian church to look at the man who, arguably, had more to do with the character and growth of the primitive church than anyone other than Jesus of Nazareth. Saul was from the city of Tarsus. This is was a fairly small city near the coast of modern-day Turkey, close to where the coast of the Mediterranean turns from East/West to North/South. Saul was a Jew who was comfortable speaking both Greek and Aramaic. All his extant letters were originally written in Greek, but many scholars claim his use of Greek shows that it was not his first language. Presumably, his first tongue was Aramaic. By Paul's own testimony, he was a Pharisee and the son of a Pharisee (Acts 23:6). Indeed, he was trained under the most influential Rabbi of his day, Gamaliel (Acts 22:3). Paul was perhaps the most promising young Jewish leader of his day. Add to this the fact that Paul was a Roman citizen (Acts 23:27), which gave him freedom of movement throughout the Roman world.

One thing we know about Paul's personality is that he was not one to compromise his convictions. He may not have been a great public speaker (1 Corinthians 2:4), but he was as tenacious as a bulldog. Taking a public stand against the new Galilean sect was not sufficient for this young firebrand. He pursued the followers of Jesus to one of their most distant outposts in Damascus to harass and arrest them, and even to see to the execution of their leaders. Later in his life, when Paul was persecuted by Greeks, by his fellow Jews and, most disheartening of all, by fellow Christians, Paul's dogged determination and willingness to take the fight to the camp of the spiritual enemy was key to his success against all odds.

This combination of two qualities made Saul of Tarsus uniquely qualified for the mission for which he was chosen by the Messiah. In Saul we have a Roman citizen who was thoroughly immersed in both the Greek and the Jewish worldview. His cultural background was particularly well suited to carry the nascent church through what was to be perhaps its most trying transition from a Jewish sect to a multicultural (but mainly Greek) religious movement. There were others besides Paul who could move easily in both worlds. But it is this quality, combined with his fearless dedication to whatever cause he took on, which made Paul an irresistible force. He was a spiritual Alexander the Great.

And then, of course, there is the event that transformed Saul of Tarsus into the apostle Paul. Perhaps, despite his zeal to destroy the church, there was a grain of uncertainty in the mind of this avowed enemy of the Jesus movement. Even as he approached Damascus to carry off the leaders of the church, the indescribable joy of Stephen, as Saul had watched him stoned to death for his convictions, must have stuck in his mind. Could this poor and poorly educated Galilean be the One? Surely not, but how to explain the lives of these misguided believers? Then, as we know, "suddenly a light from heaven flashed around him" (Acts 9:3). Saul met the one whom he was persecuting on the road to Damascus. He had a new Lord and a new mission to zealously pursue. "You will be his witness to all men of what you have seen and heard" (Acts 22:15). Clearly, Paul was faithful to this charge.

What else do we know of the man? He was not completely without financial means. Nor was he without family. Yet, he left all behind to pursue the career of an itinerant evangelist for the one he had met on the road to Damascus. Eusebius, the first Christian historian, reports to us that Paul left behind a wife in his travels. "Paul does not demur in a certain epistle to mention his own wife, whom he did not take about with him, in order to expedite his ministry the better."[2] Eusebius makes this report in about AD 324. To what epistle is Eusebius referring? We will have much to say about Eusebius. He is not always completely reliable. Clement of Alexandria[3] thinks that Paul is talking about his wife when he says in 1 Corinthians 9:5, "Don't we have the right to take a believing wife along with us, as do the other apostles and the Lord's brothers and Cephas?" It is worth noting that Paul mentions his rights here, but not an actual wife. Modern scholars lean toward the conclusion that Paul was either a widower or a lifelong unmarried man. Concerning marriage, Paul said, "I wish that all men were as I am" (1 Corinthians 7:7). In the context, he seems to be referring to the gift of celibacy. We will have to settle for being unsure whether Paul was ever married.

Paul's passion and sense of mission drove him from Damascus to Tarsus, to Antioch, to Cyprus, Asia, Thessaly, Achaia, Illyricum, Rome and probably Spain.[4] Everywhere he relentlessly preached and, where there were none, planted churches. At every point he risked death and imprisonment. Indeed, he was imprisoned at least twice that we know of. For men of such courageous and stubborn conviction, like Paul or Martin Luther King, a violent death seems almost a foregone conclusion. More reliably than his claim that Paul left a wife behind in his travels, Eusebius reports[5] that the apostle was beheaded in Rome by Nero, informing us that Paul's grave remained in a cemetery in Rome to that day.

Probably none of us will follow in Paul's footsteps. His was a unique career, molded by God for a specific historical purpose. However, even today, Christians can be inspired by his astounding faith in the providence of God. Of Paul it surely can be said that this world was not his home. More will be said about Saul of Tarsus later.

A Fork in the Road

Even as the gospel spread throughout the eastern coast of the Mediterranean, no Gentiles had yet received baptism. How many years has it been? Several, perhaps as many as ten years. The best we can tell, it was not through one of the apostles or one of the other Christian leaders reading the Scripture that the church realized the gospel of Jesus Christ was for all nations. It took a revelation from God to Peter. Here we see in evidence the intense nationalism and what to us seems the incredible narrow-mindedness of the Jews. It is therefore all the more miraculous that the gospel spread to all nations. The Jewish Christians were not unlike Jonah who, even when told directly by God to preach repentance and forgiveness to the Gentiles, strongly resisted that mission.

But let us not be too hard on our first-century Jewish brothers and sisters, and let us not be the first to throw stones. We too are tempted to reach only those like us and to conform the church to our own cultural pattern.

In any case, Cornelius was a man who was seeking God. Acts 10 records the vision in which God told Peter to get up and eat unclean food. In a Jonah-like response, Peter said "Surely not, Lord!" It took two repeats of the vision, but finally Peter got the message, and thus, reluctantly, the church began to baptize Gentiles. Even after opening the doors, in principle, to baptizing "Greeks," the churches in Jerusalem and Judea appear to have remained almost fully composed of people who were Jewish by descent. When Paul returned to Jerusalem around AD 60, he was greeted by a Jewish membership who expected him to observe Jewish customs. Perhaps it was because of this Jewish intransigence that it was on the fringe of the then-Christian world, in Antioch, that they "began to speak to Greeks also...and a great number of people believed and turned to the Lord" (Acts 11:20–21). Antioch rapidly became the second most influential church in the young movement. This important role for Antioch continued well into the Middle Ages.

By God's providence and because of the wisdom of Barnabas, Paul soon found himself in this great city, from which all three of his great missionary journeys began. We will not recount here the various journeys, the victories and the struggles of Paul and his companions, as these are common knowledge to most Christians. Those who are not familiar with Paul's missionary journeys can read about them in Acts 13–21. Suffice it to say that by his death in about AD 63 or 64, there were churches established through the work of Paul in the principal cities and many of the smaller cities as well throughout the Roman provinces of Cilicia, Cappadocia, Galatia, Lycia and Asia (in present-day Turkey). Churches had also been established in Thrace, Macedonia and

Achaia, Cyprus, Crete and Illyricum, on the east coast of the Adriatic (Romans 15:19). The Christians were by no means a majority in any of these cities. In fact, they were a small minority wherever they had been established.

Luke informs us almost exclusively about the ministry of Paul, but he was not the only missionary planting churches. Our sources on the work of the other apostles are not as reliable, but they give hints about the geographic spread of the church. Eusebius[6] has Thomas sending Thaddeus, whom he mentions was one of the seventy-two (Luke 10:1), to Edessa. This city is in the southeast corner of modern Turkey. It was the gateway to Mesopotamia and to the Parthian Kingdom. Eusebius tells us that Edessa was perhaps the very first "Christian" city. He has Mark,[7] the companion of Peter and Paul, bringing the gospel to Egypt and establishing the church in Alexandria. By the middle of the second century AD, Alexandria was home of one of the five principle churches of Christendom. A church probably existed in Rome by the time Claudius exiled the Jews from that city in AD 49, as this persecution is what sent Priscilla and Aquila to Corinth (Acts 18:2). We do not know who started this group, but almost certainly it was not Paul. Eusebius[8] informs us that Thomas evangelized in Parthia, which would be present-day Iraq and Iran. He tells us that Andrew spread the gospel in Scythia (North of the Black Sea). His mission may have included Armenia (Southeast of the Black Sea). Peter preached in Pontus, Galatia, Cappadocia and Asia, and that John ministered in Asia. In 2 Timothy 4:10, Paul, when he says that "Crescens has gone to Galatia," he may be mentioning sending the missionary to Gaul (Southern France, likely the city of Lyon). Eusebius agrees that Paul sent Crescens to Gaul.[9] Many believe that Paul established a church in far-off Spain. We know that Paul definitely had this in his plans (Romans 15:24, 28). Whether we take this view depends on our acceptance of the theory that Paul was released from the prison in Rome in which he was incarcerated at the end of Acts, only to later return to Rome where he was beheaded under Nero.

We have it on the authority of Eusebius and, even more reliably, Clement of Alexandria, Tertullian of Carthage and Dionysius of Corinth, that both Peter and Paul were executed in Rome during the reign of Nero. Let us fast-forward our history to AD 90, which is the dawn of the era from which we have writings of the church fathers. At this time we can surmise that the church was well established in Asia Minor, Palestine, Greece and Rome. Almost certainly there were churches as well in Mesopotamia, Northern Egypt, Illyricum, Spain and Southern Gaul. Most likely the gospel had also reached Carthage, Southern Egypt, Armenia and Parthia. Christianity had at least a foothold in a majority of the Roman world, and the faith had even begun to spread beyond the empire of its birth, to the East.

What is the explanation for this unprecedented expansion from a ragtag group of mostly uneducated Jewish followers who spoke little Greek and no Latin to a spiritual kingdom which, by the third century, numbered hundreds of thousands of devoted followers scattered across most of the Roman Empire and even beyond—most of whom would give their very life for the cause? Many religious leaders had preceded Jesus of Nazareth, but none before had an impact that even approached that of this Galilean Jew. How are we to explain the fantastic growth of a Jewish sect, bursting the seams of its isolated Jewish identity, planting at least a germ of faith throughout the empire—a faith that ultimately outgrew and outlasted the empire within which it grew (Daniel 2:44)? It certainly was not political patronage or financial resources. The only explanation for the growth of this powerful movement that makes sense is the personal life, character and message of the movement's founder, Jesus Christ. The answer to the mystery of the growth of the church is the transformative power released when people have personal interaction with God in the flesh. As people came to know Jesus and as they became like him, a power was released the likes of which the world had never seen. This group "conquered" Rome by the power of their righteous lives and, as we will see, by their unqualified love for one another and for the lost.

Life in the Primitive Church

In many ways, the early church serves as an ideal model for us of what the present day church should be like. This is not to say that we need to consider throwing away our cars, cell phones and cable TV. It is not the physical but the spiritual state of the primitive church that we want to reestablish. The apostles were trained directly by Jesus, so we can assume that what they created is a direct reflection of what he trained them to do. What better model could we have? But was the early church really some sort of ideal toward which we should strive? The best answer is yes…and no…. It is hard to escape the fact that God fully intended the church established in Jerusalem at Pentecost to be a sort of ideal model, as it is presented that way. If only we could be like that church!

> They devoted themselves to the apostles' teaching and to the fellowship, to the breaking of bread and to prayer…. All the believers were together and had everything in common. Selling their possessions and goods, they gave to anyone as he had need. Every day they continued to meet together in the temple courts. They broke bread in their homes and ate together with glad and sincere hearts, praising God and enjoying the favor of all the

people. And the Lord added to their number daily those who were being saved." (Acts 2:42–47)

The original church had deep faith, amazing fellowship, fantastic preaching, unequaled unity and a natural kind of evangelism by all members that led to spectacular growth.

Many have as their ideal being a "first-century Christian" or having a "first-century church." We are not satisfied with reformation; we want to restore New Testament Christianity. Not many will question this as a noble ideal. However, this leads us to a crucial question. Is the example of Christianity as lived out in the first two or three centuries a sort of extra source of inspired teaching? We will see in this section that the primitive church met in house churches. Does this mean that house churches are the ideal, God-inspired way to do church? We know that the leaders in the primitive church taught very strongly against voluntarily serving in the military. Does this provide authority to those who teach Christian pacifism and refusal to be involved in politics? The church fathers also taught in no uncertain terms that for a Christian to go to plays and other public spectacles was forbidden. If we can assume that this came from the apostles or those taught by them, does this give authority relevant to Christian behavior today and our relationship with the media?

This is not an easy question to resolve, but we had better face it now before we launch into considering the lifestyle and teaching in the very early church. Possibly this study of life in the primitive church is simply informative. Alternatively, it is very inspiring and encouraging. Or perhaps it is a source of authoritative truth about Christian life and doctrine. The simplest answer to the question of the authoritative nature of church history is that the only source of inspired truth is the Scriptures themselves. A counterargument is that if we can deduce that it was the apostles themselves who taught these things under the influence of inspiration from God, then we ought to obey what they taught, even if it is not directly contained in the Scripture. It was the apostles' guidance that led the Christians to meet in house churches, to worship God without the use of musical instruments, to take up the collection on Sunday, to take the Lord's Supper weekly, to share the love feast together, to not serve in the military unless forced…. The list can continue almost indefinitely. In some cases we know that this is what the apostles advised because it is apparent from reading the New Testament. In other cases it is a reasonable deduction that this was the policy of the apostles from the fact that our outside sources imply this is what was done from the beginning. Many of us have taught that these practices are a matter of doctrine. Are they?

One of the leading experts in our day on the primitive church is David Bercot. His writings are both scholarly and practical. Books by Bercot include *Will the Real Heretics Please Stand Up?* and *The Kingdom That Turned the World Upside Down*.[10] Another popular book in this genre is *Pagan Christianity* by Viola and Barna.[11] Bercot has thoroughly analyzed both the lifestyle and the teaching of the primitive church. His thesis is that we can know how the apostles interpreted the Bible by looking at the early church.[12] In essence, he buys in quite strongly to the idea that we can take the lifestyle, mode of worship and teaching of the early church as a sort of inspired interpretation of the New Testament. He concludes that a rather strict pacifism, withdrawal from public political life and a thoroughgoing turning away from the popular media is required of all Christians.

Is Bercot correct? The simple answer is no. Bercot is wrong because he makes an incorrect assumption. The assumption is that anything an apostle or other inspired teacher said in a limited context (the context being defined by geography, culture or time) is binding on all Christians, even outside that context. Let us suppose that one of the inspired teachers in the first century authoritatively instructed a church or group of churches to meet in house churches or to not use musical instruments in their worship or to take up their collection on the first day of the week. Can we assume that this is an authoritative instruction to us? How would we know? Perhaps God asked this group to follow this instruction for a reason that was relevant to the situation at hand. We know that Paul gave authoritative instructions to the Thessalonians (1 Thessalonians 4:1–2). Under the inspiration of the Holy Spirit, he lists some of them for our sake. There were some things that Paul taught in every church he visited (1 Corinthians 4:17), but God has not chosen to reveal all of them to us in Scripture. Which apostolic teachings, not actually recorded in Scripture, are binding?

The only reliable answer we can give is that if the Holy Spirit intended a particular instruction to be binding for all followers of Jesus for all times, then we must assume that he would have seen to that teaching finding its way into the canonical New Testament. This is a matter of faith. God knows what he is doing. Perhaps the apostles instructed the early church to meet principally in house churches because that was wise, given the persecution and the need to fly under the political radar. Perhaps there was a local cultural or practical reason to take up the collection on Sunday. The instruction to forego use of musical instruments in public worship[13] may have been a wise policy in order to help the mainly Jewish church in the first decades move away from their habits of worship. Similar arguments can be made with regard to practical things such as participation in the military, in political activities, in cultural events and so forth. If we have good reason to believe, based on church history, that the apostles gave instructions, but those instructions are not given to us in the Scriptures and we are not given the context of those instructions, we ought to be extremely hesitant to bind them on all believers. This is the bottom line.

Why, then, should we even bother to study church history and attempt to determine what was taught by the apostles and church fathers? Are these simply facts, of interest to the history buffs among us, but of little if any relevance to how we ought to act as a body of believers today? The answer, again, is no. That would be to swing the pendulum too far the other way. It is significant to us what the primitive church leaders taught their people. We have documents that tell us how the apostles and those who knew them applied what they learned from Jesus to real world situations. These documents are invaluable, but they are not the source of binding teaching. It is certainly relevant to us today to know that the church fathers, and presumably the apostles themselves, strongly advised against enrolling in the military. If nothing else, it implies permission for us to take this stand today. The lifestyle decisions advised by the church fathers and accepted in large measure by the early disciples are relevant for us. They serve as wonderful and inspiring examples to us.

Let us then take the middle road here. That certainly is my intent. Let us gaze carefully at what the early church did, let us think about the context and even consider implementing some of their policies if they might help us to become more like Jesus today. At the absolute minimum, what we can deduce the apostles taught gives us permission to do the same. Perhaps it even gives us a highly advisable way to proceed. But let us not troll church history, looking for additional laws to bind on the church today. We ought to let Scripture remain the sole standard of authority for Christian teaching.

So, what was the primitive church like? From the letters and the book of Acts we get the sense that life was relatively communal. Perhaps the church in Jerusalem in the first years was an extreme case, but Luke could say of them that "they shared everything they had," (Acts 4:32) and that "there were no needy persons among them. For from time to time those who owned lands or houses sold them, brought the money from the sales and put it at the apostles' feet, and it was distributed to anyone as he had need" (Acts 4:34). The persecutions by the Roman emperors came toward the end of the period in question, but maltreatment by Jews was a factor from the beginning. At first, before persecution broke out, the church met as a large group in the temple grounds. Later, local churches met in smaller groups in houses (Romans 16:5, 1 Corinthians 16:19). It is likely that the groups met in houses so as to avoid bringing more persecution on the Christians. As the churches matured and elders were appointed, the house church leaders were generally the elders of the local church.

The pressure on the church was incessant. Even in times of reduced persecution, the members must have felt they were in the calm between storms. Paul planned to arrest members in Damascus. Claudius, the Roman emperor, kicked all the Jews out of Rome in AD 49 because of the uproar over Jesus and the Christians. The Roman historian Suetonius, writing about AD 120, described the incident this way:[14] "Because the Jews at Rome caused continuous disturbance at the instigation of Chrestus, he [Claudius] expelled them from the city [Rome]." Most likely this Chrestus is a misspelling of the Latin Christus. Claudius had difficulty distinguishing the mainly Jewish Christian church in Rome from the other Jews there. From his perspective, it was a Jew-on-Jew argument creating the disturbance in Rome, so he kicked them all out. Luke informs us in Acts 18:2 that this expulsion by Claudius affected Aquila and Priscilla. We know of other persecutions during the first sixty years of the church. In Corinth, the Jews made a united attack on Paul and his ministry. Sosthenes, the former Synagogue ruler in Corinth, was beaten right in front of the Roman court (Acts 18:17). Jesus had such an effect in the city of Ephesus that the craftsmen who made idols in honor of Artemis started a riot (Acts 19:28–29). Paul was beaten, stoned, arrested, harassed and finally beheaded.

There is more. Nero instigated a short-lived persecution against the church in Rome in AD 64. The Roman historian Tacitus mentions this persecution, reporting that Nero tortured and killed Christians in order to draw attention away from himself over the famous fire in Rome.[15] Eusebius[16] records the words of Tertullian concerning Nero's persecution; "Examine your records. There you will find that Nero was the first that persecuted this doctrine, particularly then when after subduing all the East, he exercised his cruelty against all at Rome." As mentioned above, it is likely that Paul was executed in Rome during this persecution.

The persecutions by the Jews and Romans did not just focus on Paul. Both the apostle James and James the brother of Jesus were killed. Luke tells us about the murder of James the apostle by Herod Agrippa in Acts 12:1–2. Josephus, the Jewish historian, recorded the martyrdom of James "the Just," the brother of Jesus and the leader of the church in Jerusalem in AD 62.[17] The stoning of James was instigated by the Jewish leader Ananus. A number of Christian writers, including Origen and Eusebius, tell us that Peter was crucified upside down by Nero. Antipas was martyred for his faith in Pergamum (Revelation 2:13). Probably the persecution instigated by

Domitian was the most widespread during this time. Eusebius describes this persecution happening in the fifteenth year of Domitian, making it about AD 96, telling us that secular historians confirm the accounts of this persecution. According to Eusebius, this persecution caught up the apostle John in its net. We know from John's own testimony (Revelation 1:9) that he was exiled to the island of Patmos. We can only imagine what it was like in the primitive church to live under nearly constant threat of arrest and to have the apostles and many of the other leaders picked off one at a time. Surely one positive effect was to keep the church pure. Members of questionable commitment to Jesus presumably abandoned the faith in times of trouble.

Heresies and Other Problems

The apostolic age was a time of great growth for the nascent church, but, as we have seen, this growth inspired jealousy and persecution from outside. However, even at this early stage the greatest danger for the church came from within its ranks. Paul had warned the Ephesian elders in his farewell address (Acts 20:29–30) to beware of "savage wolves" and that "even from your own number men will arise and distort the truth in order to draw away disciples after them." To a significant extent, the organization of the church developed as a defense against those who would destroy the church from within. The acts and words of these deviant believers had a paradoxical effect on the church. Their attacks on apostolic Christianity had the effect of causing the early church leaders to more carefully formulate the Christian doctrines as a defense against people being dragged toward heretical ideas. There is good evidence that the early church tolerated a rather wide range of theological ideas in its ranks. Over the next three centuries, this tolerance was severely challenged and whittled down as attempts to push false ideas about Jesus forced the church fathers to take ever more definite public positions on the theology of Jesus (the technical term for this is Christology). We will see much more on this. We learn from church history that those who seek to destroy the church from outside can slow the growth, but they cannot destroy the church of Jesus Christ. It is only those from within who can distort the truth and destroy the unity of the body of Christ.

The first of the heresies was inspired by the so-called Judaizers. These were believers who attempted to force Gentiles to become observant Jews. The council in Jerusalem (Acts 15) was called to settle the question of binding the Law of Moses on Gentile believers. After open and heated debate, the apostles, elders and other leaders decided not to force Jewish regulations on Gentile

Christians; instead, they asked the Gentiles to forego the eating of blood and meat sacrificed to idols out of respect for the sensibilities of the Jews in their ranks. Perhaps those at the council believed they had settled the problem once and for all. If so, they were very wrong. Perhaps out of jealousy against Paul or perhaps out of a severely misguided zeal for the law, Judaizers traveled throughout the mainly Gentile churches planted by Paul preaching a distorted gospel that required adherence to the Law of Moses for salvation. Paul's reply was withering. In response to the Judaizers he said, "But even if we or an angel from heaven should preach a gospel other than the one we preached to you, let him be eternally condemned!" (Galatians 1:8). This was no mere matter of disputes over doctrine. Salvation was at stake, and Paul did not hold back, because "if righteousness could be gained through the law, Christ died for nothing!" (Galatians 2:21). About the Judaizers who taught that one must be circumcised to be saved, he sarcastically advised that they ought to take their own teaching the whole way and castrate themselves (Galatians 5:12). Whew!

These are tough words. It may be helpful to bear in mind that the situation in the first century was different than what we face today. Back then there really was just one church. This was true about the church both generally and in each city. Christians did not have a variety of churches to attend. If the Judaizers had won the day, the entire religion we call Christianity would have been destroyed. Things are different in the modern context. There are plenty of blatantly heretical teachings around us today, but such heresies do not seem so threatening to the very existence of truth. Even if such heretical groups as the LDS church get a foothold, the very existence of biblical Christianity does not seem at stake. This being true, perhaps we should still look at the passion of Paul here and consider whether we have become too comfortable with teachings that deny Jesus. We will see that this fight with those who would force law-keeping into Christianity did not end with Paul. In fact, there are groups even today, most notably that begun by Ellen G. White and her "seventh day" teaching, which attempt to link observance of Old Testament law with salvation in Jesus.

A related story is one that has been passed to us about the Apostle John. Irenaeus tells us[18] and Eusebius agrees[19] that Polycarp, who learned at the feet of John, often told the story he had heard from the Apostle. Perhaps we should take the story with a grain of salt, but it certainly tells us about the attitude of the primitive church toward certain heresies. Polycarp related that one day John was in a public bath house when he learned that the heretic Cerinthus was there as well (more on Cerinthus and his teaching below). John went running out of the building shouting, "Let us flee, lest the building fall down; for

Cerinthus, the enemy of the truth, is inside!" This admonition came from the one known as the apostle of love. Even if this story is overstated by Polycarp it tells us something about the attitude of the early church. They did not tolerate false teaching when it affected the gospel of Jesus Christ.

Another heretical group in the first century was known to later orthodox Christians as the Ebionites. The name derives from a Hebrew word meaning "the poor ones." Unlike the Judaizers, the origin and exact nature of what this group taught is somewhat obscure. Although their beginning was certainly in the first century, we do not have a New Testament book directed against this teaching (unlike the Judaizers and the Gnostics). Eusebius reported that the Ebionites were descended from the Jewish Christians who fled across the Jordan River to Pella when Jerusalem was destroyed in AD 70. We cannot take this as authoritative, but it is logical, as this was an essentially Jewish sect of Christianity that taught the necessity of obeying the Law of Moses. In this sense, of course, they were like the Judaizers, but they went much farther from the apostolic message. In the words of Eusebius,[20] "They considered him [Jesus] a plain and common man and justified only by his advances in virtue." In other words, according to Eusebius, this group denied the deity of Jesus. They also denied the virgin birth and the bodily resurrection of Jesus. They demanded observance of the Sabbath, yet they worshipped Jesus on Sundays. Eusebius' comments are polemical in nature. It is possible he exaggerates their teaching. Justin Martyr described groups much like the Ebionites in his book *Dialogue with Trypho*. Irenaeus applied the label Ebionite to Judaizing Christians in AD 180. The church fathers agreed that this group rejected most of the New Testament, using only a Hebrew translation of Matthew they called the Gospel of the Hebrews.

Liberal scholars have tried to create the impression that the Ebionites were a major movement that represents the original teaching of Jesus Christ more accurately than traditional, orthodox Christianity. Their conclusions reflect more their own anti-Christian predilections than the historical facts. Although this Jewish sect of Christianity did create a bit of a ripple in the early church, all the evidence supports the idea that from the very beginning they were a small group. In fact, their importance may have been exaggerated both in what they taught and their influence in order to serve as a foil against which the church fathers taught. There is no reliable evidence that the heretical groups that came to be known as Ebionites were ever anything other than a minor Jewish sect of Christianity that tried to hold on to their Jewish identity after AD 70 when Christianity moved decisively away from its Jewish roots.

The last heretical movement whose roots can reliably be traced back into the first century are the Gnostics. The term does not refer to a monolithic religious movement but a broad and only loosely knit set of teachings that infected Christianity at one time or another everywhere it spread. Gnosticism was more widely dispersed and continued in its influence for much longer than the Judaizers or the Ebionites. Because the peak of their influence was in the second century, we will only introduce Gnosticism in this chapter and come back to it later.

Many things have been ascribed to Gnostic teaching. The word Gnostic derives from the Greek word *gnosis* whose principle meaning is knowledge. Fundamentally, the Gnostics taught that Jesus Christ was spiritual but not human. To the Gnostics, the physical body is evil, so God cannot be intimately joined with human flesh. The physical body that was crucified on the cross was only a shell from which the spiritual emanation Jesus Christ had already left. Therefore, Jesus was not crucified for our sins. A common theme in Gnostic teaching is that the true knowledge (*gnosis*) of Jesus is a mystery only revealed to the initiates in Gnostic sects. Essentially, it was a "Christian" (using the word loosely) version of a Greek Mystery religion, complete with its Mystery cult, special hidden knowledge and saturated with Greek, not Christian, philosophy. Cerinthus, the one from whom John fled, was a Gnostic from the late first century. His is an interesting case. From Irenaeus[21] and from Eusebius[22] we learn that Cerinthus taught that Jesus will return to establish an earthly kingdom for one thousand years. He held to some classic Gnostic beliefs. For example, he claimed that Christ came into the body of Jesus at his baptism and left that body before the crucifixion. He denied that God made the physical world, because it is inherently evil. Like later Gnostics, he called the Creator a "demiurge," which is a lower level emanation from an extremely distant God. Adding to the heretical nature of his teaching, Cerinthus also taught the need to observe the Law of Moses. No wonder John was appalled at the teaching of this heretic.

The church fathers taught, and most scholars believe, that the book 1 John was written at least partially as a polemic against Gnosticism. John believed that the most dangerous enemy of Christianity in his time was this heretical belief. We can detect his care to refute Gnosticism in his preamble to the book. "That which was from the beginning, which we have heard, which we have seen with our eyes, which we have looked at *and our hands have touched*—this we proclaim concerning the Word of life" (1 John 1:1, emphasis added). John describes people who "went out from us, but they did not really belong to us" (1 John 2:19). Similarly, 2 John 7 warns against "many deceivers, who do not acknowledge Jesus Christ as coming in the flesh" who have gone out into the world. John labels such a person the antichrist. Revelation 2:24 has Jesus himself condemning the beliefs of these Gnostics who have learned "Satan's so-called deep secrets."

We will delay further discussion of Gnosticism for chapter two, but before we do, let us note that the church organization began to evolve toward the end of the first century as a response to the threat against the church from heretical teaching. They began to rely on formulaic doctrinal summaries or creeds such as the "trustworthy sayings" in 1 Timothy 1:15, 3:1, 4:9–10 and 2 Timothy 2:11–13. As with modern creeds, church leaders hoped that if they could get their members to ascribe to certain creedal statements of faith, they could protect the church against false teachings. Presumably it helped at the time. We will see that this trend to rely on creeds increased over time to the point that ultimately they became a cause, not of protecting the unity of the church, but of division. This is one of many examples we will see of a pattern that emerged in the church. What was probably a wise expedient at the time developed into a tradition that came to have an authority of its own, so that the church did not stop using it when its usefulness had passed. In the end, the church ended up with human-produced creeds that "nullify the word of God for the sake of tradition."

As another example of how the church evolved in reaction to pressure from heretical teaching, the churches as a whole moved from a leadership model that emphasized both evangelists and elders toward greater reliance on elders (*presbyteros*) and perhaps even a head elder. This head elder was separately denoted the bishop (*episkopos*). It appears that the church developed this structure as a means to protect itself from the dangers of heretics from within the church. We will see this trend extrapolated to a startling degree in the fourth through sixth centuries.

Gnosticism was not the only problem for the early church. Paul admonished Timothy to watch both his life and his doctrine carefully (1 Timothy 4:16), and the letters of Paul reflect a major problem in the early church with "life" as well as doctrine. Lest we idolize the early church, it is worth noting that they had some major sin issues. From the first letter to the Corinthians we learn that a member of the church had an adulterous relationship with his father's wife, and the church was tolerating it! They had members suing other members in the open public forum, bringing shame on the church. People were getting drunk at church and discriminating against the poorer members. The churches in Asia in the 80s AD had similar problems, as we learn from the Book of Revelation, chapters 2 and 3. We are not sure what the sin of the Nicolaitans was, but we have evidence of sexual immorality. Jesus also accuses the Christians in Laodicea of greed and materialism.

Perhaps it is discouraging to know that even in the apostolic churches there were major sin problems. But then again, perhaps it is encouraging to know that we are not necessarily any "worse" than these early Christian groups—that even in a nearly ideal church sin issues will come up. What we see in these inspired texts is how the church ought to deal with blatant public sins. They ought to be confronted, not ignored. The leadership of the early church did not tolerate open sin. Under the leadership of the apostles they publicly confronted public sin (and presumably more privately confronted private sins). From our evidence, it appears that the result was a church in the first century which, despite its occasional blatant sin problems, maintained overall a comparably righteous fellowship.

Summary

We are about to head into the second century. Here is where we will begin to pick up a good amount of firsthand information about the internal and external condition of the church from the writings of the church fathers and to some extent from the writings of the enemies of the church.

Before we do that, let us look at an event that can easily be used to mark the transition from the apostolic age to the time of the church fathers. The year is about AD 96 or 97. Domitian, the first emperor who persecuted the church, has died. Trajan has taken the throne. A time of relative peace for the church has begun. Only one apostle is left alive. John has just been released from Patmos. Eusebius tell us[23] that Irenaeus (who knew Polycarp, who knew John) related that "all the presbyters of Asia…testify that John had delivered it [sound doctrine] to them; for he continued with them until the times of Trajan." John returned to Ephesus to oversee the churches in Asia. Most likely he died in about AD 97. With that event the apostolic age ended. How are we to evaluate this age? Who would have guessed a little over sixty-five years before, when Jesus told his band of eleven apostles to "go and make disciples of all nations, baptizing them in the name of the Father and of the Son and of the Holy Spirit," (Matthew 28:19) that a little more than two generations later this uneducated and mostly ordinary band of disciples would have grown to a movement of hundreds of churches and many thousands of believers? Who would have believed that the church would include Greeks, Romans, Parthians and many others ringing the Mediterranean and beyond? John must have looked back at his own career with a sense of awe. This was a time of spectacular growth and victory. Many had died a violent death for the cause of Christ. Some serious problems such as the Jew/Gentile issue had been addressed. A strong and relatively stable leadership under church bishops had been established. Standards for dealing with sin within the church had been worked out. Copies of the four gospels had already been circulating as a group among the churches. The combined letters of Paul were also available to all the churches. With such inspired writing now available to the churches, the need for apostles and other inspired teachers lessened. But there were ominous signs of problems as well. The menace of Gnostic teaching had not been eliminated. Was it going to be possible to truly have just one church? How would the church be able to stand up to the persecution, which was sure to intensify? John had to be content to go to be with Jesus in faith that such things were in God's hands. The churches must have felt a great sense of loss with the passing of John. There was a feeling of insecurity. Can God continue to do great things through the second generation of leaders who were acquainted with the apostles?

But, unlike John, we do not have to content ourselves with leaving the future of the church in God's hands. We can learn from the church fathers how the church fared after the last of the apostles passed from the scene. Let us move on to the history of the church from about AD 95 until the end of the second century.

CHAPTER NOTES: _____

1. Note that in this book I am using the term "church fathers" more broadly that scholars traditionally do. Scholars make a distinction between the apostolic fathers, the apologists and the church fathers. The apostolic fathers are those who were influenced directly by the apostles of those who knew them. This would include Ignatius, Clement of Rome and the authors of letters such as the Didache. The apologists include Justin and Diognetus. Scholars have limited the term to church fathers to the great orthodox writers, beginning with Irenaeus.

2. Eusebius, *Ecclesiastical History* III.30.1 (Peabody MA: Hendrickson Publishers, 2006).

3. Clement of Alexandria, *Stromata* III.7.

4. Clement tells us (Clement, *Clement of Rome*, V) in about AD 96 that Paul reached "the furthest limits of the West," probably a reference to his planned visit to Spain.

5. Eusebius, *Ecclesiastical History* II.25.5 (Peabody, MA: Hendrickson Publishers, 2006).

6. Eusebius, *Ecclesiastical History*, I.13.4.

7. Eusebius, *Ecclesiastical History*, II.16.1.

8. Eusebius, *Ecclesiastical History*, III.1.1–3.

9. Eusebius, *Ecclesiastical History*, III.4.8.

10. David Bercot, *Will the Real Heretics Please Stand Up?* (Tyler, TX: Scroll Publishing Company, 1999) and *The Kingdom that Turned the World Upside Down* (Tyler, TX: Scroll Publishing, 2003).

11. Frank Viola and George Barna, *Pagan Christianity?* (Wheaton, IL: Tyndale House, 2008).

12. In his book *Common Sense*, Bercot uses the legal concept of "course of performance" as an analogy for his approach to church history. In legal circles, if the terms of a contract are not clearly laid out, then the courts resort to the "course of performance" to determine the original intent and meaning of the contract. In other words, if we know what the parties did as a result of their agreement, we can infer the intent of the agreement and that intent can be binding even if not explicitly stated.

13. Here the author is inferring that such an instruction was given by the apostles to the church from the fact that there is a striking lack of reference to the use of instruments in the church for at least three centuries after it was begun.

14. Suetonius, "Life of Claudius" in *The Lives of the Twelve Caesars*, 25.4.

15. Cornelius Tacitus, *Annals*, XV.44.

16. Eusebius, *Ecclesiastical History*, II.25.4.

17. Josephus, *Antiquities of the Jews*, XX.9.

18. Irenaeus, *Against Heresies*, III.3.4.

19. Eusebius, *Ecclesiastical History*, IV.14.5.

20. Eusebius, *Ecclesiastical History*, III.27.2.

21. Irenaeus, *Against Heresies*, I.26 and III.3, 11.

22. Eusebius, *Ecclesiastical History*, III.28.2.

23. Eusebius, *Ecclesiastical History*, III.23.3.

CHAPTER TWO

THE CHURCH FATHERS, AD 95–200

Those who hoped that the sect of Christians would quietly go away when the last of the apostles had died were severely mistaken. In fact, in the second century AD the Jesus movement made impressive strides in numbers, geographic spread and organization. This happened in spite of spasmodic but increasing persecutions from the Roman government and heretical schisms that threatened to tear the young church apart from within. The second century AD is the period when the second, third and fourth generation of Christian leaders began to produce writings of their own. Included among these church "fathers" are some truly impressive men. This is the period when the first Christian "apologists," greatest among them Justin Martyr, began to explain and defend the young faith to the intellectual elite of their day. It is also a period when we begin to have writings by pagan opponents of Christianity such as Celsus. Under the influence of heat from its intellectual opponents, the church developed a more refined and nuanced theology, using terms that the educated Greek could understand. The leadership structure of the church became more hierarchical, with influence centered around a limited number of churches and their head bishops. Traditional patterns of worship developed that were foreshadows of what later became Western and Eastern Orthodoxy.

We will focus our study of Christianity in the second century around the extant writings of the church fathers. From these we will glean knowledge of most of the important developments we know of from this period. For many of these writings we know exactly who wrote them and when or nearly when they were written. For others, especially for the earliest, we do not know the author or the exact date of writing.

The Didache (the Teaching) or The Teaching of the Lord to the Gentiles Through the Twelve Apostles

This letter, along with 1 Clement, is the leading candidate for the earliest extant Christian document. Scholars tend toward the view that it is a truly ancient document—perhaps written even before AD 90—which probably was edited into its final form some time in the second half of the second century. A manuscript of the *Didache* was discovered in 1873 in a Greek Orthodox monastery in Nicomedia. We have no idea who wrote this interesting letter. In form, it is a homily on basic Christian teaching. Many think it was used to prepare catachumens for baptism. Athanasius recommends its use for exactly that purpose.[1] Catachumen is the word that was applied to young converts who had accepted the teaching about Jesus Christ, but had not yet been baptized or admitted to the Lord's Supper. As we will see later, over the decades an ever-more-elaborate ritual was developed to prepare the new believers or catachumens for inclusion in the church.

The *Didache* was used widely in the Christian church in the second and third centuries. Eusebius mentions its use, telling us that it was a "disputed book."[2] Clement of Alexandria[3] calls it scripture. Although it was recommended for reading in many churches, it never had wide acceptance for inclusion in the canon of the New Testament. The greatest importance of this document is that it gives us a firsthand look at how the primitive church viewed such important aspects of Christianity as baptism and the Lord's Supper before the time in the early second century when monarchical bishops took control of the local Christian churches.

The writer of the *Didache* quotes from the gospels, especially Matthew, as well as from the Old Testament, especially the Book of Proverbs. It is significant for us to know that in the last decade of the first century and perhaps just a little earlier, passages from the Gospels were already being quoted as authoritative.

The content of the letter falls into three sections:

1. The two Ways. This is an exposition on Christian morality, setting forth the way of life and the way of death. To quote from the first line of the *Didache*:[4] "There are two Ways: a Way of Life and a Way of Death, and the difference between these two Ways is great.

2. A list of ordinances on baptism, fasting, the Lord's Supper and the role of various leaders in the church.

3. A final eschatology (teaching on the return of Jesus).

The middle section is probably of the most interest for us. Here we find a number of instructions familiar to us from the New Testament and some that are not. The book advises baptism "in running water," or still water if that is all that is available, or even pouring three times if no water to immerse is available. It goes further to advise that both the baptizer and the one being baptized ought to fast beforehand for one or two days. We can see already a movement toward making baptism a "sacrament." The book contains a commandment not to commit an abortion. This direct command is not found in the New Testament, although most would agree it is a straightforward application of biblical principle. The author of the *Didache* advises the young Christian to say the "Lord's prayer" three times daily. Some of us might find this a bit ritualistic, but we can imagine it helped the new convert to become familiar with the personal nature of the relation with God he or she had through Jesus Christ.

The book's description of the Lord's Supper sounds a bit like a prescribed liturgy—more ritualized than we can infer from the biblical writings but not so set in structure as it is in some Christian liturgical worship traditions today. There is evidence here that the unbaptized were excluded from the communion. The description of worship implies that the work of roving evangelists, prophets and teachers is still important at this early date in the church. Here at the end of the first century, elders and deacons are mentioned, but not a head elder or a primary bishop as leader of the church. In many ways the *Didache* represents a transitional form between the worship and practice of the first and of the second century. What we find in the *Didache* may be somewhat unfamiliar to the New Testament Christian but it marks a logical progression from worship as described in the Bible and the more liturgical worship and the monarchical episcopacy of the later second century.

Clement of Rome or 1 Clement[5]

This book may very well be the earliest noncanonical Christian writing we can date with reasonable confidence. The *Didache* may be an earlier writing, but we are less confident of its date. This makes Clement's letter very significant for our understanding of the primitive church. The book was read in most of the churches as inspired or sub-inspired (i.e. inspired by God but not canonical) from early times. Although the writer of this letter does not identify himself, our sources are unanimous that it was written by Clement, bishop of Rome. He was an elder of the church in Rome from AD 88–99. Eusebius[6] tells us, upon the authority of Origen, that the author was Clement, the third bishop of Rome and, less likely, that this was the same Clement mentioned by Paul (Philippians 4:3). Irenaeus tells us[7] that Clement was personally acquainted with the apostles. The most commonly mentioned date for the book is about AD 96—the year Domitian died. This date is used because

Clement mentions the church's "recent misfortunes"—a likely reference to the persecution under Domitian. The book is written from the church of Rome to the church in Corinth. Clement quotes from or alludes to the New Testament books of Romans, 1 and 2 Corinthians, Ephesians, Titus, 1 Peter, James and Hebrews. Here we have good evidence that an informal list of inspired writings was already circulating among the churches during the last decade of the first century.

From the content of the letter, we get the idea that there was no bishop/chief elder yet in Rome or in Corinth. Clement does not speak as a monarchical bishop, but as one of the elders in Rome. He speaks of the leadership in Corinth as the elders, not the bishop. If so, then Eusebius' reference to Clement as "bishop" may be his reading a later form of church leadership into earlier history. This is strong evidence for an early date of writing as by the time Ignatius wrote (a bit before AD 120) he could assume that the churches with whom he communicated were lead by a single monarchical bishop/head elder.

The theme of Clement is the danger of the twin sins of pride and jealousy. Hotheaded younger Christians in Corinth had rebelled against the elders of the church and deposed them without apparent cause. Clement strongly rebukes these rebels. There is an emphasis on personal righteous living and salvation through such righteous living. Significantly, Clement refers to what later became known as the "trinity." "As surely as God lives, as Jesus Christ lives, and the Holy Ghost also" (1 Clement 58).[8]

The Epistle of Barnabas

The Epistle of Barnabas was considered by many in the early church an inspired letter. We do not know the date when this letter was composed, but we can be assured that it was not written by Barnabas the companion of Paul on his first missionary journey. The content of the book narrows the date of composition down somewhat, but not to our satisfaction. Scholars seem to agree that it was written some time between the destruction of Jerusalem in AD 70 and the Bar Kochba rebellion in AD 132, after which any hope of a rebuilt temple in Jerusalem was almost certainly lost. Most likely it was written after AD 100. The book takes a strongly allegorical view of the Old Testament, which is why scholars tend to think the author may have been from Alexandria, where allegorical interpretation became dominant at a very early date. The author cites Matthew and Mark and quotes extensively and rather freely from the Old Testament, along with IV Esdras and Enoch—apocryphal books which many in the early church took to be part of the inspired Old Testament canon. Along with the *Shepherd of Hermas* (see below), the Epistle of Barnabas was included at the end of the manuscript known as Codex Sinaiticus. Sinaiticus is, arguably, the most reliable manuscript we have, being an entire Greek copy of the Old and the New Testaments from about AD 350. This fact shows the importance given to the Epistle of Barnabas by the early church.

The theme of the book is that Jewish forms of religion have never been what God had in mind. The purpose of the author seems to be to oppose any tendency for the church to maintain a Jewish identity. Two rather strong trends in the second century are easily detected in this book. The first is the tendency of the church fathers, especially those in the school of Alexandria, toward free allegorical interpretation of Scripture. Allegorical interpretation allows one to read between the lines of the obvious literal historical meaning of texts to find hidden symbolic meanings. The problem with this spiritualizing of the Scripture is that it allows the imaginative interpreter to read just about anything desired into the biblical text.

There is a second tendency in the second- and third-century church that is represented in the Epistle of Barnabas. The writer of Barnabas wanted the church to almost completely repudiate its Jewish roots. This tendency only increased after the second Jewish rebellion, also known as the Bar Kochba rebellion, in AD 132. After this tragedy all hope for a revitalized Jewish state in Palestine seemed to have disappeared. Eventually we will be able to extrapolate this trend to an embarrassing anti-Semitism within the church. This distinctly unchristian behavior included church leaders laying the blame for the death of Jesus on the Jews. The writer of the Epistle of Barnabus did not go this far. The lack of strong and clear reasoning as well as the unfounded allegorizing of the Old Testament text make one wonder that many in the early church considered the possibility of including this book in the canon of the New Testament.

The Shepherd of Hermas or the Shepherd

Along with the *Epistle of Barnabas*, the *Shepherd of Hermas* was considered by many in the early church to be inspired and to belong in the canon of accepted writings. Irenaeus and Tertullian considered it inspired or sub-inspired. It was included with the Epistle of Barnabas at the end of the Codex Sinaiticus. Its reference to Clement of Rome (Shepherd 2:4) has caused some to date the book somewhere between AD 88 and 97. However, the Muratorian Fragment (AD 170, an early partial listing of inspired Christian documents) has:

But Hermas wrote the Shepherd very recently, in our times, in the city of Rome, while bishop Pius, his brother, was occupying the chair of the church of the city of Rome. And therefore it ought indeed to be read; but it cannot be read publicly to the people in church either among the Prophets, whose number is complete, or among the Apostles, for it is after their time.

If this is true, then the book is from as late as the 140s AD.

The content of the book is five visions granted to a person named Hermas who was a former slave. The five visions are followed by twelve rules for holy living and ten similitudes (simple stories with a moral point). The book alludes often to the Old Testament as well as the synoptic gospels and the Gospel of John. Its interpretive style is highly allegorical, which has prompted scholars to associate the book with the church in Alexandria. The book emphasizes morality and ethics and does not mention Jesus, except perhaps allegorically. It has female characters with names such as Fortune, Chance, Knowledge, Happiness and Deceit. Here we see a trend in the second century that continued through the following centuries. The church tended to strongly emphasize morals—a list of dos and don'ts—without much context connecting it to forgiveness or mercy or to Jesus Christ. This was not unlike the kinds of moralistic literature of the Greeks at that time.

Christian Writings Before AD 150

Title	Author	Date Written	Subject
Didache	Unknown	90–100?	Baptismal preparation
First Clement	Clement of Rome	96?	Righteous living
Epistle of Barnabas	Unknown	Before 132	Warning against Judaism in the church
Shepherd of Hermas	Unknown	Early 2nd Century	Holy living
Letters of Ignatius	Ignatius	117	Obey the bishop
Letter of Polycarp to the Philippians	Polycarp	About 120	Righteous living, warning against Docetism
Martyrdom of Polycarp	Unknown	155 or 156	Martyrdom of faithful Christians
Second Clement	Unknown	Before 150	Righteous behavior
Letter to Diognetus	Unknown	About 120	Defense of Christianity

The Letters of Ignatius

Do nothing without the bishop.　　—Ignatius of Antioch

Ignatius was bishop of Antioch. This is the same Antioch where the first significant number of Gentile conversions happened (Acts 11:19–22). It was one of the pillar churches in the second century. Ignatius wrote seven letters of admonishment to the churches. The seven letters were written to the churches in Ephesus, Magnesia, Tralles, Rome, Philadelphia and Smyrna, as well as a personal letter to Polycarp, bishop of Smyrna. These letters were written under duress, while Ignatius was traveling toward his own execution in Rome. This execution occurred in or perhaps slightly before 117, during the reign of Trajan. This makes the letters of Ignatius one of the earliest glimpses into primitive Christianity we have. We can be certain that Ignatius knew the apostle John. The style of the letters is very earnest and personal. The letters were collected and preserved by Polycarp who was bishop of Smyrna in Asia at the time of Ignatius' march toward Rome. One gets the strong impression from the letters of Ignatius that he considered the Gospels and the letters of Paul to be inspired and that these letters were already beginning to be part of an informal canon. He quotes from Matthew, John, Romans, 1 Corinthians, Acts, Ephesians, Philippians, Colossians, 1 Thessalonians, 1 and 2 Timothy and Hebrews.

In the letters of Ignatius we find a forerunner of a number of trends we will find in second-century Christianity. Perhaps foremost of these is his emphasis on the prime role in the church for the bishop. One subtle distinction between Ignatius and those who followed him is that he does not prove the authority of the bishop by succession from the apostles. Ignatius says in Magnesians 6,[9] "Let the bishop preside in the place of God and [the presbyters] in the place of the Apostolic conclave." Unlike what we see in the *Didache*, where the elders/presbyters were referred in the plural, without mention of a principal elder or bishop, Ignatius was a strong advocate of what is known as the monarchical episcopate (from the Greek *episkopos* or overseer). From his letters it is not hard to detect why he felt this was important. He has many warnings against heretical influences from the Judaizers and Docetists (more on this teaching below). Apparently Ignatius felt that the best way to guard against churches falling into heretical teaching was to have a single bishop overseeing all important aspects of the teaching and life of the church in each city. If a whole group of leaders fell into apostasy, this was an intractable problem, but if a single bishop were to advocate heretical ideas, he could be replaced and order reestablished in the church. The striking authority Ignatius assigned to the bishop and its connection in his mind to preventing heresy can be seen from the following passages:

> Flee from schism as the source of mischief. You should all follow the bishop as Jesus Christ did the Father. Follow, too, the presbytery as you would the apostles; and respect the deacons as you would God's law. Nobody must do anything that has to do with the church without the bishop's approval. You should regard the Eucharist as valid which is celebrated either by the bishop or by someone he authorizes. Where the bishop is present there, let the congregation gather, just as where Jesus Christ is there is the Catholic [i.e. the universal] Church. Without the bishop's supervision, no baptism or love feasts are permitted. (Ignatius to the Smyrnians 8)

and

> Let the bishop preside in the place of God and his clergy [the presbyters/priests] in the place of the Apostolic conclave, and let my special friends the deacons be entrusted with the service of Jesus Christ. (Ignatius to the Magnesians 6)

It is hard to see this granting of unbridled authority to one person in the local church as consistent with what was taught and practiced in the New Testament church. It is also not hard to understand why Calvin and other Reformation theologians did not like Ignatius, as his letters were used by Rome to support its strong hierarchical structure. On the other side of the debate, the Roman Catholic Church has used the writings of Ignatius as strong support for their hierarchical and authoritative leadership structure. From the Roman perspective, the earlier an authority, the stronger the tradition. Ignatius certainly represents an early authority upon which one can build a tradition.

How should we think about this? One perspective is that under the pressure from some rampant false teachings the temporary granting of increased authority to a chief elder may have been a wise expedient. However, what may have been a wise direction to move in for a difficult situation eventually became a tradition that took the weight of authoritative doctrine in the Catholic Church of the Middle Ages. Here is one lesson of church history we will do well to remember: We must always let church practice reflect the doctrines and the principles taught in the inspired Scripture. Jesus was clear that the qualities of a Christian leader are humility and service, not lording it over others. Ignatius represents a radical view of the role of bishop at his time, but his ideas eventually became common practice—cementing the separation between clergy and laity that has plagued the church ever since.

Another concern of Ignatius is related to the first. He gave many warnings against the false teachings that were threatening to destroy the church of Christ. Ignatius' concern is that of a person who is near death thinking that all they have fought for might be lost. It reminds us of Paul's concern expressed to the elders from Ephesus that savage wolves would rise up from among the flock (Acts 20).

It appears from Ignatius' letters that there were two paths to heresy about which he was particularly concerned. One of these is the tendency to incorporate Jewish ideas about law-keeping into Christian teaching. He has strong words about the Judaizers who had, apparently, not yet disappeared from the churches.

> Do not be led astray by wrong views or by outmoded tales that count for nothing. For if we still go on observing Judaism, we admit we never received grace.... It is monstrous to talk of Jesus Christ and to live like a Jew. (Ignatius to the Magnesians 8:1, 10:3)

This seems to be hyperbole to us. Christ himself lived like a Jew. Paul did not outlaw "observing Judaism." What Paul opposed was the forcing of Mosaic Law on those who were not from a Jewish background. It is an irony of church history that the very tendency that Paul opposed in Galatians and Colossians—the tendency to seek salvation through observance of ritual—became the hallmark of later Western and Eastern Orthodoxy. Indeed, there is evidence that Ignatius moved in the direction of replacing the Jewish Sabbath with a "Christian" Sabbath on the Lord's Day (Magnesians 9). His advice moved the church toward replacing the Jewish clergy with "Christian" clergy and to some extent transformed the Christian remembrance at the Lord's Supper into a kind of a sacrifice at an altar. With Ignatius the deacon's role began its transition from servant of the physical needs of the poor to servant of the priest at the Eucharist. All these tendencies were to increase with time.

An even greater concern of Ignatius is the teaching of Docetism. The docetic heresy got its name from the Greek word for appearance, *dokesis*. This teaching entered the church through the influence of Greek philosophy, which taught that the physical creation is essentially evil. To the Greek philosopher and to the Docetist believer in Christ, Jesus could not have occupied a physical body. He only appeared to be a physical person. His body was a mere phantom; and thus the name *dokesis*. Of course, if Jesus did not occupy a real body of flesh this would do damage to the doctrines of the Incarnation and the bodily resurrection of Jesus. To do this is to tear the heart out of

Christianity. Cerinthus, whose teachings were discussed in chapter one, was a Docetist. Passages that show Ignatius' concern over these doctrines include the following:

> [Concerning the Docetists] Guard yourselves carefully against men of that sort. You will be safe enough so long as you do not let pride go to your head and break away from Jesus Christ and your bishop and the Apostolic institution. To be inside the sanctuary is to be clean; to be outside it, unclean... I can see the devil's snares ahead. So let submission and unselfishness be your weapons against them; take a fresh grip on your faith (the very flesh of the Lord)... He [Jesus] was verily and indeed born and ate and drank... and indeed crucified, and gave up the ghost in the sight of all heaven and earth... It is asserted by some who deny God—in other words who have no faith [in other words the Docetist teachers and their followers] that his sufferings were not genuine. If this is so, then why am I now a prisoner? (Ignatius to the Trallians 7–10)

> All this He submitted to for our sakes, that salvation might be ours. And suffer He did, verily and indeed; just as He did verily and indeed raise Himself again. His Passion was no unreal illusion, as some skeptics aver who are all unreality themselves. The fate of those wretches will match their unbelief, for one day they will similarly become phantoms without substance themselves. For my own part, I know and believe that He was in actual human flesh after his resurrection. (Ignatius to the Smyrnaeans 2–3)

Here we see both a warning against those who deny that Jesus occupied the flesh and Ignatius' solution, which is to remain inside the church and in submission to the bishop.

The third theme that runs through the letters of Ignatius is his desire for martyrdom. This very brave disciple of Jesus was not only willing to give his life rather than offer sacrifice to the pagan Roman god, he sought martyrdom. Essentially he said, "bring it on." This desire of Ignatius is found in all the letters, but especially the one to the Romans. In Ignatius' own words:

> For my part, I am writing to all the churches and assuring them that I am truly in earnest about dying for God—if only you yourselves put no obstacles in the way, I must implore you to do me no such untimely kindness; pray leave me to be a meal for the beasts, for it is they who can provide my way to God. I am his wheat, ground fine by the lions' teeth to be made purest bread for Christ.... Still their ill-usage [i.e. his ill-treatment at the hands of Roman soldiers] does at least enable

me to make some progress in discipleship; *though that is not to say that my sins are yet wholly absolved.* How I look forward to the real lions that have been got ready for me! All I pray is that I may find them swift.... This is the first stage of my discipleship; and no power, visible or invisible, must grudge me my coming to Jesus Christ. Fire, cross, beast-fighting and quartering, splintering of bone and mangling of limb, even the pulverizing of my entire body—let every horrid and diabolical torment come upon me, provided only that I can win my way to Jesus Christ! (Ignatius to the Romans 4–6, emphasis added)

What an inspiration this faithful disciple of Jesus must have been to his fellow Christians! Surely many were strengthened in the face of severe persecutions by his powerful convictions. On the other side of the coin, Ignatius seems to have an almost unhealthy fascination with death. He gives a hint of the thinking that his salvation will somehow be completed by his "sacrifice." We can see a foreshadow of what later became a cult of martyrs and saints in the Middle Ages.

In his letters Ignatius comes across as an amazing Christian approaching the end of his days. His theology of Jesus is that of the New Testament writers. How can we not admire this church father? His tendency to stress the authority of the bishop, the forms of worship and his zeal for martyrdom are reasonable responses by Christianity to the stresses of persecution from without and false teaching from within. We can only regret that these trends were extrapolated to an unwarranted extent over the following centuries.

The Old Testament: Church Leadership and Organization

As previously mentioned, we can think of the Old Testament as an inspired source of commentary on "church history." One of the important roles church history can play for the modern church is in applying its lessons to questions about organization and leadership of God's people. How should we organize the work of the ministry? What should be the balance between strong leadership under a principal leader versus a shared leadership structure? How should the church be organized and its leadership structured in order to utilize the special gifts of each member? How should leaders be chosen and trained?

We should think of Old Testament examples of leadership and organization principally as description, not prescription. In other words, we will not find commandments about how the New Testament Church should be organized and led. However, Paul says of the Old Testament stories that "these things happened to them as examples and were written down as warnings for us, on whom the fulfillment of the ages has come" (1 Corinthians 10:11). In other words, we can assume that the examples in the Old Testament are a good source of experiential advice from which we can gain wisdom and guidance in how we should do church today.

A few useful examples for us today come to mind. One pattern in the Old Testament seems inescapable. When Israel lacked a strong, godly, visionary leader, God's people suffered disgrace and defeat. A solid case can be made from Old Testament example that the local church and perhaps the church in a larger sense must have a godly man providing vision, a direction and an example to God's people. There is no example of "group leadership" bringing victory and spirituality for God's people. This is not to say that shared leadership under a godly man is not to be advised (see below). However, every time His people did well, God used a man of strength and spirituality to bring victory. Examples such as Moses, Joshua, Caleb, David, Hezekiah, Josiah, Ezra and Nehemiah come to mind immediately.

The converse is true as well. When Israel or Judah lacked a strong, visible, godly leader, the result was sinful behavior gone rampant and defeat for God's people. This was true even if there were many spiritual individuals in Israel, but they were excluded from taking on a leadership role. When Israel suffered shame and wallowed in idolatry in the time of Elijah, there was no shortage of men who had not bowed to Baal. In fact there were 7,000 righteous men in Israel, but one key element that was lacking was a spiritual leader (1 Kings 19:18). The theme passage in the book of Judges is: "In those days Israel had no king; everyone did as he saw fit" (Judges 21:25). On the other hand, "when the princes in Israel take the lead, when the people willingly offer themselves—praise the Lord! (Judges 5:2).

What can we conclude from these examples? In order for the church to be spiritually strong and to grow, she must give attention to programs to develop strong leaders. Wise leaders will seek input from the people and will try to create a consensus, but God's leader must take the lead. Godly leadership will always come from the heart of a servant (Mark 9:35), but this servant leader must step out and lead the people. It is human nature that when we do not have a sense of direction, chaos ensues. The Scripture is sufficient to thoroughly equip the man of God for every good work (2 Timothy 3:16), but even those who are spiritual need to be part of a group that is being led somewhere in order to thrive.

The need for strong individuals leading God's people is not the only lesson for church leadership and organization we can glean from the Old Testament. Another lesson is that worldly models for leadership have no place with God's people. Strong leadership alone is not the key. In fact, it can be a recipe for disaster if it is not spiritual. Throughout the time of the Judges, Israel learned well the need for some kind of strong leadership. Unfortunately, they looked to the world for their leadership model. They begged Samuel, "appoint a king to lead us, such as all the other nations have" (1 Sam 8:5). Samuel warned them, not of the danger of having a strong leader per se, but of setting over themselves a man chosen by the standards of the world. The people did not listen to the warning—they did not trust in God. They chose to use the weapons of the world to defend God's kingdom (2 Corinthians 10:4). Saul fit the model for leadership of the Egyptians, the Hittites and of those who were great in the eyes of the world. He was young, strong, handsome and charismatic. Samuel granted their request and the rest is history. Saul relied on self and pandered to the will of the people (1 Samuel 15). Fortunately for Israel, God replaced Saul with a leader after his own heart.

The lesson for today's church is that strong, godly leadership is needed, but we need to be careful to avoid the seductiveness of the ways of the world when we choose whom to place in principal leadership roles. Our models are not Alexander the Great, Winston Churchill or Steve Jobs. Our model for leadership is Jesus. Moses, David, Hezekiah and other biblical models for God's leader have a number of traits in common. Moses was "more humble than anyone else on the face of the earth" (Numbers 12:3). David had a heart fully devoted to God. "Hezekiah trusted in the Lord, the God of Israel. There was no one like him among all the Kings of Judah, either before him or after him" (2 Kings 18:5). Profound humility, deep devotion and a surrendered trust in God are hallmarks of godly leadership.

Positive Old Testament models for leadership and organization of God's people include more than just examples of reliance on a main spiritual leader. There are a few iconic biblical examples of settings in which God was able to bless his people greatly. The Golden eras for the Jews include their time in the wilderness under Moses, Israel during the reign of David, and the restoration of God's people to the promised land under the leadership of Ezra. In all of these cases, we see examples of God putting people with special gifts in supportive roles to share the burden of leading God's people. Moses had his "capable men from all the people." The elders who shared the work of ministry were trustworthy, they feared God and they hated dishonest gain (Exodus 18:17–26). David had his mighty men (2 Samuel 23:8–39) whose loyalty was unquestioned and whose zeal for God was a reflection of David's own heart. He had Asaph to oversee the worship ministry. Asaph's legacy in the temple worship and his poems influenced God's people even long after his death. Unfortunately, David's example of choosing men to support his service of Israel was not without blemish.

In some cases, David chose unwisely—appointing men with selfish ambition such as Joab to head his armies. The result was disastrous. Ezra had perhaps the best leadership team in the history of Israel. He was the preacher and teacher—the spiritual leader of the people. Ezra had Nehemiah—a man of deep convictions—as his governor. To inspire the people and call them to repent, he had Zechariah the visionary and Malachi the messenger of righteousness. To oversee the worship, Ezra had Joshua the High Priest who was perhaps the greatest high priest in the history of Israel. Jewish history, then, informs us that wise leadership structure will put spiritually strong men and women in places of influence where they can use their God-given gifts to the glory of God.

Polycarp of Smyrna

Our next snapshot of the Christian church in the second century comes from the life, the pen and the martyrdom of Polycarp, the humble bishop of Smyrna. Shortly before his execution in AD 155 or 156, Polycarp speaks of himself as having served the Lord these "eighty and six years." This is more likely to indicate his age and his having grown up in a Christian home than having actually served as a minister or bishop for that long. In any case, his life spans from about the time the temple was destroyed in Jerusalem until past the midpoint of the second century. Truly he is an important transitional figure. According to Irenaeus, Polycarp had been "instructed by Apostles and had had familiar intercourse with many who had seen Christ."[10] Perhaps we should be a bit skeptical of the claim, but Tertullian tells us[11] that Polycarp received his appointment as bishop of Smyrna by the apostle John himself. Whether this is true or not, Polycarp is an invaluable link between apostolic times and the second half of the second century when Irenaeus and others began to write the first important systematic theologies.

Irenaeus knew Polycarp personally. For this reason he can give us very reliable information about this man who knew at least one of the apostles. Irenaeus[12] tells us that he learned under Polycarp and that the great bishop traveled at his great age to Rome in about AD 154. The purpose of the visit was to confer with Anictetus in order to discuss a dispute about the date of Easter. Irenaeus also informs us that during his visit Polycarp persuaded many who had fallen under the influence of the heretical teaching of Marcion and Valentinus (more on them below) to return to the orthodox faith. His success against the heretics was partly due to the fact that Polycarp could claim to have learned from the apostles themselves. Soon after Polycarp returned to Smyrna a fresh round of persecutions broke out. Because he was the bishop of Smyrna, Polycarp was arrested and executed as a martyr. We do not know a lot of details about the life of Polycarp, but from what we can glean, we get a picture of a humble and gracious man, yet one who had no toleration for those who brought false teaching to the church. According to Irenaeus, it was Polycarp who often repeated the story of the Apostle John running out of the bath in Ephesus when he found out the heretic Cerinthus was inside. When meeting Marcion face to face, rather than giving the customary Christian greeting "I acknowledge us," Polycarp is reported to have said, "I acknowledge the first-born of Satan."[13] Unlike his contemporary Justin Martyr, he was not highly educated. His Greek is not that of a philosopher or one trained in rhetoric, but his mind was saturated in the teaching of the apostles.

Polycarp wrote a letter to the church in Philippi. We do not know the exact date of the letter, but likely it comes from not long after the martyrdom of Ignatius in AD 117. The text has many New Testament allusions, providing clear evidence that he considered these works inspired. He quotes from Matthew, Acts, Romans, 1 Corinthians, Galatians, Ephesians, 2 Thessalonians, 1 Timothy and 1 Peter. He mentions the letters of Paul, telling us that "if you study them attentively, [they] will enable you to make progress in the faith which was delivered to you.[14] His is a plea to simple, righteous living;

especially a call to avoid every kind of greed. He puts in a short warning against the Docetist teaching between two longer discourses on godly living. "To deny that Jesus Christ has come in the flesh is to be Antichrist" (Polycarp 7). In Polycarp's letter we do not see Ignatius' strong call to submit in everything to a monarchical bishop, although we assume that Polycarp occupied such a position.

We also have in our possession a gripping firsthand account of the arrest and execution of the octogenarian bishop Polycarp.

The Martyrdom of Polycarp

Eighty and six years have I served Him, and he has done me no wrong. How then can I blaspheme my King and my Savior?"

—Polycarp

The church in Smyrna produced an account of the execution of Polycarp in AD 155. The account was delivered to the church in the small city of Philomelium. This wonderful little eyewitness report of the martyrdom of Polycarp represents in many ways what was beautiful about the Christian church in the second century. As we see the events leading up to his execution we can see in vivid detail the humility, the kindness, the compassion and the passion of Polycarp, companion of the apostles and respected leader of the churches in Asia at this time.

A fresh round of persecutions broke out in Smyrna soon after the aged Polycarp returned from his mission to Rome. A younger disciple named Germanicus was arrested. He exhibited amazing bravery before the animals who were to devour him. The response of the crowd was to yell, "Down with the infidels [atheists]! Go and find Polycarp!"[15] Spineless government officials hunted down Polycarp to satisfy the crowd, despite his advanced age. His friends urged Polycarp not to volunteer for execution. They carried him out of his own home under cover of darkness. Applying torture to find his whereabouts, the soldiers arrested Polycarp in the middle of the night at another farmhouse. The venerable man could have escaped, but instead he said, "God's will be done." Graciously, Polycarp fed the soldiers before being led off to Smyrna. When the soldiers demanded that Polycarp offer incense and say, "Caesar is Lord," he refused. When demanded to say of the Christians, "Down with the infidels," Polycarp pointed to the crowd who hoped to see him burn, saying, "Down with the infidels."

The Governor, however, still went on pressing him. "Take the oath and

I will let you go," he told him. "Revile your Christ." Polycarp's reply was, "Eighty and six years have I served Him, and he has done me no wrong. How then can I blaspheme my King and my Savior?"

Persisting in his attempts, the Governor then said again, "Swear by the Luck of Caesar." Polycarp answered, "If you still think I am going to swear by Caesar's Luck, and still pretend not to know what I am, let me tell you plainly now that I am a Christian; and if you want to know the meaning of Christianity, you have only to name a day and give me a hearing."

After threatening wild beasts did not sway Polycarp, the magistrate switched tactics. "If you do not recant, I will have you burnt to death, since you think so lightly of wild beasts." Polycarp rejoined, "The fire you threaten me with cannot go on burning for very long; after a while it goes out. But what you are unaware of are the flames of future judgment and everlasting torment which are in store for the ungodly. Why do you go on wasting time? Bring out whatever you have in mind to do."

With this the magistrate announced to the arena, "Polycarp has admitted to being a Christian." The crowd responded in fury, "That teacher of Asia! That father-figure of the Christians! That destroyer of our gods, who is teaching whole multitudes to abstain from sacrificing to them or worshipping them!" A unanimous outcry went round to burn Polycarp alive. Immediately citizens, including the Jews, built a pile of wood. Polycarp was tied to a stake at the center of the wood, and the fire was started.

Imagine for a moment being a member of a church for which this kind of treatment of its leaders was common. If we imagine ourselves a Christian in the city of Smyrna at the time of this persecution, we can get a feeling for the kind of family atmosphere and dedication to Christ and one another that pervaded the church. This was no social club.

On a side note, the same letter reports a young enthusiast named Quintus from Phrygia who turned himself in voluntarily to be martyred. Under pressure and without the support of his companions, Quintus' courage failed him at the sight of the beasts. He relented and offered the sacrifice to the "Luck of Rome." This detail was given by the author Marcion as a cautionary tale followed by advice for disciples not to volunteer for execution. In later years, this advice was not accepted by all.

Second Letter of Clement

The document commonly known as the Second Letter of Clement was almost certainly not written by Clement of Rome, the author of 1 Clement.

The story of how it got its name is a bit complicated. It is thought to have been written in the first half of the second century. From its style, scholars speculate that the letter was written in Alexandria or a church under its influence. One thing about this letter makes it of particular interest to us. What makes this document unique is that it is probably a transcript of an early sermon—very likely the earliest Christian sermon we have, other than the Book of Hebrews. If this is true, then it provides us with an instructive if limited glance at how Christian leaders explained the gospel to their own community.

The style of the letter/sermon is highly moralistic. It may be that we are taking too much from one sermon, but the impression it gives is that holy living is stressed with relatively little mention of grace and the security of salvation. The doctrine of baptism appears to be moving in the direction of what later became the Roman "sacrament" of baptism. For example in 2 Clement 6:9[16] we find:

> If even such upright men as these cannot save their children by their upright-
> ness, what assurance have we that we shall enter God's kingdom if we fail to
> keep our baptism pure and undefiled? Or who will plead for us if we are not
> found to have holy and upright deeds?"

Another example of this kind of thinking is found in 2 Clement 8:6: "This, then, is what he means: keep the flesh pure and the seal [i.e. your baptism] undefiled, so that we may obtain eternal life."

The author quotes from an apocryphal letter—probably the Gospel of the Egyptians. This is some of the evidence that the letter was written in Alexandria. We find in 2 Clement 12:3–4:

> "For when someone asked the Lord when his Kingdom was going to come, he
> said, 'When the two shall be one, and the outside like the inside and the male with
> the female, neither male nor female.'"

This appears to reflect a dualistic/Gnostic influence; somewhat surprising in a letter that is otherwise orthodox in its theology.

A works salvation mindset can be found in the letter. Perhaps we can infer that this kind of thinking was creeping into Christian teaching in general as well. Salvation by works certainly became a hallmark of the Western church in later centuries. 2 Clement 16:4 has:

> But fasting is better than prayer, and charity than both. Love covers a multitude
> of sins, and prayer, arising from a good conscience, rescues from death. Blessed

55

is everyone who abounds in these things, for charity lightens sin.

Like Polycarp's letter of about the same time period, the monarchical episcopate is not emphasized, but rather the writer emphasizes the work of the elders of the church.

The Philosophical Attack on Christianity and the Intellectual Response: The First Apologists

In the first century—at least before AD 70, it appears that neither the Greeks nor the Romans made a distinction between the Nazarenes (Christians) and Jews. The young church was treated as a sect of Judaism. As we head into the second century, this changed significantly. By the time of the Jewish Bar Kochba rebellion (AD 132), Christianity and Judaism were viewed as two different religions. Christianity had distanced itself from Judaism to the point that mainstream Christians were repudiating and even attacking Judaism. They did so to an extent that would seem unrighteous and unloving to us. Besides, by the middle third of the second century Christianity was already reaching the point that both its numbers and geographical reach were surpassing that of Judaism. It is at this time that we find pagans began to mount a pointed philosophical attack on this upstart religion. The philosophical attack was in addition to the blunt political attacks, which took the form of persecution. In this section we will be looking at the nature of these intellectual criticisms of the church and the first defense offered by early Christian writers. Our antagonists will include the likes of the pagan philosopher Celsus, while our protagonists will include one of the heroes of the early Christian movement, Justin "Martyr."

The religious and philosophical atmosphere in the Roman Empire was quite eclectic. As a rule, the Roman government was tolerant of any idea that allowed its adherents to also give nominal honor to the Roman god. There were two groups which adamantly refused to pay homage to the Roman cult; the Jews and the Christians. It is striking how much the two monotheistic religions stuck out in the polyglot of religions in the Roman Empire. From the Roman perspective, the Jewish refusal to participate in the common Roman religion was forgivable to some extent. This is because they recognized that their practice was based on a truly ancient tradition—one which predated the foundation of Rome itself. When the followers of Jesus threw off their Jewishness, they became exposed to an even more aggressive attack because they could no longer claim to represent a truly ancient tradition. The intellectual assault against Christianity was not long in coming.

The list of pagan writers who opposed Christianity in the second century include Fronto, Tacitus, Lucian and Celsus. The most notable of these was probably Celsus. He was a highly educated Roman who may have been raised in a Christian home. As an adult he turned toward Greek philosophy. It is worth noting that Celsus had the ear of the Roman Emperor at the time, Marcus Aurelius. Aurelius was known as the philosopher emperor. He was an ardent supporter of the pagan philosophers, especially of the Stoics. Celsus' critique of Christianity was summarized in a work titled *The True Word: A Discourse Against the Christians*, written somewhere between AD 175–180. This work was sufficiently influential that Origen of Alexandria wrote an entire treatise titled *Against Celsus* in AD 248 in which he defended Christian belief against the arguments of Celsus. In his book, Origin refuted Celsus nearly line-by-line. For this reason we have virtually the entire document of Celsus' polemic. This treatise is particularly helpful to understanding the pagan view of Christianity. It also gives us a unique insight into how outsiders viewed some of the actual practices and teachings of Christians at that time. Much of what we know of what the opponents of the orthodox church said comes from the Christian response to their enemies. Experience tells us that polemical responses to an antagonist tend to exaggerate the argument of the opponents, so it is nice to have the original work of Celsus. For this reason we will let the work of Celsus represent the more or less "typical" response of the intellectual community of the Greek and Roman thinkers in the second century to the Christian church.

Celsus opposed Christianity primarily on philosophical grounds. He kept away from the spurious charges of others that Christians were performing bloody rituals and child sacrifices. Essentially, he argued that Christian belief was superstitious, foolish and irrational. According to Celsus only the uneducated and unsophisticated could possibly accept this upstart religion. To be a Christian required blind faith, unsupported by evidence or reason. The readers will recognize that this is strikingly similar to the arguments intellectuals make against the Bible and Christianity today. The pagan ideas Celsus attempted to paint as superior to Christianity were a blend of the philosophical thinking of the followers of Plato and the Stoics. Celsus, like many of the Greek philosophers, was a monotheist. He argued for what he called "The True Doctrine." One thing we can be confident of from reading Celsus is that the pagans believed the early church taught that Jesus was God in the flesh. This flies in the face of the claims of some modern scholars that the church did not teach that Jesus was God until later. Here is Celsus on the subject:[17]

Now if the Christians worshipped only one God they might have reason on their side. But as a matter of fact they worship a man who appeared only recently. They do not consider what they are doing a breach of monotheism; rather they think it perfectly consistent to worship the great God and to worship his servant as God. And their worship of Jesus is the more outrageous because they refuse to listen to any talk about God, the father of all, unless it includes some reference to Jesus: Tell them that Jesus, the author of the Christian insurrection, was not his son, and they will not listen to you.

About the Christian idea that Jesus is deity he said:

It cannot be the case that God came down to earth, since in so doing he would have undergone an alteration in his nature.[18]

This was the crux of the philosophical challenge to Christianity from the second all the way through the fifth century. More than one Christian apologist rose to counter this argument. The Greek philosophers, whether of the school of Plato, Aristotle or the Stoics, all believed in a kind of "God" who is a distant, pure, undivided, spiritual entity. To them it was blasphemy that God could take on a physical form, because the physical world is essentially evil. God cannot have two natures, and to them the central Christian claim required God to change his nature. The Christian response to this philosophical argument had huge ramifications, as we will see. In forming a response, especially in the third and fourth centuries, Christian apologetics had its birth.

With this brief introduction, let us now look at some of the writings of the early Christian apologists.

The Letter to Diognetus

The earliest Christian document we have that has been described as an apologetic is known as the *Letter to Diognetus*. The Greek manuscript of the letter contains twelve chapters. Scholars believe that the first ten chapters of the Greek text are most likely a genuine letter of defense of Christianity from a writer in Asia in the second or third decade of the second century. This is followed by two additional chapters of material from a different writer toward the end of the third century. The author of the epistle does not identify himself. The essay is addressed to a person, real or not we do not know, named Diognetus. It is not so much a philosophical or theological defense of

Christian teaching as one based on the character of the church itself and its role in human history. This gives useful insight into how the church viewed itself at this early date. The book can be described as an apologetic because, unlike the other letters we have considered, it is not a defense of Christianity to believers. It does not address problems within the church. The *Letter to Diognetus* is addressed to outsiders.

The book begins with a description of the "foolishness" of idolatry that sounds much like those found in the Old Testament. It mocks the worshippers of chunks of wood that are rotting even as they are worshipped. The letter contains a sarcastic attack on Judaism, with its attention to ceremony and sacrifice. This ungracious treatment of Judaism would hopefully make most Christians today blush. "Are they not asking for ridicule when they boast of the mutilation of the flesh as a sign of their choice by God, as if for this reason they were especially beloved by him" (Diognetus 4:4). Such an attack may have earned points with his Greek hearers, but it was not a worthy polemic against Jews who had faithfully obeyed God.

The author gives a beautiful and moving description of the early church that has every feeling of a genuine (if somewhat idealized) description of the church as it was at that time. "Every foreign land is their fatherland, and yet for them every fatherland is a foreign land. They marry, like everyone else, and they beget children, but they do not cast out their offspring.... It is true that they are "in the flesh," but they do not live "according to the flesh" (Diognetus 5:5–8). The Christians are described as the nearly invisible leaven in the entire Greek and Roman world that dramatically improves the moral wealth of everyone. One gets the sense that the writer is confident the hearer cannot possibly deny the absolutely exemplary lives of the Christians, as it was common knowledge. We can only wish such were the case with believers today. Along with the author of the *Letter to Diognetus* we too can be proud of our brothers and sisters who so wonderfully spread the aroma of Christ in the second century.

Justin, "Martyr"

> Whatever things were rightly said among all men, are the property of us Christians.
>
> —Justin, "Martyr"

The second Christian apologist we will look at is Justin. To some he is known as the father of Christian apologetics. Many argue that he was the greatest of all the apologists in the early church. As the work of Freud defined all psychology that followed him, so the work of Justin defined the work of Christian apologists who followed him. Even if we do not agree with Justin on everything, his work was seminal in its defense of the faith.

Justin was born in Palestine in the city of Flavia Neapolis, which is ancient Shechem and modern Nablus. He was not Jewish, but it seems likely that early exposure to Judaism influenced his heavy reliance on Old Testament Scripture in his defense of Christianity. Some have speculated that he came from a Christian home. It is likely that he left Christianity as a young adult, only to return to it later. In any case, one thing we can say with confidence is that Justin was culturally Greek. He was trained as a philosopher. He was most strongly attracted to Platonism, although exposure to the Stoics is evident. According to Justin himself, he was attracted to the deep wisdom of the prophets of Israel long before his conversion to Christianity. Also decisive to his conversion to the Jesus movement was Justin's exposure to the Christian martyrs. He said that their amazingly courageous and "philosophical" willingness to face death rather than deny their beliefs was what impelled him to consider Christianity as having the true philosophy and Jesus Christ being the true Philosopher.

According to Eusebius, Justin wore the philosopher's robe even after his conversion. To him this must have been a statement that, despite what its critics might say, Christianity is not just a religion for the poor and uneducated—it was a religion for the philosopher. We can assume that some of his fellow Christians were uncomfortable with this style of dress as we know some felt Christians should have nothing to do with philosophy (Tertullian will be a prominent example of this). To them the philosopher was the natural enemy of the church, and not without reason as we have seen that many pagan philosophers attacked the church. These Christians felt that a simple belief, sometimes known as fideism, was to be preferred to a faith that required the support of reason or evidence. Of course, even today many Christians are skeptical of philosophy in general and prefer a simple kind of faith divorced from intellectual reflection.

After his conversion, Justin began to apply his philosophical training to defending the beliefs of Christianity. Up to this time, few Christians had put much energy into considering the philosophical implications of the biblical teaching about the nature of God. The concept of the "trinity" had not yet been fleshed out. Christian theology was in its infancy. A surprisingly wide range of beliefs about God and the relationship between the Father, the Son and the Spirit was tolerated in the church. We will see in the next two chapters that this situation changed radically. By the fourth and fifth centuries fights over minutiae of the philosophical implications of the incarnation tore the church apart. Pressure both from without and from within brought philosophy into the Church in a big way.

Justin arrived in Rome about AD 150 and began to teach and defend Christianity there. While in Rome, Justin authored a number of works. Of these, three have come down to us. In the writings we have, he not only provided a defense to those who ridiculed Christians on intellectual grounds, but he laid the groundwork for later Christian theology.

His *First Apology* was addressed to the Roman Emperor at the time, Antoninus Pius. Given some of the dignitaries mentioned in the work, scholars have estimated it to have been written in AD 155. The impetus for this, the *First Apology of Justin*, was the martyrdom of Polycarp. As in the *Letter to Diognetus*, Justin points out the stellar moral behavior of the Christians. "We are in fact of all men your best helpers and allies in securing good order."[19] Justin makes the rational argument that Christians have such good civic behavior because Christians teach that all are subject to eternal judgment for everything they do in this life. The pagans have no such motivation toward moral behavior.

We who took most pleasure in the means of increasing our wealth and property now bring what we have into a common fund and share with everyone in need; we who hated and killed one another and would not associate with men of different tribes because of their customs, now after the manifestation of Christ live together and pray for our enemies.[20]

In his *First Apology* Justin pointed out much in common between Christian teaching and that of Plato. Famously, and shockingly to many, he described Plato's mentor Socrates as a "Christian before Christ." Justin implied that although much of Greek mythology and philosophy are false teaching, their underlying concepts were derived from ideas first given to the Jews through Moses. According to Justin:

We have been taught that Christ is the First-begotten of God, and have previously testified that he is the Reason [logos] of which every race of man partakes. Those who lived in accordance with Reason [logos] are Christians, even though they were called godless, such as, among the Greeks, Socrates, Heraclitus and others like them; among the barbarians, Abraham, Ananiah, Azariah and Mishael [i.e. Shadrach, Meshach and Abednego] and Elijah and many others.[21]

Here we find that for which Justin is most famous. He equates Jesus, the first-begotten of God, with the Greek philosopher's idea of logos. To the Greek philosopher, logos meant the ineffable word, design, argument, truth, reason. Along with John (John 1:14), Justin identifies Jesus as the *logos* of the one God. He is anticipating the Greek argument that God cannot take on flesh because to do so requires God to change his very nature. To the Platonist or Stoic this is not possible. To the Greek, God was immutable and unchanging. For God to be affected by emotion was anathema to the Hellenist philosopher. Justin also claims that both the godly Jews and the godly Greeks such as Socrates and Heraclitus who displayed knowledge of Jesus (*logos*) were at least in a sense Christians. Justin is attempting to "baptize" Greek philosophy.

This is Justin's philosophical apologetic. His chief evidence to support the claim that Jesus is in fact God-in-the-flesh comes from fulfilled messianic prophecy in the Old Testament. This argument seems very modern to us. Justin notes prophecies that the Messiah would tie his colt to the vine and wash his robe in the fruit of the vine (Genesis 49:10–11), that he would be the Branch to grow out of the root of Jesse (Isaiah 11:1), that he would be born of a virgin (Isaiah 7:14), that he would be born in Bethlehem (Micah 5:2), be crucified (Psalm 22:16) and ride into Jerusalem on a donkey (Zechariah 9:9). He quotes and applies the entire fifty-third chapter of Isaiah to Jesus.

Justin also proves that the God of the Jews gave mankind free will, using Deuteronomy 30:15 and 19 to support his argument. He then proceeds to claim that Plato got his own idea of free will from Moses![22] Justin exposes the Christian heretic Marcion of Pontus, telling the emperor that this false teacher claims that there is a God greater than the Creator God of the Old Testament. We will have more to say on Marcion below.

Justin's second extant work is the *Second Apology of Justin*. Eusebius tells us that the second apology was produced early in the reign of the emperor Marcus Aurelius, in about AD 162. In this letter, Justin expands on his apologetic, again referring to the Greek philosopher and explaining in more detail the idea that Jesus is indeed God-in-the-flesh. As in his first apology, Jesus is the divine *logos*.

I confess that I both boast and with all my strength strive to be found a Christian; not because the teachings of Plato are different from those of Christ, but because they are not in all aspects similar, as neither are those of the others, Stoics, and poets, and historians. For each man spoke well in proportion to the share he had in the spermatic word [logos] seeing what it was related to.... Whatever things were rightly said among all men, are the property of us Christians.[23]

Here we see the Greek idea of logos applied to Jesus. We also see the idea that there is truth in all philosophy, but the *Truth* is found in Christian philosophy because it comes directly from the Word of God who became flesh in the man Jesus Christ.

The third work we have from Justin is known as *Dialogue with Trypho the Jew*. It was also composed in about AD 162. It is different from the other works in that it is styled as a dialogue with a Jewish philosopher Trypho who was active some time before the rebellion of Bar Kochba in AD 132. It also contains an autobiographical reflection on the part of Justin concerning his journey from follower of Plato to Christianity. In this letter, Justin explains to Trypho why the incarnation is consistent with monotheism. Trypho was an actual philosopher who ridiculed Christianity as a rejection of monotheism. Justin claims that the Jews had removed certain portions of their Scripture in order to be able to deny that Jesus fulfilled the prophecies of the Messiah.

Of course, Justin is known to history as Justin Martyr. Martyr was not his last name! He earned this label through the means of his death. Justin anticipated his execution in his own writings. His bold proclamations of the absurdity of pagan beliefs may well have spelled his own doom. Eusebius tells us[24] that Justin became Justin Martyr in AD 162. He was tortured by a certain philosopher-opponent named Crescens. When he refused to make an offering to the Roman god, his fate was sealed. Surely the life, the writing and the mode of death of Justin all gave great encouragement to the Christian community in his time.

Many Christians have hesitated to endorse the theology of Justin Martyr. It is fair to say that in his zealous attempts to make Christianity palatable to the Greek intellect he went too far to accommodate human philosophy to Christian ideas. To find truth in all the philosophers but all truth in the Gospel alone is reasonable, but to attempt to baptize the philosophies of Socrates and Plato seems to go too far. Justin was not the only one to make such a mistake. We will see that Clement of Alexandria and Origen also made too great a compromise with Greek philosophy. Let us learn from Justin's mistakes, but surely there is far more to admire than to avoid in this inspiring philosopher for Christ who laid down his life for the cause.

Athenagorus of Athens

Athenagorus is, arguably, a better writer and a clearer thinker than Justin, so why is he less well known to Christian history? The answer is that Justin was first great apologist, because he was the more original of the two and, perhaps most important of all, because Justin proved to the whole world the sincerity of his belief by willingly dying for Jesus Christ.

We know less of the life story of Athenagorus than of Justin Martyr's. Undoubtedly, he was thoroughly immersed in Greek philosophical thinking. Likely he lived in the most Greek of Greek cities—Athens—as he calls himself an Athenian in his apologetic. We do not know when or where he was born, but there is good reason to believe that the more important of his two extant writings, *A Plea Regarding Christians*, was written in AD 176 or 177, as it appears to be set about the time of the great persecution at Lyon and Vienne. The other apologetic work of Athenagorus that has come down to us is a defense of the resurrection of Jesus of Nazareth.

His *A Plea Regarding Christians* is addressed to the Emperor Marcus Aurelius and his son Commodus. Athenagorus addresses the emperor as a fellow philosopher, appealing to his reason and good sense at every point. His writing is quite elegant and his reasoning is clearer than that of Justin. His sources are more eclectic than Justin's as well, drawing his cosmology from Pythagoras, arguing for monotheism from the Stoics, Plato and Aristotle and quoting extensively from the Iliad. Theologically, Athenagorus is nearly identical to Justin, drawing liberally on his original thinking. With Justin he argues that Jesus Christ is the *logos* of God.

Athenagorus defended the Christians against the three offenses with which they were most often charged in the second century. "Three charges are brought against us: atheism, Thyestean feasts and Oedipean intercourse."[25] Christians were falsely charged with atheism because they refused to acknowledge the gods of Rome. Remember that during the events surrounding the burning of Polycarp, the crowd chanted, "Down with the atheists." By "Thyestean feasts" Athenagorus refers to the accusation of cannibalism—the ludicrous charge that the disciples sacrificed and ate their own children. This charge was able to flourish in part because in the second century the church excluded all the unbaptized from their Eucharist (Lord's Supper). The third common accusation at the time is obliquely referred to by Athenagorus as "Oedipean intercourse." This is the charge of incest. The exclusive nature of Christian worship services gave cause to the pagans to assume sexual rites were included. This was not completely unreasonable, because a number of the secret Mystery cults in the Greek world did indeed include sexual promiscuity.

In defending against the charge of atheism, Athenagorus makes the point that the real gripe of the Romans against Christianity is not lack of a belief in God but lack of willingness to worship through the offering of sacrifices. Here our Christian philosopher hit the nail on the head. What distinguished

Christianity from pagan religions was its rejection and even derision of the idea of buying off God by offering sacrifices. The thing that brought a death penalty—proof of atheism to the Roman authorities—was refusal to offer sacrifice to the "Genius" of Rome. The modern equivalent is this: What marks Christianity as different from all world religions even today is that it rejects works salvation. We are not saved by anything we can offer to God, but only by accepting the sacrifice offered by God himself. This is done, not apart from works (James 2:24), but through faith in the work of God. Like Athenagorus, we should never back down or apologize for this wonderful Christian doctrine.

Athenagorus offers a litany of charges against the foolishness and self-contradiction of all the pagan gods, goddesses and idols, knowing that his philosopher reader will agree with this to some extent. Having gained an ally in attacking the silliness of pagan belief, he proceeds to show that the more spiritual-sounding beliefs of the Stoics and the followers of Plato are really a more sophisticated version of the same kind of polytheistic belief in a created entity. Athenagorus provides an explanation of the "trinity" as follows:[26]

> Indeed we say that the Holy Spirit himself, who inspires those who utter prophecies, is an effluence from God, flowing from him and returning like a ray of the sun. Who, then, would not be astonished to hear those called atheists who admit God the Father, God the Son and the Holy Spirit, and who teach their unity in power and their distinction in rank?

Athenagorus debunks the charges of immoral behavior, including cannibalism and incest. He claims, quite reasonably, that these false charges are motivated, not by any evidence, but by a desire to bring down the wrath of the authorities on the church. He confidently asserts the moral character of the Christians.

> The injury we suffer from our persecutors does not concern our property or our civil rights or anything of less importance. For we hold these things in contempt, although they appear weighty to the crowd. We have learned not only not to return blow for blow, nor to sue those who plunder and rob us, but to those who smite us on one cheek to offer the other also.... But when we have given up our property, they plot against our bodies and souls, pouring upon us a multitude of accusations which have not the slightest foundation, but which are the stock in trade of gossips and the like.[27]

Again, we get the sense that the Christians as a group held to a moral standard that would be the envy of any philosopher. Regarding the charge of incest, our apologist points out that Christians are commanded to not even offer a lustful glance—that for us a glance is considered as evil as the act of adultery. Of those who charge the Christians with sexual impurity, he quotes the proverb: "The harlot reproves the chaste."[28] Christians, with their refusal to divorce and their teaching on purity, were the most chaste of all peoples in their day. We can only hope that the sexual purity of Christians today will rise above those around us as did the behavior of the church in the second century.

Concerning cannibalism, Athenagorus is proud to point out that the Christians refused to even attend the public spectacles of violence, which was the favorite form of entertainment for the Romans and Greeks. We find evidence that participation in such public entertainment was prohibited by Christian teachers from many other early sources in addition to Athenagorus. Here is one area in which modern-day believers ought to take note from our brothers and sisters in the second century. Have we partaken too deeply at the well of worldly entertainment, with its glorification of violence and sexual impurity? In addition, Athenagorus points out that the Christians refused to partake in abortion or the exposure of unwanted children—accepted practices in their day. How could anyone, he argues, accuse of cannibalism those who most valued life?

Gnosticism: Marcion and Valentinus

The Christian church faced many challenges during the second century. One question we can ask is: What was the greatest danger to the church? Another is: What was the greatest *perceived* danger? Was it persecution? Was it a drift toward worldliness and a loss of conviction about sin? While these may have been the greatest *actual* danger to Christianity, the church leaders in general did not perceive things this way. If we take the writings of the early church fathers at face value, they perceived the greatest threat to the church to be the attempts by heretical teachers to hijack the Christian movement. One of the themes of this church history is that the church's reaction to heretical teachings was the greatest single cause of changes in the teaching, practice and organization in the church in the first few centuries—for better or for worse.

There is one thing about the primitive church that is so distinct from the modern situation that it is difficult for us to conceive how truly different the dynamic was. Until somewhere near the end of the second century, there was literally one church. In other words, despite some widely variant ideas about theology and church practice, in any one city there was only one Christian church. There was not an Ebionite church on one street corner, a Gnostic church on another and an orthodox church on still another. In the modern context, if we strongly disagree over basic doctrine or practice of the group we worship with, we simply agree to meet separately and, hopefully, to live at peace with one another in our own sphere. This alternative simply did not exist for the early church. For this reason, if a group in a local church taught the necessity of following the Law of Moses or if some disciples who were attracted to the "deeper" teaching of the Gnostics became part of the church, there was real danger of the entire church in an area being no longer truly Christian. The option of agreeing to disagree and forming a separate fellowship was not available.

This dynamic had several effects that will seem strange to us. First, in the early church there was in many cases a surprisingly broad spectrum of ideas about Jesus to be found among the members. The church was more tolerant of heterogeneous ideas than we might suspect. The leaders were generally quite orthodox, but the members might have been fairly heterodox. For example, the evidence is that all or virtually all the bishops were publicly strongly opposed to Christians being involved in the military, yet members who chose to be in the military were tolerated. By the way, this tolerance of heterodox ideas did not survive into the fourth and fifth centuries under increased pressure for theological unity from the Ecumenical Councils. Second, the leadership structure and many of the practices of the church were created, not because of biblical mandate, but to prevent the church from being overtaken by the heterodox believers within the ranks of the church. The move toward the monarchical bishop, the increasing use of formulaic creedal statements, the exclusion of the unbaptized from worship are all symptoms of this self-protective stance leading toward questionable theology that was present within the church.

There is little doubt which heretical movement within the church offered the greatest challenge to Christianity during the second century. This was Gnosticism. We have seen that Gnosticism was already a concern in the first century. The threat actually increased in the second. Let us review what Gnosticism is, discuss the different strains of thinking that it included and describe the response of orthodox Christianity to Gnostic teaching.

Gnosticism was far from monolithic. Remember that there was not a separate Gnostic "church" around which a unified idea could crystallize (although this changed with some Marcionite churches by the end of the second century). Gnostic groups tended to form around individual teachers, not unlike the way Hindu groups tend to gravitate around certain gurus. Having said this, second-century Gnostic movements had certain characteristics in common. One was a denial of the incarnation of Jesus Christ. To the Gnostic, Jesus had a spiritual but not a physical nature. This thinking was derived from Greek philosophical ideas, such as those of Plato, which taught that the physical world is evil. The god of the Old Testament, *Yahweh*, created the physical world and therefore Yaweh is not a good god. Jesus is an emanation of good, therefore he could not be defined by a physical body. To the Platonist (and therefore to the Gnostic), God is not personal. God is unimaginably distant from humans. Because they denied that Jesus was human, Gnostics denied the incarnation and the crucifixion of Christ. A second general characteristic of these Gnostic movements was a belief that the real gospel is characterized by a deeper, hidden meaning that underlies the literal sayings of Jesus. This belief in a deeper, symbolic, spiritual meaning behind the message of Jesus is the genesis of the name Gnostic, which comes from the Greek *gnosis*, meaning knowledge. The emphasis on secret knowledge, revealed gradually to the initiate, was a characteristic of the Greek Mystery religions.

Gnostic believers created their own "gospels" and other writings. Until this century, we knew about Gnostic writings principally from the church fathers who described them and even quoted from them in order to show why they were in contradiction with apostolic teaching. Because the mainstream Christian writers were so strongly opposed to teaching that they considered as Gnostic and heretical, we ought to be hesitant to completely accept their characterization of their enemies. Our near-complete reliance on church fathers to understand the Gnostics changed dramatically with the discovery of the Nag Hammadi Library in the Egyptian desert in 1945. This manuscript discovery provided a wealth of original Gnostic writings. These include the most famous of them all, the Gospel of Thomas, as well as the Gospel of Philip, the Gospel of the Egyptians, the Apocryphon of John and many others.

A Sample List of Gnostic Texts

Title	Subject/Content	Date/Source
Gospel of Thomas	Sayings of Jesus	AD 100–140
Gospel of Philip	Collected writings	Early 3rd, Valentinian
Gospel of the Egyptians	Asceticism	120–150, Sethian
Gospel of Judas	Gnostic cosmology	170, Sethian
Gospel of May	Gnostic dialogue	129–180
Apocryphon of John	Origin myth	120–180, Sethian
Hypostasis of the Archons	Gnostic cosmology	3rd, Sethian
Gospel of Truth	Gnostic philosophy	140–180, Valentinian

The documents in the Nag Hammadi collection are in Coptic—the language of Egyptian Christianity—but almost certainly all or nearly all were originally composed in Greek. Some of them are pseudo-Christian Gnostic writings, others are Gnostic but without the veneer of Christianity. It is beyond the scope of a church history to analyze all these writings, but suffice it to say that in general they confirm what we know of this heretical teaching from other sources. To give an example of Gnostic teaching, let us look at a statement from a Gnostic document that was first published in 2006: *The Gospel of Judas*. In this "gospel" (which is surely not a gospel at all), Jesus tells Judas that he will do him a favor by betraying him to the Jews. The crucifixion will allow him to be free of the body in which he is imprisoned. "But you [i.e. Judas] will exceed all of them. *For you will sacrifice the man that clothes me.*"[29] We can see that the writer of this document does not believe Jesus had a physical nature, but that he was imprisoned in the body of the person we know as Jesus. In this "gospel" Judas is Jesus' favorite apostle because he is the one who is privy to the deeper, secret truth underlying the simplistic gospel message. "Come, that I may teach you about [secrets] no person [has] ever seen. For there exists a great and boundless realm, whose extent no generation of angels has seen."[30]

The *Gospel of Judas*, like other Gnostic documents, has a bizarre cosmology. The ineffable "God" is too distant to have any interaction with humanity. From this esoteric deity come several levels of emanations, such as aeons. Characters in Gnostic cosmology include the likes of Sophia, Nebro, Yaldabaoth, Saklas, Galila, Yobel and Adonaios. In the Gospel of Judas, Jesus is also known as Seth, and he is one of the five rulers over the underworld (this is why the Gospel of Judas is labeled as a Sethian Gnostic writing in the table above). Gnosticism was clearly not an alternative kind of Christianity. It was a Greek philosophy/religion masquerading as Christianity.

At the risk of oversimplifying, Gnostic practice was based on the Mystery religions, its theology was based on dualistic religion (such as Mithraism), its philosophy was based on Platonism or Neoplatonism, and its story was based on Christianity. To provide some modern perspective, there is much parallel between self-centered Gnostic pseudo-Christianity and New Age religion as practiced in the West. New Age writers such as Elizabeth Clare Prophet use the Nag Hammadi Library extensively to argue that the Gnostics were the true Christians.

It should be no surprise to us at all that during the second and third century the bishops and Christian teachers vigorously opposed this non-Christian religion. In fact, the response of the orthodox Catholic Church to the threat of Gnostic teaching largely shaped the history of the church from this point forward. The Church developed a well-defined systematic theology, not because the members of the church or its leaders were calling for it but in order to protect the church from such deviant ideas. Catachumens (candidates for baptism) began to be required to make a formulaic statement of faith before baptism. The oldest such baptismal confession we know of is called the Old Roman Symbol. In these confessions the creation of the physical world by God was stressed, as well as the physical incarnation and death of God's Son, Jesus Christ. Many of us are familiar with the Apostles' Creed, which is a direct descendent of these early faith statements.

The church fathers traced Gnosticism back to the influence of Simon Magus. Justin Martyr[31] and Eusebius[32] agree that after his rebuke by Peter (Acts 8:18–24), Simon moved to Rome where he started the counter-Christian Gnostic movement. It is difficult to judge the accuracy of this view, but we know that the two most significant Gnostic movements in the second century originated in Rome. There is a confusing mix of Gnostic leaders and Gnostic movements in the second century. In order to narrow this swath of information to a manageable quantity, let us consider as exemplars of the Gnostics in general the two most influential teachers of Gnosticism in the second century, Marcion and Valentinus.

Marcion

Marcion was probably from Sinope on the north coast of Asia Minor, the son of a wealthy merchant. He began his movement in about AD 144 in Rome. It is surely not a coincidence that he began this anti-Jewish movement soon after the Roman suppression of the Bar Kochba rebellion. Consistent with Gnostic thinking, Marcion concluded that the god of Judaism, Yahweh, was an evil god. Marcion said that the Jewish deity was a *demiurge*—a lesser emanation of the unknown and unknowable God. This Hebrew *demiurge* was essentially evil because he was responsible for creating the physical world. According to the Gnostic worldview, anything physical is inherently evil. The evil god of the Old Testament was jealous, vengeful and genocidal. He created a world of suffering and pain from which followers of Jesus could escape through special knowledge imparted by Marcion. For this reason, he declared Christianity to be separate from Judaism and completely rejected the Hebrew Scripture.

Marcion created his own unique canon of Scripture. He rejected the gospels of Matthew, Mark and John as too "Jewish" and published his own edited version of Luke as the only gospel. From what has already been said about Gnosticism, we should not be surprised that Marcion's Luke excludes the story of the incarnation and the baptism of Jesus, as well as references to his fulfillment of messianic prophecy. Marcion was particularly enamored of the teaching of Paul, with its emphasis on grace and love versus law and judgment. His canon included ten of Paul's letters, rejecting the Pastoral Epistles (those to Timothy and Titus), Hebrews, James, the letters of Peter and John and Revelation. It is significant that Marcion does not include any of the Gnostic gospels or other writings in his canon. As far as we know, even the Gnostics did not have the nerve to compare the "gospels" of Thomas and Peter and others to the four pillar gospels. Some believe that the first authoritative lists of New Testament books were published as a reaction to the bogus canon of Marcion. The oldest published canon we have is the Muratorian Fragment from about AD 170. This document lists the four canonical gospels and all the books now contained in the New Testament except Hebrews, James and 1 and 2 Peter.

There is some evidence that under the influence of Marcion we have for the first time examples of there being separate "Christian" fellowships. In a few places, there were identifiable Marcionite and mainstream Christian churches in the same city. Marcion and his followers were excommunicated. Polycarp may well have met Marcion personally. He called him "the firstborn of Satan."[33] Eusebius tells us that Justin wrote a work against the teachings of Marcion. The Marcionite teaching was denounced both by Irenaeus in *Against Heresies* in 180 and by Tertullian in a work titled *Adversus Marcionem* in 208. The Marcionite movement continued into the fourth and perhaps even the fifth century, after which they were oppressed by the state church.

Valentine

Some do not classify Marcion as a Gnostic. This is because, although much of his theology was in common with the other Gnostic movements, he did not stress occult Mystery practices. Valentine (Valentinus in Latin) will represent for us more of the classical Gnosticism. His religious system definitely included the secret rites common to most Gnostic groups. Valentinus made the dubious claim that his deeper hidden knowledge was handed down to him by oral tradition directly from Jesus to Paul to Theudas and then to Valentinus. Eusebius tells us[34] that Valentine brought his demonic teaching to Rome during the episcopate of Hyginus (AD 138) and that he lived until the time of Anicetus (AD 160). Tertullian tells us[35] that Valentine began as an orthodox teacher but when he was unsuccessful in his bid to attain the bishopric of Rome in 143 he turned to Gnosticism. "Just like those (restless) spirits which, when roused by ambition, are usually inflamed with the desire of revenge, he applied himself with all his might to exterminate the truth; and finding the clue of a certain old opinion, he marked out a path for himself with the subtlety of a serpent."

Valentine taught that people fall into three categories. Those who attain the highest level were called spiritual. Below them in attainment were those called psychic. The lowest level—the common people—were called material. The spiritual people were those who had access to the secret *gnosis* from Valentine and through this knowledge access to the divine Pleroma (a concept of God derived directly from Platonism). The regular, orthodox Christians could have a lesser kind of salvation. These were the psychics. The rest of unenlightened humanity were considered material. These material people were lost. Valentine's theological system included a confusing array of emanations, aeons and syzygies. Christ did not have a physical nature and he did not suffer. Irenaeus tells us that Valentine wrote a work titled *The Gospel of Truth*. The Nag Hammadi Library (discovered in 1945 as mentioned previously) included a book of this name, making it likely that we have access to some of Valentine's writing, or that of one of his disciples. In this work, we are told that Jesus gave the mysterious, unknown name of the Father to his disciples. Knowledge of this hidden name (which, of course, is not included in the New Testament and is not known by the more physical regular Christians) allows a person to penetrate the veil of ignorance that separates us from the Pleroma. Jesus has revealed this name through a complicated language of abstract elements.

The followers of Valentine and his Gnostic ideas were numerous, especially in Rome. As with New Age teaching today, this self-focused religious movement appealed to the pride and itching ears of its hearers (2 Timothy 4:3). The church desperately needed a champion of pure, biblical, apostolic teaching who could match the charisma and personal magnetism of Valentine. Irenaeus of Lyon fit this bill well, as we will see below.

There were many other Gnostic groups operating in the second and even the third century. Eusebius identifies some of the better known, such as the Carpocratians, Basilidians and Saturnalians. Let us now move to the last of the important heretical movements of the second century we will be studying.

Montanus and Montanism

The last heretical movement of the second century we will discuss is Montanism. The Montanists were also known as Phrygians because their movement began in Phrygia (central Asia Minor). Their movement was sometimes known as the New Prophecy. In a sense this movement represents the opposite of Gnosticism. Whereas Gnosticism appealed to the rational and the intellectual mind, Montanism appealed to the emotional part of human nature.

The movement was begun by Montanus and two prophetesses, Maximilla and Prisca (Priscilla) around AD 150. The essence of this movement was an emphasis on ecstatic utterance and prophecy. Montanus was a recent convert to Christianity. Perhaps he became disillusioned with what he saw as worldliness in the church and a lack of spiritual fervor. Montanus and his prophetesses claimed to be possessed by God himself or by the Holy Spirit and to provide fresh revelation. They spoke while in a trance. Montanus was quoted as saying, "I am come neither as an angel, nor as an ambassador, but as God the Father."[36] Didymus has Montanus saying, "I am the Father, the Word, and the Holy Spirit."[37] The prophetess Maximilla said, "Hear not me, but hear Christ."[38, 39]

It is not hard to see parallels between Montanism and the modern-day Charismatic/Pentecostal movement, with its ecstatic utterances, modern-day revelation and speaking "in the Spirit." Both movements are essentially conservative and appeal principally to the emotional rather than intellectual needs of its members. Montanism met a legitimate desire of Christians to have an emotional connection with God, which may have been lacking in the more hierarchical and formalized Catholic church. It can also be viewed as a legitimate reaction against wordliness in the church. The same can be said for the modern Pentecostal movement.

Despite the strengths of the Montanist movement, it is easy to understand why the Christian church as a whole reacted very strongly against this group. The key issue in this case was authority in the church. Here we have young Christians with relatively little knowledge of the Bible, but with their aura of authority, being able to trump the sound doctrine of the church. They did not acknowledge the authority of the bishop. Montanus, Maximilla and Prisca claimed authority because, according to them, they spoke for God himself. Montanus accused the church of being spiritually dead. The bishops responded rightly that Christian revelation was complete. They were extremely skeptical of ecstatic teaching in which the speaker completely lost the control of human reason.

To Montanus and his followers, one piece of evidence that the mainstream church was dead was its lack of miraculous spiritual gifts. The bishops responded by denying this charge. By the second century there is relatively little mention of continuing miraculous gifts of healing and tongues. However, the church defended itself by saying that there still were miraculous prophets in the church at this time (mid-second century). Eusebius tells us that "even down to his [Justin's] time gifts of prophecy shone forth in the church."[40] He reports Quadratus saying that some with the gift of healing and other "true miracles" were present in the church down to the time of Trajan (AD 117). "Some of them have also lived to our own times."[41]

There is some evidence that Montanus did not intend to veer from correct doctrine—that his movement in its earliest phase in fact did not include any truly heretical teaching. His emphasis was on a vigorous asceticism including many prescribed fasts and a strong discouragement of marriage. His movement welcomed martyrdom as a sign of true Christianity. Tertullian himself, one of the most influential of the church fathers, is said to have held to the Montanist teaching toward the end of his career.

Montanus, Maximilla and Prisca began a commune in Phrygia in a town called Pepuza, which they declared to be a "New Jerusalem." They preached the imminent return of Jesus; a teaching that was not necessarily in conflict with the orthodox church, although they gave greater emotional energy to this teaching.

It is an irony of church history that the long-term effect of the Montanists on Christianity was to impel the church even more strongly toward instituting the monarchical bishop, the canonization of Scripture and the tendency to trace ecclesiastical authority by direct line to the apostles. The Montanists' attempt at making Christianity more personal and spontaneous had the exact opposite effect.

The First Systematic Theologian: Irenaeus

He became what we are so that we might become what he is.

—Irenaeus of Lyon

Although we have more to say about Christianity in the second century, our discussion of Irenaeus to some extent marks a transition. His is the last biography of a second-century church "father" we will look at. His literary work marks an end and a beginning. With Irenaeus we can mark the end of truly primitive Christianity and the beginning of the age of systematic theology and what became known as Christendom.

The term Christendom has been used to refer to the idea and to some extent the reality of a Christian world. Christendom was a dominant political and religious institution from the end of the Roman Empire, through the Medieval period, the Renaissance and the Reformation. The vision of Christendom was a political and social world dominated by Christian ideals—a theocracy. It saw the marriage of political power and religion to be a natural one. Arguably, Augustine was the greatest visionary of Christendom, but as early as Irenaeus we see a Christian leader dreaming of a Christian world governed by bishops, whose values and institutions are Christian, guided by the Christian tradition, handed down by the successors to the apostles.

Irenaeus ruled as bishop in Lugdunum (present day Lyon), a leading military and trade city on the Rhone river in Gaul (roughly France today). He was born in the 120s AD. According to Irenaeus himself,[42] he was taught by Polycarp in Smyrna. Irenaeus, the great champion of church and apostolic tradition, saw this as quite significant. When he wrote his great works he spoke as one who knew Polycarp who in turn had learned from the apostle John. Irenaeus was in Rome at the time of Polycarp's martyrdom in Smyrna. Because he often used phrases reminiscent of Justin in his writings, it is likely that Irenaeus studied at Justin's school while in Rome. He was sent by the church in Rome to serve in Lugdunum. He lived in a primarily Latinized city, but his culture and language were Greek. The church in Lyon was making the transition from a primarily Greek-speaking subculture in a Latin/Roman city to a primarily Latin church. We know from Eusebius and others that a vicious persecution broke out in that city in 177. Pothinus, the bishop of Lyon, was executed. Most likely, Irenaeus would have been killed as well, except that he happened to be on a mission as a presbyter of Lyon to the church in Rome. On this mission he helped the bishop of Rome at the time, Anicetus, work out a compromise with the Eastern churches over the date to celebrate Easter. Upon his return to the city he was selected to the rather dangerous position of bishop of Lyon in 177. He became, in effect, the head of the Christian churches in Gaul. In the last written material we have from Irenaeus he admonished Victor, the bishop of Rome, for his divisive attempt to disfellowship the Eastern churches because they observed Easter on a different date from the Western churches (more on this below). Victor ruled from 190–198. Irenaeus probably died somewhere between 198 and 202.

Irenaeus was fairly well educated, but he was not an intellectual. Through his writings, he created a somewhat systematized theology. However, he did this not so much because he was a theologian, but as an effective way to help Christian teachers answer the attacks of the Gnostics and other heretics. This is a key feature of early Christian theology. To a large extent the direction it took reflects not a systematic working out of Christianity and a doctrine of Jesus Christ, but a response to pressures on the church from pagan persecutors and even more so to attacks from heretical groups (especially Valentinus and Marcion in this case).

His great work was *The Refutation and Overthrow of the Knowledge Falsely So Called*, also known as *Five Books Against the Heresies*. This writing came to be known simply by the title *Against Heresies*. In the book, he mentioned the

Roman bishops down to Eleutherus, who died in 189 or 190, giving us a good idea when it was written. *Against Heresies* was divided into five books. Its principle subject was a systematic refutation of the heretical teachers of his day—especially the Gnostics. It was not written as theology but as a practical source of material Christian bishops could use to oppose the followers of Marcion, Valentine and others in their cities. Irenaeus' chief concern was to preserve and protect the Christian tradition as spoken by Jesus and as passed down to us through the apostles and the church fathers. Arguably, one of his mistakes was to overemphasize the importance of tradition in determining what is true, even if that tradition was not necessarily found in canonical writings. If one thing characterizes Irenaeus, it is that he was zealous for tradition and the authority of "the Church." He saw in this the antidote to Gnostic teaching. As Ignatius played an important role in creating the monarchical bishop, Irenaeus played an important role in raising "apostolic tradition" (which included the traditions of the church fathers such as Irenaeus) to an authority on par with the New Testament.

Many Christian groups claim Irenaeus as their own as a theologian and a Christian teacher. Restorationists, Reformers, Roman Catholics and Orthodox believers find him supporting their ideas. Understandably, Restorationists love quoting from Irenaeus, because his doctrinal stance is wonderfully in line with their understanding of biblical doctrine—especially his teaching on salvation. Mainline Protestants appreciate his relatively unadorned Christianity, which seems on the face of it to be more like their practice than the Roman church's. Arguably, though, the Roman Catholic and even more so the Eastern Orthodox Church own Irenaeus more than the rest because he is a direct link between primitive, apostolic Christianity and a church based on canon, creeds and church tradition. Irenaeus says:

> Having received this preaching and this faith...the Church...carefully preserves it, as if living in one house. She believes these things [everywhere] alike, as if she had but one heart and one soul, and preaches them harmoniously, teaches them, and hands them down, as if she had but one mouth. For the languages of the world are different, but the meaning of the tradition is one and the same.[43]

and

> We appeal again to that tradition which has come down from the apostles and is guarded by the successions of the elders in the churches.[44]

Going perhaps still further in assigning authority to tradition, he says:

Even if the apostles had not left their Writings to us, ought we not to follow the rule of the tradition which they handed down to those to whom they committed the churches?[45]

Irenaeus finds authority seated not only in the canonical writings, he finds truth and even salvation in "the Church." Let us see how he has adapted what Jesus said in John 10:7–8:

Since there are so many clear testimonies, we should not seek from others for the truth which can easily be received from the Church. There the apostles, like a rich man making a deposit, fully bestowed upon her all that belongs to the truth, so that whoever wishes may receive from her the water of life. She [i.e. the Church] is the entrance to life; all others are thieves and robbers.[46]

Here Irenaeus substitutes the Church for Jesus as the gate to life. We can see where he is headed here and where the hierarchy of the church headed in the following centuries.

Irenaeus uses an argument that foreshadows Roman Catholic claims for supreme authority as "the Church" today. He assigns to Rome a preeminent role in preserving the traditions of the apostles. To support this, he lists the bishops of Rome beginning with Peter, down to his own time. He then dismisses the followers of Valentine and Marcion in the following manner: "For there were no Valentinians before Valentinus and no Marcionites before Marcion."[47] One can hear echoes of this argument today from Catholic apologists. Were there any Lutherans before Luther or Presbyterians before Knox? Interesting from a historical perspective is that the argument had some validity in Irenaeus' time.

Why did Irenaeus ascribe so much to church tradition, over and perhaps even above the authoritative Scripture? Was it because he wanted to use tradition as an excuse to ignore what the Scriptures taught? Certainly not. The reason he stressed tradition and the rule of faith more than Scripture in his arguments was that the invocation of an uninterrupted tradition provided the bishops of the church one of their strongest arguments against Gnosticism and other false teachings. Marcion and Valentinus were able to use, or abuse, the New Testament Scriptures quite effectively to their own ends, especially among those who were not so well acquainted with the Bible and were susceptible to strange interpretations. When Irenaeus invoked apostolic tradition, bolstered by apostolic succession of the bishops of Rome, Ephesus, Alexandria and Antioch, he was able to provide what seemed a solid leg on which to base the orthodox faith he professed. That this leg of tradition was to prove a stumbling block to biblical Christianity in the long run was not envisioned by Irenaeus.

In *Against Heresies*, Irenaeus described the teachings of about twenty different identifiable heretical groups. With a biting humor he pointed out the ludicrous cosmology of these mainly Gnostic teachers that was so obviously a creation of human imagination. For example, when listing the cosmological speculation of the Gnostic Secundus, he says:

> Iu, iu, and pheu, pheu! Truly we may utter these exclamations from tragedy at such bold invention of ridiculous nomenclature, and at the audacity that made up these names without blushing. For when he says "There is a certain Pro- arche before all things, above all thought, which I call Monotes," and again, "With this Monotes there reigns a Power, which I call Henotes," it is obvious that he admits that he is talking about his own inventions, and that he has given names to his inventions which no one else had given them before.[48]

Irenaeus sarcastically makes up his own names for such aeons. Why not call one "Gourd" or "Cucumber" or "Superemptiness?" He informs us that Marcion called the God of the Old Testament evil. He describes in great detail the speculations of Valentine.

Irenaeus had ideas about salvation in common with all the early church fathers. He saw salvation as the forgiveness of sins, provided through the blood of Jesus, activated in the life of the believer by faith and repentance. Like the writers of the *Didache*, the *Shepherd of Hermas*, the *Epistle of Barnabus*, and like Justin, as well as the church fathers who came after him, including Tertullian and Origen,[49] Irenaeus taught that the consummation of one's relationship with God occurred in the water of baptism.

> When we come to refute them [the Gnostics], we will show in its proper place that this class of men have been instigated by Satan to a denial of that baptism which is regeneration to God. Thus, they have renounced the whole faith.... For the baptism instituted by the visible Jesus was for the remission of sins.[50]

Irenaeus' New Testament is our New Testament. His use of the canon is as conservative Christians use it today. For Irenaeus, to quote from the Old Testament or from the New is to assign equal authority. He quotes with the implication of full authority nearly every New Testament book, including those for which there was still some controversy in the second century. He uses Titus, Hebrews, James, 1 and 2 Peter, 1 and 2 John and Revelation. He mentions and even quotes from noncanonical writings such as 1 Clement and

Justin, but does not treat them as authoritative. Irenaeus is quite sure that there are exactly four gospels, finding prophetic indication that four is the natural number of gospels, as there are four cardinal directions and four beasts in Ezekiel 1. He is the first we know of to let the four creatures in Ezekiel symbolize the four gospels. The ox is a symbol of Luke because of his emphasis on priestly things. The man in Ezekiel 1 is Matthew because he stresses the human birth of Jesus. For Irenaeus, the lion represented the gospel of John, while the eagle represented Mark. In late Roman and Medieval artwork, the association of John with the lion and Mark with the eagle were reversed. The eagle of Ezekiel 1 came to represent John, while the lion symbolized the Gospel of Mark. Irenaeus also sees an analogy to the four gospels when he identifies the four covenants God has made with mankind: the covenants with Noah, Abraham, Moses and Jesus Christ. Given the evidence from Irenaeus, we can agree with Hans von Campenhausen that "it is undisputed that both Old and New Testaments had in essence already reached their final form and significance around the year 200."[51]

The theology of Irenaeus is not as fully developed as that of Tertullian or of writers from the fourth and fifth centuries. He does not delineate fully the nature of Jesus or of the Holy Spirit. The idea of the "trinity" is not fully spelled out. Nevertheless, his is a step in this direction. To Irenaeus Jesus is God incarnate in the flesh. This is in opposition to the teaching of the Gnostics, who believed either that the Spiritual Christ came into the body of the physical Jesus at his baptism or that Jesus was never a physical being. Jesus, "on account of his abundant love for his creation submitted to be born of a virgin, himself by himself uniting man to God."[52] Irenaeus famously and beautifully said, "He became what we are so that we might become what he is."

Irenaeus sees Christ as a new Adam, as does Paul (Romans 5:12–17). However, Irenaeus goes beyond this biblical teaching. He hints at the direction the Western church was to head in the following centuries with some highly speculative theology. In passing, he mentions that Mary is the new Eve, because the obedience of Mary began to repair the damage done by the disobedience of the mother of all the living (i.e. Eve). "The Virgin Mary [became] the advocate of the Virgin Eve."[53] Do we see a hint of a later doctrine of Mary, the Mother of God? Might Irenaeus even be affected by the Gnostic speculation about Mary and the Mother Goddess? This seems less likely. Centuries later, however, the doctrine of Mary was to take the place of the Mother Goddess in the hearts of many converted to Catholicism from pagan beliefs.

We have spent a lot of time looking at the life and writing of Irenaeus. This is well justified as he represents to us so many transitions. His is the transition from a Greek and Asiatic church to a Latin and Roman church. His is the transition from leaders who knew those who knew the apostles to those who had to rely fully on oral tradition and writings rather than personal testimony. His is the transition from primitive to institutional Christianity—to Christendom. And for us, he is the transition from chapter two to chapter three, but a few important items must be raised before we leave this chapter.

Other Developments in the Church During the Second Century

Thus far, we have let the life and teaching of the second-century church fathers and the heretics they opposed tell the story of the church during this period. There are a number of other trends that ought to be traced before we pass to the history of the church in the third century and beyond.

The Church and the Pagan World

There is one key feature of the primitive church in the second century that is hard to miss when we look at how they viewed themselves and how they were viewed by outsiders. The Christian church was radically different in their lifestyle from the pagan world in which they lived. This stark difference was, unfortunately, to fade in subsequent centuries, but it was maintained to a remarkable level through the second century. The members of the church viewed themselves as holy, set apart, saints. If anything, they reveled in their differentness rather than fleeing from it. Pressure due to persecution could have caused the church to back down and become more like "the world" in order to lower their public exposure to criticism, but as a rule it did not have this effect. Why this is so can be debated, but surely it was due at least in part to the personal ministry of Jesus. The person Jesus Christ and the life he himself lived, as seen in the four gospels and as exemplified and taught by the apostles (in the first century) and by those who knew the apostles and those trained by them (in the second) served as a living model to Christians everywhere.

What were some of the features of this differentness—this unique Christian holiness? For one, the church was strongly admonished by its leaders to boycott public entertainment. Christians did not attend public plays, or if they did it was not sanctioned by their leaders. Neither did they take part in the public spectacles in the arenas such as gladiatorial fights or chariot races. It is likely that his execution was Polycarp's first visit to a Roman arena. The way Tertullian put it at the end of the second century:[54]

All excitement that invokes violent excitement is forbidden to us. Therefore, we are barred from every kind of spectacle—especially the circus. For violent emotions preside over the circus, as though they were at home there. See the masses thronging to the circus, their violent emotions already aroused! They are already riotous, already blind with hysteria, already agitated about their bets! The master of the races is too slow for them. Their eyes are already rolling, as though they were among the lots in the master's urn. Everyone hangs on the edge of his seat, waiting for the signal. There is the united shout of a common madness.

Tertullian's views on public entertainment may have been somewhat more extreme than other bishops' as he moved toward asceticism later in his life, but they reflect the general admonishment that can be found in the church fathers who addressed this issue. His argument that such entertainment was sinful included the emotional and spiritual effects of worldly entertainment on the Christian mind, as well as the dubious participation in idolatrous ceremonies. Does this mean that Christians today should not go to movies or plays and should remove all televisions and the Internet from their homes? Let the reader decide. Paul's admonition against relying too heavily on man-made regulations to support spirituality (Colossians 2:20–23) may serve as a word of caution against the excesses of Tertullian, but it seems that at the very least we should let ourselves be challenged by the hard-line teaching about participation in worldly activities we find in the second-century church leaders.

The disciples were challenged to avoid luxury in possessions and in their way of dress. Women were advised not to wear wigs or to dye their hair or use makeup. Men were advised not to pull out their hairs. Why should tables have ivory legs and knives have jeweled handles? Christians were advised to wear simple clothing that had not been dyed. To what extent the members accepted such admonitions we do not know. The fact that writers felt the need to give such admonitions suggests that some were behaving in a worldly way, at least from the point of view of the teachers.

Without exception, the evidence points toward the early church fathers being strongly against Christians voluntarily taking part in military service. The early church was decidedly pacifist. To them, the killing of other humans, even if sanctioned by a governing authority, was sinful.[55] Church fathers in the second and early third centuries who mention this stance of the church include Tertullian, Hippolytus, Origen, Lactantius and Clement of Alexandria. The refusal of Christians to join the military is proved by the pagan Celsus' criticism that if all men were like the Christians, the empire would be overrun by barbarians. This policy was to change dramatically after Constantine, as we will see. Again, we can ask how the policy of the church as a whole in the second and third century with regard to pacifism should affect our view of the question today. Was this the natural response of a religious minority that was suppressed by the very same military institution some wanted to join, or was it a reflection of a tradition handed down directly from the apostles? John the Baptist's advice to some soldiers who came to him was to be content with their pay, but it did not include a command that they quit their commission as soldiers. What we can say with confidence is that for the first two centuries of its existence, the influential leaders of the Christian church were solidly pacifist.

Worship in the Second Century

What was worship within the church like in the second century? We do not have any systematic treatises from this period describing Christian worship. However, taking into account both the instructions and the offhand references of the church fathers concerning worship in this period, we can get a fairly good idea of how the primitive churches conducted their assemblies. One feature we can discover is a gradual but profound change over time in the general tone of worship.

Let us remind ourselves of the picture we have already established of life and worship in the church in the first century. The implications of developments in the second century are best understood in light of how they marked a change from the apostolic period. To the New Testament writer, the church was a family of believers. It certainly was not a building, and it was not even a strongly organized institution. Modern-day commentators on the early church tend to read their own philosophy into the evidence. Some see an organized church with qualified, ordained leadership and a well-defined and dignified worship service. Others see a highly spontaneous, "organic," nearly structureless meeting with no hierarchical leadership overseeing it, either in the assembly or in the church in general. Both views are exaggerated, as the truth appears to lie somewhere between these extremes. Perhaps our most detailed picture of worship in the first century is provided by Paul in 1 Corinthians. This is just one data point, and we ought to be cautious in assuming that this one snapshot precisely characterizes the churches in general.

Having said this, we find evidence that the meeting in Corinth and elsewhere was a celebration, not a somber assembly. It included an intimate, communal "love feast" which was a meal, connected in some way with the commemoration of the sacrificial death of Jesus we call the Lord's Supper.[56] The common term for the church meal was *agape*, which explains why in

English we call it the love feast. Some say that the meal itself was the Lord's Supper, but this is not likely. The meal was taken, followed by singing, praying, prophesying and finally the sharing of bread and wine as a remembrance of the Lord's death and resurrection (Luke 22:19, 1 Corinthians 11:24).

In 1 Corinthians, Paul warned that the worship should be conducted in a fitting and orderly way (1 Corinthians 14:40), but this instruction serves to emphasize for us the fact that the meetings were relatively spontaneous, with participation by many of the celebrants. It does not seem that there was a single worship leader who carefully choreographed every event in the service; rather, various prophets and teachers were given opportunity to speak and to pray. Paul does not mention preaching in his description in 1 Corinthians, but from an abundance of other New Testament data, we know preaching was part of the regular worship. For example, we find in 2 Timothy 4:3: "Until I come, devote yourself…to preaching and to teaching" and in Acts 20:7 we learn that Paul apparently spoke to the church for several hours. From these we can infer that worship often included something akin to a modern sermon and/or Bible teaching.

The meetings of the Christian family included "psalms, hymns and spiritual songs" (Colossians 3:16). This communal singing did not include the use of musical instruments—making the worship of the church distinct from that of both Jews and pagans. All the early church fathers who mentioned the subject agreed that instruments were not used. The evidence from the first century does not contradict this conclusion. We do not have a biblical explanation of the lack of use of instruments in worship from the first century, but Clement of Alexandria (third century), Ambrose and Augustine (fourth century) and Jerome (fifth century) all associated the use of instruments with pagan worship.

Acts 2:42–47 describes Christian fellowship and worship happening on a daily basis. We can assume that to some extent the tendency to meet often continued, but we know that a principal weekly meeting was held on Sunday, also called "the Lord's Day" (Revelation 1:10), or known as "the first day of the week" (Acts 20:7) or as "the eighth day,"[57] to mark it out as the day after the Jewish Sabbath. Paul tended to meet with the Jews on the Sabbath to proclaim Jesus to his people, but we can be sure this was not the same as and did not conflict with the Christian fellowship on Sunday. We cannot prove from the evidence that from the very beginning the communion was always observed weekly on Sunday (not less and not more often), but the biblical and extra-biblical data supports this conclusion.

All the evidence points toward worship in the first century happening in "house churches."[58] Depending on the situation, these individual house churches may have been overseen by the appointed elders/overseers in each city. The large worship in the temple courts in Acts 2:46–47 appears to be an exception, but it was not unique. Nevertheless, small, family-like meetings were the rule. There certainly were no large church buildings at this time. The "church" in any one city could be thought of as a collection of the smaller groups which met in various homes. Whether meeting in relatively small groups was by design or as an expedient given the pressure of persecution is debatable.[59]

With this backdrop, let us consider how Christian worship changed in the second century. As a rule, the forms described above were maintained throughout this time. The love feast continued into the second century. However, over time the communal meal gradually disappeared from the Sunday meeting. Some church leaders were sufficiently frustrated with the tendency for this meal to lead to debauchery that they felt it best to have the Christians eat in their own homes. At the end of the second century Tertullian mentions the love feast, but does not associate it with the communion. Rather it took place in the evening. There is some evidence of the love feast continuing even into the fourth and fifth centuries, especially in Egypt, but by the third century it was not a feature of most Christian Sunday morning assemblies.

Most other elements of the first-century worship were continued in the second, including the Lord's Supper, singing of psalms, prayer and teaching/preaching. There was a subtle, gradual, but in the end profound change from a spontaneous participatory worship to a very predictable worship directed by an ever-more-hierarchical leadership. Spontaneous prayer and instruction gradually gave way to Liturgy and prescribed forms of worship. Most members played a more passive role in the services.

Let us look at some evidence supporting this description. Irenaeus was the first we know of to call the communion an "offering."[60] Here we see the language of sacrifice, whether taken from the Jewish or the pagan idea. The Lord's Supper gradually became less a communal remembrance of the resurrection and more of a priestly offering for the sins of the people. Of course, as the communion became an offering, the focus tended more toward the bishop who made the offering and less on the communal aspect. Gradually the idea of the priesthood of all believers (1 Peter 2:9) subsided as a result. This shift was subtle in the second century but became much more pronounced by the fourth and fifth, as we will see. We find the first use of the word "church" to mean a meeting place for the assembly rather than a reference to the body of Christ in Clement of Alexandria about 190.[61]

The move toward formalization of worship in the form of a church calendar is evidenced in a relatively small way (small compared to what became of the church calendar in later centuries) by the second century controversy over the timing of the celebration of Easter. The churches in Asia Minor were called Quartodecimans (fourteenthers) because they celebrated Easter as a remembrance of the crucifixion of Jesus on the fourteenth day of the Hebrew month Nisan. The churches in the West had Easter as a celebration of the resurrection of Jesus and celebrated it on a day of the week rather than a day of the month. For them, it always fell on a Sunday, specifically the first Sunday after the first new moon following the Spring Equinox. Some Christians were feasting while others were fasting. To many this was a scandal. Eusebius tells us[62] that Polycarp representing Ephesus and Anicetus representing Rome disagreed over this issue as early as 155. He also relates that Polycrates from Asia Minor argued sharply with Victor the bishop of Rome over this question. In AD 190 Victor excommunicated the Eastern churches over the timing of Easter. Irenaeus of Lyon had to be called on to mediate this dispute. It seems that Victor lost sight of the admonition of Jesus that one should not "break the commandment of God for the sake of your tradition" (Matthew 15:3). For instance, the command to keep the unity of the spirit in the bond of peace was certainly violated (Ephesians 4:3). Sadly, we in the modern church has not put this tendency entirely behind us.

Creeds and Catechumens

Other shifts in practice during the second century bear noting at this time. One was the tendency to use more or less standardized creeds as a basis both for unity among the faithful and for division from the heretical. Such creeds were probably recited before the baptism of converts. The tendency to have a uniform standard creed rose earlier in the West than in the East. One example is what is known as the old Roman creed:

> I believe in God, the Father Almighty;
> And in Jesus Christ, his only begotten Son, our Lord;
> And in the Holy Spirit, the holy church and the resurrection of the flesh.[63]

One can see immediately that having to publicly state this creed may have served to combat the teaching of adoptionists, docetists, gnostics and other groups. Bear in mind that creeds at this point were still flexible and did not carry the strong theological implications or authority of later examples such as the Nicene Creed. There is no evidence at this early date that differences in creeds were the cause of divisions within the church. Differing creeds as a cause of division is a much later phenomenon.

Such creeds were intimately connected with the instructions of candidates for baptism, known as catachumens. This brings us to the question of instruction of those converted to faith in Jesus Christ in the pivotal second century. It is difficult to define a linear connection between the mode of instruction of those baptized on Pentecost in Acts 2, that which is hinted at in the *Didache* (approximately the end of the first century) and the practices at the close of the second century. What we can say for sure is that there was a dramatic formalization and standardization in the teaching of candidates for baptism. Our best source for this is the *Apostolic Tradition* of Hippolytus[64] and *On Baptism* by Tertullian. By this time (near the end of the second century), the catachumen had a lengthy time of preparation before being immersed. The *Apostolic Tradition* suggested a three-year period of instruction. One can imagine this probationary stage serving more than one purpose. First, the moral convictions of the candidate could be well tested. Former prostitutes, actors in pagan plays, practitioners of magic arts, gladiators and so forth had to refrain from their former activities and means of employment this entire time. Joining the army was prohibited. Bear in mind that the church of the second century had quite strict (from our perspective) standards of morality and separation from the world. In addition, this lengthy time of examination was useful to prevent the entrance of young, impressionable believers who would later succumb to heretical teachers. Third, false converts—spies intent on persecuting the church—were not likely to pass this rigorous period of inspection. Remember that the catechumens were excluded from the communion service.

Baptisms generally were held off until Easter except in special cases such as imminent death. Baptism was preceded by appointed days of fasting, prayer, instruction and confession of sin. The day of the baptism began with prayer. Catechumens removed their clothing (which explains why male and female were baptized separately). Candidates made a final verbal renunciation of "the Devil, his pomp and his angels." They were anointed with oil. There was a series of questions, the creed was stated, and a bishop or elder laid hands on the one to be baptized. At this time, there was a triple immersion in the names of the Father, the Son and the Holy Spirit. After the baptism, there was an additional anointing with oil. Again, the bishop or presbyter laid hands on the one baptized. Tertullian (but not Hippolytus) tells us that this is when the Holy Spirit was received. This was followed by a special baptismal eucharist (eucharist being the common name at the time for the Lord's Supper). The *Apostolic Tradition* has this baptismal communion including a cup of water, symbolizing the washing of sins that had just occurred, as well as a cup of milk and honey, symbolizing the spiritual food the Jews ate while sojourning in the wilderness.

Baptism was by immersion, but some made accommodation for pouring in the case of those in a sickbed or on the point of death. Allowance for pouring, as previously noted, was made as early as the *Didache*. Baptism of children (not infants) was described by Hippolytus and discouraged by Tertullian. The very strong role for personal confession of faith in Jesus included in the ceremony precluded baptism of infants, at least for a time. Tertullian is the first we know to mention infant baptism. He acknowledged the existence of the practice in about AD 220, but he opposed it. By the middle of the third century we find both Origen and Cyprian of Carthage supporting infant baptism.

The doctrinal and practical implications of such a lengthy delay of baptism as well as the additions to biblical teaching of such practices as anointing with oil, laying on of hands and drinking of water as well as milk and honey is interesting to contemplate. It is easy to see that the anointing with oil and laying on of hands gave emphasis to the fact that the sinner was being cleansed of their sins. It is also possible to see how this increased pomp and ceremony may have detracted from attention to the importance of the individuals coming to faith in the blood of Jesus. Already by this time, baptisms were only done by bishops and presbyters (whose title morphed into the word priests) and the laying on of hands took on a spiritual significance. One can see already where this was to lead. Eventually, baptism was to become a sacrament that had no effect unless performed by an ordained priest.

Growth and Persecution

Two hallmarks of the first-century church were fantastic growth and the persecution that accompanied this growth. We will not have a lot to add to this here, as this continued in the second century. During the second century the growth was probably more in numbers than in geographic reach. We noted previously that by the end of the second century Christianity had at least a foothold in Britain, Germania, North Africa, the Mesopotamian territory of the Parthian empire and possibly even Armenia and Georgia. It is too early and there is too much doctrinal unity to speak of a separate church of the East at this time.

As a general rule, persecution against the Christian church was relatively mild, at least compared to what we will see in the third century. Of course, for the thousands of followers of Jesus martyred during the second century calling the persecution "mild" may not seem like an appropriate description. Our evidence is a bit thin, but the general impression one gets is that Trajan (98–117), Hadrian (117–138) and Antoninus Pius (138–161) did not purposefully attack the church. Instead, they seemed to want to minimize the persecution. Rather than promulgate a new basis for charges against those known as Christians, they simply continued the policy handed down to them, perhaps all the way back to Nero, at which time the charge against the believers was refusing to deny the name Christian.

A letter from Pliny the Younger, historian and governor of Bithynia to Trajan in 112, and Trajan's response will give a sense of the kinds of persecution and the legal status of the church in this period. Pliny inquired of Trajan what the official policy of the emperor was. Apparently, he had never taken part in legal proceedings against the sect. Perhaps his lack of knowledge of the procedures indicates that such legal procedures against Christians, though not rare, were also not exceedingly common. Pliny stated that the basis of any charge was holding to the name "Christian." In other words, the members of the church were not accused of sedition or treason, but of steadfast loyalty to Jesus, a man who had been executed by the Roman Empire for claiming to be king/messiah. Pliny reported to Trajan that his policy was to execute those brought before him who steadfastly held to their confession of Christ. Those who recanted and offered a prayer to the gods and incense to a statue of the emperor were released. Pliny said that denying the name of Christ and offering pagan sacrifice were "things which those who are really Christians cannot be made to do." In his reply, Trajan approved of the policy of his governor, adding that Christians were not to be sought out for punishment and that anonymous accusations were not to be pursued. Roman government did not include a public prosecutor. The policy, then, was consistent with the general situation in the empire, which was that in such cases, law was only resorted to when a citizen made formal charge to a magistrate. Another Roman policy was that only provincial governors could pronounce a death penalty. For this reason, the persecutions were concentrated in the provincial capitals. It was during the reign of Antoninus Pius that Polycarp was executed in Rome in 156.

The remarkable exception to the reticence on the part of Roman emperors in the second century to persecute the church was the reign of Marcus Aurelius (161–180). It is ironic that the most virulent persecution of the Christian church in the second century came from Aurelius, who was known for his piety and mildness in general. He was a Stoic philosopher in his own right and very well educated. The *Apology* of Justin Martyr was written during the reign of the philosopher-emperor. It indicates that those who attacked the church based their opposition at least in part on philosophical questions, which is consistent with the spirit of the age and what we know of Marcus Aurelius. Whether or not Justin's letter ever even reached Marcus Aurelius, we do not know, but one thing we know for sure is that Justin was martyred.

There was a major, albeit local persecution of the church in Lyons and the Rhone Valley (the southern part of modern France) in 177. We have the entire *Letter of the Churches of Vienne and Lyons* in Eusebius' *Ecclesiastical History* book V.1 to provide details of this intense attack on the church. The letter mentions "blows, plundering and robberies, stonings and imprisonments." The action of the government and the soldiers was dictated by the rage of an anti-Christian mob. Here we have reported the torture and execution of Blandina who, after she had experienced a full day of torture still declared, "I am a Christian, no wickedness is carried on by us." Sanctus experienced "beyond all measure and human power, the various torments devised by men," finally being accosted with "fastened red hot plates of brass to the most tender parts of his body." In the end, he simply declared "in the Roman tongue, 'I am a Christian.'" He was roasted on the iron chair. Certainly dozens but more likely hundreds were killed in this outbreak. Pothinus, the bishop of Lyons, was past ninety years of age and "very infirm in body," but his weakness did not spare him the fate of brutal beatings which led to his death. In this letter, the martyrs are called "wrestlers," as they wrestled with Satan.

Eusebius reports the reign of Commodus (180–192) was relatively mild, although a leading teacher in Rome, Appolonius, was accused and executed for the faith. Perhaps the most famous of what was to become known as the "Acts of the Martyrs" comes at the beginning of the third century in 203. It is *The Passion of Perpetua and Felicitas*. This is one of the earliest Latin sources we have. It describes the martyrdom of Perpetua, a daughter of the elite in Carthage, and her slave Felicitas. Perpetua was twenty-two years old and was nursing a child at the time of her arrest. She was still only a catachumen, although she was baptized before her execution. Felicitas gave birth while imprisoned, awaiting her execution at the hands of the Roman authorities. Part of the *Passion* is a diary of her experiences and the visions she had while in prison. This moving and emotional account must have served as a great motivation to the Christians at the time. A passage from Perpetua's diary in which her father passionately begs her to renounce her discipleship in order to save her life will give a sense of how emotional the letter is.

> "Father," said I, "do you see, let us say, this vessel lying here to be a little pitcher, or something else?" And he said, "I see it to be so." And I replied to him, "Can it be called by any other name than what it is?" And he said, "No." "Neither can I call myself anything else than what I am, a Christian."[65]

One aspect of the church in the second and even the early third century comes out strongly in this document. Both the church leaders and its members had a strong sense that the return of Jesus was imminent. All the way back to the writings of Paul, one gets the sense that the early church felt that the "second coming" of Jesus was to be in their generation. Some have given this out as evidence that the apostles were mistaken. If they personally believed this, then they apparently were mistaken, but as far as we know, none of the apostles publicly taught this while claiming inspiration. Jesus did not say when he would come back. He even admonished his followers that anyone who says they know the day or the hour is to be ignored. Presumably the persecutions of the church helped to maintain this sense that the last days were about to end. The editor who wrote the preface to *Perpetua and Felicitas* felt that the visions of Perpetua were evidence that the end of the last days were upon the church.

Another novel tendency in the church at the end of the second century is revealed by this pious letter. This is the honoring of the martyrs above other Christians. By the end of the second century the word "saint" was applied, not to Christians in general (which is the biblical use of the word) but to the martyrs (literally witnesses), the confessors (those who were persecuted and confessed Jesus, but were not killed) and very godly bishops and presbyters. It is too early at this point to describe this as a cult of the saints, but we can see the beginnings of this trend in the Acts of Perpetua and Felicitas:

And we therefore, what we have heard and handled, declare also to you, brethren and little children, that as well you who were concerned in these matters may be reminded of them again to the glory of the Lord, as that you who know them by report may have communion with the blessed martyrs, and through them with the Lord Jesus Christ, to whom be glory and honor, for ever and ever. Amen.

Here we can see that already Christians were being taught that through the martyrs, one could have a more profound communion with Jesus Christ.

Conclusion

This chapter has covered developments in the Christian church from approximately AD 95–200. We have passed from the time of the apostles and their close associates to a time when memory of those who had met disciples who knew the apostles was passing away. The second century was a time of great growth and many victories for the cause of Christ. Persecution was significant, for sure, but if anything this seemed to purify and strengthen the church rather than undermine it. Although the church was still fairly small numerically compared to the population of the entire Roman Empire, it had become like a leaven that was present in the entire loaf. Basic facts about the Christians, such as their refusal to take part in rites normal to the Roman society and their amazing love for each other and deeds to help the poor and oppressed, were becoming a matter of common knowledge in the empire. The church began to defend its teaching, not to its Jewish competitors, but to the Greek and even to the Roman world. From the point of view of the church fathers at this time, the biggest threat to the legacy of Jesus Christ was from false teachers. They may well have been right, but in our study of these times, through the lens of history, we discover that what seemed like a practical and reasonable expedient in response to these attacks on the Christian faith was often a double-edged sword. Some of the trends of the day, created in response to the pressure of opponents to biblical Christianity, became the seeds of degradation of the primitive Christian faith. The implications, subtle in the second century, will become profound in the time leading up to the first general council of the church in Nicaea. It is to this pivotal chapter in Christian church history that we now turn.

CHAPTER NOTES:

1. Athanasius, *Festal Letters*, 25.
2. Eusebius, *Ecclesiastical History*, III.25.4.
3. Clement of Alexandria, *Stromateus*, I.20.100.
4. Using a translation from Maxwell Staniforth, *Early Christian Writings* (New York: Penguin Books, 1982).
5. There is a book known as 2 Clement. This book was probably not written by Clement of Rome and it was not even a letter, but rather a transcribed sermon from about the 140s AD.
6. Eusebius, *Ecclesiastical History*, III.15, 16.
7. Irenaeus, *Against Heresies*, III.3.
8. Translation from Maxwell Staniforth, *Early Christian Writings* (New York: Penguin Books, 1982).
9. This and other translations from the letters of Ignatius are taken from Cyril C. Richardson, *Early Christian Fathers* (New York: The Macmillan Company, 1970).
10. Irenaeus, *Against Heresies*, III.3.4.
11. Tertullian, *Praescript*, 32.
12. Irenaeus, *Against Heresies*, III.3.4; also mentioned in *Eusebius Ecclesiastical History*, V.20.4–8.
13. Eusebius, *Ecclesiastical History*, IV.14.7.
14. The *Letter of Polycarp to the Philippians*, 3, taken from the translation of Maxwell Staniforth, *Early Christian Writings*, (New York: Penguin Books, 1982).
15. All quotes from the *Martyrdom of Polycarp* are from Maxwell Staniforth, *Early Christian Writings* (New York: Penguin Books, 1982).

16. Translations from the Second Letter of Clement are taken from Cyril C. Richardson, *Early Christian Fathers* (New York: The Macmillan Company, 1970).

17. Celsus, *The True Doctrine: A Discourse Against the Christians*, translated by R. Joseph Hoffman (New York: Oxford University Press, 1987), p. 116.

18. Ibid., p. 78.

19. Justin, Martyr, *First Apology of Justin*, 12, translation from Cyril C. Richardson, *Early Christian Fathers* (New York: The Macmillan Company, 1970).

20. Ibid., 14.

21. Ibid., 46.

22. Ibid., 44.

23. Justin, *The Second Apology of Justin*, 13, translation taken from Roger E. Olson, *The Story of Christian Theology* (Downers Grove, IL: InterVarsity Press, 1999).

24. Eusebius, *Ecclesiastical History*, IV.16.7–9.

25. Athenagoras, *A Plea Regarding Christians*, 3, translated by Cyril C. Richardson, *Early Christian Fathers* (New York: The Macmillan Company, 1970).

26. Ibid., 10.

27. Ibid., 1.

28. Ibid., 34.

29. Translation taken from *National Geographic*, May 2006, p 56, emphasis added

30. Ibid., p 47.

31. As cited by Eusebius, *Ecclesiastical History*, II.13.2.

32. Eusebius, *Ecclesiastical History*, II.1.11–12.

33. Unknown author, *The Martyrdom of Polycarp*, 23.3.

34. Eusebius, *Ecclesiastical History*, IV.11.1.

35. Tertullian, *Adversus Valentinianus*, 4.

36. Epiphanius, *Heresies*, xlvii.11.

37. Didymus, *On the Trinity*, III.41.

38. Epiphanius, *Heresies*, xlvii.11.

39. The modern church is not without its Montanus, Maximilla and Prisca. We have Joseph Smith, Mary Baker Eddy and Ellen G. White, all of whom claimed to be prophets, to offer new revelation—to be the direct spokesperson for God. Both Eddy and White had a kind of ecstatic utterance. We should assume that they will not be the last.

40. Eusebius, *Ecclesiastical History*, IV.18.8.

41. Ibid., IV.3.2.

42. Irenaeus, *Against Heresies*.

43. Irenaeus, *Against Heresies*, I.10.2, translation by Cyril C. Richardson, *Early Christian Fathers* (New York: The Macmillan Company, 1970). Citations of Irenaeus below are from the same translation.

44. Ibid., III.2.1.

45. Ibid., III.4.1–2.

46. Ibid., III.4.1.

47. Ibid., III.4.3.

48. Ibid., III.11.4

49. Blessed are they who, placing their trust in the cross, have gone down into the water... We indeed descend into the water full of sins and defilement. However, we come up, bearing fruit in our heart, having the fear [of God] and the trust in Jesus in our spirit (*Epistle of Barnabas*).

Before a man bears the name of the Son of God, he is dead. But when he receives the seal, he lays aside his deadness and obtains life. The seal, then, is the water. They descend into the water dead, and they arise alive (*Shepherd of Hermas*).

As many as are persuaded and believe that what we teach and say is true, and undertake to be able to live accordingly, are instructed to pray and to entreat God with fasting, for the remission of their past sins. The rest of us pray and fast with them. They are brought by us where there is water, and are regenerated in the same manner in which we were regenerated ourselves. They there receive the washing with water (Justin Martyr, *First Apology*).

Now, the teaching is laid down that "without baptism, salvation is attainable by no one." This is based primarily on the ground of that declaration of the Lord, who says, "Unless one is born of water he has not life." However, when this is laid down, there immediately arise scrupulous (or rather, audacious) doubts on the part of some (Tertullian).

50. Irenaeus, *Against Heresies*, I.3.4–6.

51. Hans von Campenhausen *The Formation of the Christian Bible*, translated by J. A. Baker (Philadelphia: Fortress Press, 1972), p. 327.

52. Irenaeus, *Against Heresies*, III.4.2.

53. Ibid., V.19.1.

54. Tertullian, *The Shows*, 16, translation from David Bercot, *A Glimpse of Early Christian Life* (Tyler, TX: Scroll Publishing, 1991).

55. It is worth noting that even in the fourth and fifth centuries, when Christians serving in the military became rather common, believers were still required to make a confession and acknowledge their sin when they killed their enemies in the line of duty. The idea of just war for God was to remain an idea for the distant future.

56. Biblical evidence that the love feast was a common part of Christian worship includes Acts 20:11, 1 Corinthians 11:17–34, which is decisive that this was an actual meal, and Jude 12.

57. And we too rejoice in celebrating the eighth day; because that was when Jesus rose from the dead (*Epistle of Barnabas*, 15).

58. Greet also the church that meets at their house (Romans 16:5).

59. Whether it was by design, i.e. part of God's plan for his people to meet in house churches, or an expedient is not a small point. Some have argued that house churches are the "biblical" way to do church. I will argue that this is not the case. Unless we can find direct evidence to the contrary, the simple fact that in most cases the early church met in smaller groups is not prescriptive for today. What is prescriptive is that however the meetings of the church today are designed, the family-like, relational, one-another, Jesus-honoring loving relationships between those in the church must be fostered and maintained.

60. Irenaeus, *Against Heresies*, IV.18.5.

61. Clement of Alexandria, *The Instructor*, III.11.

62. Eusebius, *Ecclesiastical History*, V.24.

63. Adapted from the reconstruction of Hans Lietzmann, H. Lietzmann, *The Founding of the Church Universal*, trans. B. L. Woolf (New York: Scribners, 1938).

64. This letter is ascribed to Hippolytus of Rome in about 215. It reflects practices from the late second century or perhaps even earlier as Hippolytus wrote in order to defend traditional practices against what he saw as innovations in his time.

65. Perpetua, *The Passion of Perpetua and Felicitas*, I.1; this and other quotes taken from a translation by Roberts-Donaldson at www.earlychristianwritings.com.

CHAPTER THREE
A STORM OF PERSECUTION YIELDS
TO TOLERATION OF CHRISTIANITY
AD 200–325

The third and early fourth centuries of the present era was the time of by far the greatest persecution of the Christian church. Many who are not initiated in the facts of church history have the mistaken notion that Nero and Domitian were the greatest persecutors of Christianity. This is far from the truth. Emperors such as Diocletian, Decius and Valerian attempted through an absolutely vicious campaign to completely suppress the Christian church as a force within the Roman Empire. Those experiencing the results of the edicts of Diocletian or Decius must have felt that their very existence as an organized family of followers of Christ was at stake. Many fled to the desert. Even more apostatized from the faith. Many thousands were executed. In some sense, even more problematic for the church were the thousands who yielded under persecution but who later, in times of relative peace, relented and wanted to return to the fold. Of course, we have the advantage of knowing the end of this story. Our present chapter includes what seemed at the time the happiest possible ending with the Edict of Milan in 312, providing official government toleration of Christianity.

Of course, persecution and later toleration are not the only important historical trends we will follow in this seminal period in church history. In fact, this chapter does not end with the Edict of Milan. Instead, we end the present chapter with what is now considered by most to be the first general council of the Christian church at Nicaea in 325. This council was called by Emperor Constantine. For us the fact that Constantine (rather than the bishops) called this council will at least symbolically be a very important point of departure. Such demarcations are always too arbitrary, but with the Council of Nicaea, we will mark the end of the period of the primitive church fathers and the beginning of what came to be known as Christendom. This was the joining of governmental and spiritual power—the marriage of church and state—which was to be the dominant political religious and cultural force in Europe for well over one thousand years.

That is not all. The second century is the time of the first systematic Christian theologians. The Nicene Creed could not have been written at the end of this period if not for the systematizing of Christian theology by the great authors and teachers of this era such as Tertullian, Clement of Alexandria, Origen and Cyprian. In the long run, one can argue that the work and writings of these great church fathers is the most important legacy of the third century of the Christian faith. This, too, is the period when asceticism became a small but growing movement within Christianity. Thousands fled the growing worldliness in the church to a life of total separation from the world in the desert. It is also a time when the dramatic distinction between the Western and Eastern churches emerged. The West, with its reliance on Latin as its principle language and its largely Roman culture and mindset, began to drift doctrinally and theologically from the Eastern Church, which remained Greek both linguistically and culturally.

Important Church Fathers in the Early Third Century

Church Father	Date	Location	Chief Importance
Tertullian	157–220	Carthage	First Latin father, first to use the word trinity
Clement of Alexandria	152–215	Alexandria	"Plundered the Egyptians" by justifying Greek and Christian philosophy
Origin	185–254	Alexandria, Caesarea	Apologist, wrote *Against Celsus*; most influential theologian in the East before Nicaea
Cyprian	200–258	Carthage	Defined church organization

The Church Grows in Numbers and Influence, Is Perceived as a Threat, and Is Persecuted

We will skip for now the crucial role Tertullian and Clement of Alexandria played in the early third century and focus instead on the phenomenal growth of the church and the persecution that it brought in the second half of the third century and the first decade of the fourth. As in the second century, growth of the church in the third century was more numerical than geographical.

Relatively small outposts in Spain, North Africa, Britannia, Germania, Illyricum, Phrygia (central Asia Minor), Ethiopia and Syria became larger churches with their own bishops. Tertullian[1] mentions Christians in Britain in the early third century. We have reports of bishops in Aquitania, Toulouse, Vienne, Rheims, Bordeaux, Paris and Metz (all in Gaul of Germania) from the third century. During the second and third centuries, North Africa, centered around Carthage, became one of the most important strongholds of the church. It was here rather than in Rome where Latin first replaced Greek as the primary local language of the church. Carthage and North Africa were the home of Tertullian, Cyprian and later, Augustine. Rome was the source of important leaders of the church, but not of influential writers and Christian intellectuals.

Although our records are scanty, the exception to this rule of numerical rather than geographic growth seems to have been in the East. This is the only place where Christianity had spread outside the borders of the Roman Empire. From a foothold in Edessa (northwest Mesopotamia) at the end of the first century, the faith spread to the north and east. It may have been helpful to this process that Edessa passed back and forth between Roman and Parthian control. In any case, here the language of the church was Syriac rather than Greek. Some historians[2] have proposed that Edessa may have been the first city to be predominantly Christian, by as early as the third century. It was at this time that the Parthian Empire fell apart. Perhaps the lack of a strong empire in the region allowed Christianity to spread to the East. By 225 more than twenty bishoprics (i.e. churches with a bishop as their head) were in place in Mesopotamia and the Western part of Persia.[3] Churches were known in Adiabene, near the Caspian Mountains and on the Bahrein Islands in the Persian Gulf. It is in the city of Dura-Europos, on the Tigris River, that the first building dedicated to use as a place of Christian worship has been identified. It had been used for worship at least since 232. There is some reasonably good evidence that Christianity even reached as far as Bactria (present-day Afghanistan) and India by the third century. Reports in Christian literature of the apostles Thomas and Bartholomew bringing the gospel to India and Southern Arabia respectively are possibly true, but not sufficiently supported by hard evidence. In any case, it seems that in the third century the missionary spirit was stronger in these churches in the East than in the Greek or Latin churches.

The first state to officially accept Christianity as its religion was Armenia. The ancient country of Armenia served as a buffer state between Parthia and the Roman Empire. It was located in present-day northeastern Turkey, Armenia and northwest Iraq. Christianity entered Armenia by the late second century or earlier. Records are a bit sketchy, but apparently the Armenian ruler

Tradt (Tiridates to the Romans) converted in the late third century. He was influenced by the Christian missionary Gregory "the Illuminator." It is possible that Tiridates, like Constantine after him, was at least partially influenced to convert for political reasons. By this time a new and vigorous dynasty, the Sassanids, had been established in Persia. Sassanid power was accompanied by the Persian state religion, Zoroastrianism. Tiridates may have wanted to counteract Persian political power by being baptized into this non-Persian religion. As was later the case with the conversion of Constantine, the people of Armenia were brought into the Christian fold only gradually. Even when people were baptized *en masse*, without a true Christian conversion of the heart and mind they remained essentially pagan in mindset for a long time.

In addition, Christianity spread across the Caucuses in the third century to what eventually became the Christian country of Georgia. Native Georgian claims that Andrew passed through here are not to be believed, but by the late third century there is good evidence of a Christian church in a country that was later to become a bastion of Christianity against the onslaught of Islam. A question to remain for a future chapter is why did Christianity, which spread so quickly into Central and South Asia, fail to take root there and why did it ultimately virtually disappear?

But back to the Roman Empire and to our story of growth and persecution. Statistics, of course, are not possible to be obtained. It was not in the spirit of the time to collect detailed data on religious affiliation. However, a general picture can be gleaned from Christian and non-Christian sources. By the middle of the third century, the Christian faith was beginning to be a quite significant proportion of the total population. This was especially true in Asia Minor, Syria in the area around Antioch, Egypt and the region of Alexandria, and in North Africa around Carthage. This growth was enabled at least in part because of a time of relative peace for the church. Under Septimus Severus (193–211) there were some fairly significant persecutions on an order similar to those during the reign of Marcus Aurelius. Initially the rule of Severus was actually favorable to Christianity. He had many Christians in his personal household. There was a rumor that he was healed miraculously through the help of a Christian slave. His son and future emperor Caracalla was raised by a Christian nurse.[4] For unknown reasons his lenient policy changed in 202. He outlawed conversions to Judaism and Christianity. One example of the results of persecution at this time is the martyrdom of Perpetua and Felicitas, which was already described. Another is the death of Leonides, the father of Origen, who was martyred during the persecution under Severus in 202–203. Following the severe reign of Severus, between 211 and 250, there was an extended period of peace for the church. At this time, small buildings for

Christian worship began to emerge (not to be confused with the large basilicas built under Constantine). A number of prominent converts were brought to the faith. The emperor Philip the Arabian (244–249) was so favorable in his policy to the church that Eusebius (probably falsely) thought him to be a Christian.[5]

All this changed in the most dramatic fashion under the emperor Decius (249–251). He took the imperial mantle in October 249. By late December 249 or very early in the year 250, he issued edicts that radically changed the relationship between the Roman state and the Christian church. A persecution like no other the church had ever experienced ensued. Decius adopted a policy that seemed intent on completely destroying Christianity's influence within the Roman Empire. He had the chief bishops of the church arrested in all the cities. He is the first emperor who ordered that all Roman citizens must make a public sacrifice to the gods of Rome, to include the burning of incense, the pouring of an offering to the god of Rome and the sharing in meat sacrificed to an idol. Those who did so were given a certificate testifying to their compliance. Those who refused were subject to dismissal from their jobs, arrest, exile and execution. The church, accustomed to relatively favorable treatment, was not prepared for this vicious attack. Great numbers, perhaps the majority who were put to the question, publicly denied their faith. Some did so immediately, others only after a period of imprisonment or torture.[6] To all outward appearances, this was a time of great defeat for the Christian church.

Why? Why did Decius take on this policy? To the church it must have seemed very sudden and unexpected. One explanation can be found in the political situation in the Roman Empire. Through all of the second century and even well into the third, the empire had experienced a time of relative prosperity and peace. The "barbarians" were generally either repulsed in the North and the Northeast or were successfully incorporated into the empire. A tense peace was generally maintained with the chief enemy to the East, Parthia. The fortunes of Rome appeared to turn in the middle of the third century. Famines became more common. Although likely not true, people became convinced it was a time of more earthquakes and other natural disasters. Military defeats occurred at the hands of Germanic tribes in the North and the Goths in the Northeast, not a familiar thing for the Romans. The emperors at this time were often military leaders who had risen through the ranks. As political disasters mounted for the empire, unity of religion seemed to be more crucial to the emperors. Decius in particular wanted to inspire the Romans to return to an earlier greatness that included a stronger reverence for the specifically Roman pagan gods. Perhaps the problems in the empire were due to laxity in sacrificing to these gods. That is how Decius perceived the situation. The stubbornness of the Christian church really stuck out here. Epicureans, Stoics, Neoplatonists and Manichaeans could fairly easily accommodate a bit of Roman pagan religion as part of their practice. Their beliefs were largely philosophical, not religious. It was a time of much syncretistic thinking about religion. This was certainly not the case with the Christians. With the defeat of the Bar Kochba rebellion in AD 138 and the scattering of the Jews throughout the empire, Christians became the only obvious target as a religious scapegoat. When things go very badly for a political state, one of the most common tactics of the leaders is to point the finger of blame at a group that is not well integrated into the society. Unfortunately, history tells us that the majority usually go along easily enough with the persecution of the out-group. This is what happened to the Christian church at the time of Emperor Decius.

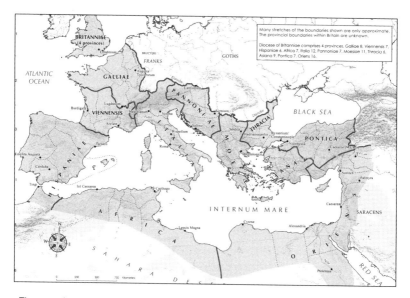

The map shows the domination and influence of the Roman Empire during the time of the Roman Caesar, Emperor Decius.

The Old Testament:
Relying on God in Times of Persecution

God did not leave his people unprepared for the great persecutions in the first three centuries. In the Book of Daniel he left wonderful examples of men of faith bearing up under the worst persecution. Shadrach, Meshach, Abednego and Daniel were real people who lived real lives. Even as youths, they held up despite great temptation to compromise their faith. Nebuchadnezzar tempted them with riches and worldly honor, but Daniel and his friends resolved not to defile themselves (Daniel 1:8). Shadrach, Meshach and Abednego refused to bow to an idol, even upon pain of death in a fiery furnace. "If we are thrown into the blazing furnace, the God we serve is able to save us from it, and he will rescue us from your hand, O king. But even if he does not, we want you to know, O king, that we will not serve your gods or worship the image of gold you have set up" (Daniel 3:17–18). The faith of these youths, separated from family and fellowship, must have served as a tremendous encouragement to the Christians when asked to make a similar sort of compromise during the reign of Diocletian. Being offered the third place in the kingdom by Belshazzar held no attraction to Daniel. "You may keep your gifts for yourself and give your rewards to someone else" (Daniel 5:17). Daniel was unfazed when commanded not to worship his God. He prayed, as usual, with the windows open, which resulted in a night in the lion's den.

These are not just entertaining stories. They are intended by God to serve as an example to those who are being tempted to compromise their convictions under pressure from pagan religion or political opposition. They are intended to encourage those who will be persecuted to the point of death for their faith. How were Daniel and his friends able to remain faithful despite a relatively weak support system? They believed that God is in control, even when the circumstances seemed impossibly dire: "The God we serve is able." "There is a God in heaven who reveals mysteries" (Daniel 2:28).

The prophecies in Daniel served the purpose of helping to encourage the Jews and later the church when suffering extreme attacks from pagan enemies. The Jews suffered the worst persecution in their long and difficult history under Antiochus Epiphanes in 167–164 BC. The Greek king sacrificed pigs in the temple, smearing defiled blood all over the holy things. He put a statue of Zeus in the Holy of Holies—right where the cherubim were placed—and the face on the statue was that of Antiochus. This desecration of the temple was the "abomination that causes desolation" spoken of through Daniel. Sacrifice to God was outlawed. Those who circumcised their sons were threatened with the execution, first of their child, then of their wife, then of themselves. All of these things are recorded in the *Histories of the Jews* by Josephus, as well as in I and II Maccabees, in the Old Testament Apocrypha. Many of the Jews compromised their faith. They were willing to be half Jewish and half Greek. Only a small remnant remained faithful and refused to compromise their holiness and convictions about righteousness.

All these things were prophesied in minute detail by Daniel, almost four hundred years before the events. He prophesied of Antiochus that he would "set [him]self up to be as great as the Prince of the host" and that he would take away the daily sacrifice and bring the sanctuary low (Daniel 8:11). Why did all this happen? Was it because God had lost control of the situation? Absolutely not! It happened "because of rebellion" of God's people (Daniel 8:12). It happened so that God's people "may be refined, purified and made spotless until the time of the end, for it will come at the appointed time." As Daniel prophesied, "some of the wise will stumble" (Daniel 11:35). Many seemingly faithful Jews lost their faith in God. However, the true believers did not compromise, no matter the cost. The parallels to what happened under the persecutions of Decius and Diocletian are uncanny.

What must have been encouraging to the church is that God had prophesied that the persecution would only be for a limited time, after which God would judge the enemies of his people. In fact, he was quite specific. It was to last for "2300 evenings and mornings; then the sanctuary will be reconsecrated"(Daniel 8:14). This is exactly what happened. The abomination of desolation happened in November 167 BC. On December 25, 164 BC—1150 days later—the troops of Antiochus were defeated by the Jewish army under Judas Maccabeus and the temple was rededicated. This event is still celebrated by the Jews in the holiday known as Hanukkah. God foretold all these persecutions and the subsequent victory for God's people hundreds of years before the events. We can assume that the Jews in the time of Antiochus took courage from the book of Daniel. They understood that God is in control, even in times of great persecution—that God can use such struggles to purify and strengthen his people. In fact, this is precisely what occurred. In the immediate aftermath of the great persecutions, the Jewish kingdom had a renaissance of faithfulness to God under the Hasidim.

God also prophesied through Daniel the persecution of the early church. Daniel 7 has a vision of the eleventh king of Rome. He will be a boastful king who will change the set times and laws. He will speak against the Most High and oppress his saints. The saints will be handed over to him for a time, times and half a time. In other words, the persecution will be temporary (paraphrasing Daniel 7:23–25). Naturally, given the track record of Daniel, this is precisely what happened. The eleventh king of Rome was Domitian. His was the first systematic persecution of the saints. He demanded to be addressed as "my Lord God Domitian." He changed the set times, changing October and November to Domitianus and Germanicus (his middle name). He overturned Roman law as well, setting up his own Domitian law, exactly as foretold by Daniel. What is the point of all this? God wants to assure us about those who persecute his people. He says of the Roman persecutor, "The court will sit, and his power will be taken away and completely destroyed forever" (Daniel 7:26). Yes, there will be persecution. It will get intense. This does not mean that God is not in control. God rules the nations. No matter the temptation, no matter the intimidation, the saints who trust in their God will be vindicated in the end.

We can assume that the early Christians were well aware of the prophecies in Daniel. We can also assume that they could count to eleven. The book of Daniel served as a great encouragement to remain faithful in the face of withering persecution.

It can serve the same purpose for the church today. I have traveled to many countries, including ones in which the Christian message is not welcomed. I have shared fellowship with brothers and sisters who have been beaten for their faith—some of them more than once. A sister once shared about a brother who was thrown in jail for studying the Bible with her. When I asked the brother about the story later, he responded, "Which time was that?" I have shared with sisters in Christ who have had their lives threatened, yet they refused to compromise their faith.

How should the church respond to attacks from religious or political opposition? We should respond as did Daniel, Shadrach, Meshach and Abednego. We should not attack our attacker. We should trust in the God who is able. We should maintain our righteous example no matter the pressure to compromise. God is in control. We should refuse to defile

> ourselves with the things of the world. We should trust in our God for
> salvation. We should remember that in the end, the court will sit, and the
> power of those who oppose our message will be destroyed forever.

The church must have felt a sense of relief and even vindication when Decius was killed in battle with the Goths in 251. Despite the attacks, or perhaps because of them, there was actually a renewed vigor in the churches. Bishops were appointed to replace those who had been martyred and exiles returned to the cities. Unfortunately, the death of Decius brought only a relatively brief respite to the intense attacks on the church. The political situation for the empire remained the same. The reign of Valerian (253–260) began with tolerance. During this time a sharp disagreement came to the fore in the church. What to do with those who had lapsed in their faith during the persecution and who had made a sacrifice? Could they be readmitted to fellowship? Was a period of works of penitence required? Could those who had lapsed ever be accepted as leaders in the church again? This became a key issue for the rest of the third and well into the fourth century. Such issues of church discipline and standards of discipleship are clearly relevant today. Much perspective can be gained as we look at how the third-century church approached these issues. Two schismatic groups arose, largely over this dispute. One was the Novatians and the other was the Donatists. The Donatist controversy was to serve a principal role in the formation of the theology of Augustine. We will get back to the Novatians and the Donatists, but let us return to the story of persecutions and times of relative peace for the church.

There were renewed plagues and further defeats at the hands of the barbarians on the frontiers. Whether this caused Valerian to change his attitude toward the church we cannot know, but in any case, in 257 he began a fresh and even more violent attack on the church than that of Decius. Valerian went beyond the edicts of his predecessor. He ordered the most powerful bishops in the church to travel to Rome to give public honor to the Roman gods. Those who refused were exiled or killed. Followers of the Christian cult were warned that execution awaited those who met in churches or Christian cemeteries. A second edict promulgated by Valerian in 258 required that those bishops, presbyters (priests) and deacons arrested in 257 were to be executed. Christian members of the imperial household were to suffer confiscation of their goods and be sent into slavery. The edicts of Decius had not worked, as the church was actually strengthened. Noting this, Valerian hoped to behead the church. Cyprian, the bishop of Carthage, had fled to the desert in 250, not out of fear for his personal safety, but because the church begged him to do so. He was arrested in 257 and martyred in 258. Sixtus, the bishop of Rome, was captured and executed along with four of his deacons.[7] The bishop of Tarragona, the Roman capital of Spain, was burned at the stake. The list could continue for some time. The suffering of the church and especially its leaders continued until the capture of Valerius by the Sassanids in 260.

Again, a period of relative toleration ensued, initiated by Gallienus, the son of Valerian. Gallienus was a Neoplatonist and an enthusiast of Plotinus, the leading teacher of this philosophy. He put forth an edict of tolerance for Christianity (not to be confused with the Edict of Toleration in 312). The next forty-three years was another period of relative peace for the church, at least from their Roman persecutor. Spotty persecutions continued and a number of martyrdoms are reported, but these were the exception, not the rule. The controversy over how to deal with the lapsed did not lapse. Despite these issues, the church seemed to emerge from persecution stronger than ever. Eusebius reports that in some cities, Christians made up a majority of the council. "Spacious churches" were erected in many cities.[8] A brief respite of relative political and economic prosperity for the empire ensued. The reign of Diocletian (284–305) was particularly auspicious as this great emperor restored order and vigor to the empire.

In this period of relative peace Christians probably reached a majority in some regions. The church was now the most powerful group in the empire outside of the Roman government and armies. Such power naturally led to suspicion and jealousy. Near the end of his reign, Diocletian suddenly completely reversed his policy of tolerance. Some believe he did so reluctantly, under pressure from his subordinate and the future emperor of the East, Galerius. Galerius was an ardent pagan. In any case, in 303 Diocletian published an edict calling for the destruction of all the Christian churches, burning of all copies of the Christian Scriptures, and the removal of all followers of Jesus from places of power in the Roman state. Soon, this order was followed by another. Now all the rulers of the church were to be imprisoned. A third edict later ordered those who refused to renounce their faith to be tortured. Many, of course, died under torture. Eusebius recorded all these edicts for us.[9] Bear in mind that at this point in our history he is an eyewitness to the events of this persecution, already being an important figure in the church hierarchy.

In 305, Diocletian willingly (as far as we know) stepped down from the role of emperor, handing off power to co-emperors Galerius in the East and Constantius in the West. Galerius pursued the persecution of the church ferociously, while Contantius did so only halfheartedly. We have detailed accounts of the persecutions of Diocletian and Galerius from both Eusebius and Lactantius.[10] Eusebius saw with his own eyes churches being torn down, Scriptures burned and Christians given to wild beasts.[11] In one case, the beasts refused to prey upon the Christians but attacked those who goaded them. Entire towns in Asia Minor were surrounded and burned to the ground, killing all inhabitants.[12] This was the most intense and widespread of all the Roman persecutions. Many refused to deny their Lord under the most horrendous circumstances. Against the advice of their leaders, some came forward of their own accord and suffered martyrdom. As in the persecutions under Decius and Valerian, many could not stand the test and apostasized.

The politics in Rome at this time are confusing, as up to four men ruled parts of the empire at one time. When Constantius died in 306 his son Constantine took his place in Gaul, Spain and Britain, continuing his father's lenient stance toward the church. Constantine is the hero of Eusebius' *Ecclesiastical History*, and the one to whom principal credit is given for legalizing Christianity and making Rome an officially Christian state. It was not until 323 that he overcame his rivals and gained power over the entire empire. Constantine took Rome from Maxentius in 312. Intense persecution continued in the East under Galerius until 311, and under his successor in the East, Licinius. The persecution in the East lasted for a total of ten years.

A culminating event in the history of Christianity was the so-called Edict of Milan published by Constantine in 313. Feeling sufficiently strong after defeating Maxentius he gave full legal status to the Christians, restored to them their properties and legalized Christian conversion. Licinius acceded to this decree in his territories in the East, bringing a virtual end to persecution of the Christian church under Roman rule. It is difficult to overstate the implications of what happened under the reign of Constantine. For better or for worse, the entire course of the history of Christianity (ignoring the church of the East for a moment) was irrevocably and radically shifted. The career of Constantine marks quite neatly the beginning of Christendom and the end of the second phase of the history of the Christian church (the first two being the apostolic age and the age of the persecuted church and the church fathers).

Why did the leaders of the Roman Empire, even those who were at heart fully pagan, give up the policy of trying to defeat Christianity? Even Galerius and Maxentius agreed to legalize or at least tolerate this unpopular religion. Unlike Constantine, neither was personally supportive of this outsider group. Although still a decided minority, the church had become the single most significant force in the empire outside the state. Competitors had two choices. They could either see this power as a threat and try to defeat it, or they could work with it. Bottom line, the policy of persecution did not work. Cutting off the head resulted in new and often even more vigorous bishops and other church leaders coming forward. Notable intellectuals and philosophers continued to embrace this teaching despite the persecution. As Tertullian said, "The more we are cut down by you, the more in number we grow; the blood of the martyrs is seed."[13] Whether Constantine got fully behind the church because he came to faith in Jesus or simply as a political expedient will be debated indefinitely. No doubt, his sponsorship of Christian institutions was decisive, but it is likely that even without this support, the empire probably would have come to terms with Christianity eventually. Persecution did not have the desired effect of slowing the advance of this radical new teaching.

The natural thing to do at this point is to offer a biography of Constantine, but we will not do this now as we have gotten ahead of ourselves. Having covered the political history of the church up to the Edict of Milan in 313, we will return all the way back to the beginning of the third century and trace the course of Christian theology, of internal victories and struggles, the schisms of the Novatians and the Donatists, and the life of the Christian church in the third century. The great figures during this time will be Tertullian of Carthage, Clement and Origen of Alexandria and Cyprian of Carthage. Clement and Origen will personify for us changes and developments in the Greek East, while Tertullian and Cyprian will represent developments in the Roman West in the third century.

Tertullian: The First Great Teacher in the West

What has Athens to do with Jerusalem?
—Tertullian of Carthage

Tertullian is the great writer, teacher, apologist and theologian of the Western church at the end of the second and beginning of the third century. He is arguably the first influential leader we can label as Western. Up until this time, the language of the church, even in Rome, Gaul and Spain, had been principally Greek. Irenaeus ministered in Lyons, but he was Greek in language and temperament. An overarching theme for the next three chapters will be the division between the Eastern and Western churches. Language— Latin versus Greek—will be significant, but ultimately it will not be the chief distinction. We will see a growing division in outlook, emphasis, doctrine and theology. The West emphasized hierarchy and organization. The East emphasized philosophy and theology. The West was concerned with doctrine. The East was concerned with religious experience. The West was practical. The East was mystical. In essence, this is the distinction between the Greek/

Hellenistic mindset and that of Rome, and with it Gaul, Spain and North Africa. As we look at the life and teaching of Tertullian, and as we compare him to Clement and Origen, we will see this distinction already fully realized both in their theology and in the practical Christian issues they emphasized.

Most of the readers of this book are Western in their mindset. The author counts himself in this group. We are prejudiced in favor of our view of things. We, too, tend toward the practical and show concern over doctrine rather than theology. We are more focused on being right than on a personal, mystical experience of God. We are absolutely perplexed as to how our Greek, Russian or Syrian Orthodox friends can find their version of Christianity fulfilling. Their worship services are a complete enigma for us. I would like to propose that we have much to learn from the Eastern way of thinking about Christianity. Experiencing the divine is a key aspect of biblical Christianity. God is to be worshipped in spirit and in truth. Perhaps we need to reconsider our definition of "in spirit" in this quote from Jesus (John 4:24). One can make a strong argument that the mindset in the primitive church was more Eastern than Western. Not that we will necessarily join an Eastern Orthodox church, but we should try to understand their experience and incorporate some of their ways of thinking into our own philosophy of how to experience a relationship with God through Jesus Christ.

But back to the subject at hand. Tertullian was born in Carthage around AD 157. He was trained as a lawyer and, though Latin in language and mindset, he was well acquainted with the Greek philosophers. He became a Christian at a relatively advanced age for that time, being baptized some time after the year 190. From the time of his conversion he rose rapidly in influence as a writer. He devoted his considerable skill in rhetoric as a lawyer to defending and explaining the Christian faith. He was married and may have served as an elder in Carthage. One way of thinking about Tertullian and his legacy is as a "Christian conservative." At risk of applying a modern label anachronistically, we can see Tertullian as representing the conservative point of view and his orthodox counterpoints Clement and Origen as "liberals." It is probably more useful to think of Tertullian as representing the Roman West versus the Greek East. As with all human beings, labels can be helpful, but in the end do not explain the person. This is particularly true with Tertullian, who was a complex person.

One piece of evidence for his moral conservatism is that in his later career Tertullian swung all the way toward the Montanist sect, especially after 207. Remember that this group was not necessarily heretical in its theology (although some would have labeled it that way) but the Montanists emphasized a stricter moral position and a more experiential spiritual life than did the mainstream church. The Montanists were among the first to voluntarily seek out martyrdom in the persecutions of Decius and Valerian. They denied the possibility of forgiveness of certain sins for Christians, even upon repentance. Their stricter moral stance was very attractive to Tertullian, who viewed the Church as too lax on many issues. He was a supporter of asceticism before it had become a major movement and advocated a fairly extreme position on sex and marriage. It is debated whether Tertullian ever became a schismatic or merely supported Montanism in the abstract. Two hundred years later, Augustine labeled the Montanists in North Africa Tertullianists. It is perhaps because of the stain of Montanism that Tertullian was never made bishop or canonized by the Roman church. Although hesitant about Tertullian, the church embraced his writings wholeheartedly, especially in the West.[14]

His important writings are many. *Apologeticus*, or *Apology*, is a defense of Christianity and a cutting and sarcastic criticism of paganism. Tertullian is one of the first to argue for the Christian Scripture based on fulfilled prophecy. He argued for the natural right of freedom of religion for all humans. He vehemently called for the right of Christians to stand trial, noting that they were not charged with actual crimes, but only with taking the name Christian. Here we find his famous statement "Christians are made, not born."

Against Marcion, a treatise against the Marcionite heresy, is a defense of the goodness of the Law of Moses and of the still greater Law of Christ. Much of what we know of this heretical group comes from Tertullian's polemic. Tertullian wrote a number of other polemical works against heretical teachings, including *Against Valentinian*, in which he discharges this version of Gnosticism. We will not treat these letters in detail, because the subject was covered in the last chapter.

In his *Prescription Against Heretics* Tertullian follows Irenaeus. He dismisses all the heresies of his day on the basis of apostolic succession and the rule of faith. How can they say they have the truth when they cannot claim that a single one of the apostles or their successor bishops in the great churches taught their version of Christianity? There is no doubt that these teachings are innovations. The Scriptures belong to the Catholic Church and are not to be interpreted by those without apostolic authority or line of descent through the bishops. In *Prescription* Tertullian is categorical in his rejection of philosophical speculation about God. He absolutely rejects the methodology of such Christian authors as Justin, Clement of Alexandria and Origen who sought to borrow from Plato and Aristotle. Here we see coming to the forefront Tertullian's Western mindset, dispelling the philosophical and seeking the practical approach to Christianity. He said quite famously, "What has Athens to do with Jerusalem? What accord is there between the

(Platonic) Academy and the Church? What harmony is there between heretics and Christians?"[15] Here he is quite uncompromising, implying that those who appeal to Greek philosophy are courting heretical thinking. Such vain intellectual curiosity is not conducive to Christian growth, at least according to Tertullian.

The most important polemical writing of Tertullian was *Against Praxeas*. This became perhaps his most quoted work. He was cited by Jerome, Augustine and many more. It is here that he most clearly describes his theology of God and his Christology. The document was written in order to oppose the teaching of Praxeas. We know little of this particular person, other than the fact that he was teaching in Rome. Tertullian accuses him of teaching modalism. This is the belief that there is only one person in the godhead, but three aspects or manifestations of that one person. There is no Son or Spirit separate from the Father. Tertullian coined the word *patripassianism* to describe this false theology. To quote Tertullian on Praxeas, "He says that the Father Himself came down into the virgin, was Himself born of her, Himself suffered, indeed was Himself Jesus Christ."[16] Experience tells us that Tertullian may well be somewhat overstating the view of Praxeas, setting up a bit of a straw man, but we know that modalism was a common teaching in the churches in the third and early fourth centuries.

Whatever one thinks of Tertullian, he was a brilliant and original thinker; one who could produce a great turn of phrase. His creative phrases to describe God and the relation between Son and Father became standard usage more than one hundred years after his death. Tertullian is the one who coined the word "trinity" (Latin *trinitas*). Of course this word does not appear in the New Testament. If the creation of this theological term was the only contribution of Tertullian, this alone would have made for an important legacy. What was Tertullian's view of the "trinity"? Tertullian held to the idea of one substance in three related persons[17] (*tres personae, una substantia*). The Greek translation for his Latin statement here is *tres hypostases, homoousios*. Although Tertullian wrote in Latin, the Greek words *hypostasis* and *homoousios* were destined to become very significant in the theological debates more than a century after him. Here he was well ahead of his co-theologians in moving toward the Nicene theology. The three persons of the godhead are different "not in condition, but in degree; not in substance, but in form; not in power but in aspect."[18] No Christian author was to use so prescient a phrase in describing the godhead for one hundred years. Tertullian argues from Scripture for three distinct persons. He quotes Jesus, who said to the Father, "Not as I will, but as you will" (Matthew 26:39). Tertullian used an analogy for what he called the trinity—one which is imperfect, as are all illustrations of the godhead. He described the Father as the tree, the Son as the branch and the Holy Spirit as the fruit. He saw the trinity as a Monarchy, with the Father over the Son and the Spirit, even though they are of the same substance.[19]

Tertullian was ahead of other church theologians by two hundred years in his Christology as well. He described Jesus as having both a divine and a human nature, yet as one person. Tertullian anticipated the argument of the Greek philosophers, as well as that of Clement and Origen, that it is impossible for God to suffer or change in nature. This made it very difficult for people raised in a Greek way of thinking to accept that God limited himself in the form of a little child and that he suffered on the cross. Tertullian's response was that in his divine nature Jesus did not suffer, but in his human nature he not only suffered, but died. The two natures were "conjoined" in Jesus.[20] We will see in chapter four that if only the church had accepted this view in the third century a lot of struggle and division could have been avoided. It is hard to exaggerate the importance to the Greek mindset of this philosophical imperative that God not suffer or change. We will return to this with Clement and Origen.

If Tertullian was the first to get it "right" with regard to his doctrine of God and of Jesus, and if the church as a whole was not to completely incorporate something like his view for almost two hundred and fifty years, this raises an obvious question. Were the believers before or even immediately after Tertullian wrong? Were they therefore heretics and not saved? After all, John implied in 1 John 2:18–25 that he who does not have a proper understanding of the Son does not have the Father as well. This is an important question. We should bear in mind that a number of modern heretical groups (Jehovah's Witness and Mormons, for example) stake a claim to be the only saved people based on an argument that the early church became completely apostate. We need to think carefully here. The answer is that the church as a whole did not have incorrect teaching. Rather they had a view of the Father, Son and Spirit that was not spelled out and defined as carefully as we have in Tertullian or the later ecumenical creeds. We have already mentioned that there was a wider range of views about the nature of Jesus in the early church than we might expect. Is it possible for a saved believer to be a bit fuzzy about the exact nature of the relationship between Father and Son and about the conjoining of the human and the divine in Jesus? Obviously, the answer is yes. So, why, one might ask, all the yelling and screaming and dividing over these issues in the third, fourth and fifth centuries? It is when teachers publicly defined and taught a specific description of God or the Son or the Holy Spirit that violated the clear sense of Scripture and the assumed (though not necessarily clearly defined) apostolic view of Jesus that a response was required. It seems that the church fathers were not strongly inclined to give exact definition to God. They preferred to keep the mystery at the forefront. In the end, human reason cannot fully explain the godhead. Generally, it was only when the church was forced to do so by what appeared to be false teaching that it narrowed down its definition of orthodox theology. Remember this point: The mainstream church defined its theology, not in order to remove the mystery, but to defend the mystery.

Tertullian's writing covered almost every conceivable subject relevant to Christianity, and we are not done with him yet. Like others at the time, he was not concerned all that much with a doctrine of salvation. We have already seen in chapter two that in his treatise *On Baptism* he had a very well defined teaching that baptism is the point at which one receives forgiveness of sins. He did not teach that the Holy Spirit was actually received at the point in time of the baptism, but rather that it prepared the recipient, who received the grace of the Holy Spirit with the laying on of hands after the baptism. Tertullian was more concerned with the purity of life of a person after baptism than were his contemporaries. We already know his view on Christians in military service and involvement in public spectacles. He took what will seem a rather extreme view on the veiling of women (*On the Veiling of Virgins*) and on second marriages, even of those whose spouse had died. This will foreshadow for us the tendency of the West toward legalism when compared to the East (and when compared with Scripture, in many cases). Roman culture was a culture of law, and it is not surprising that Western churches came to reflect this concern with law. This emphasis on law and insistence on rules of conduct was to lead to much division, particularly in the West.

This trend is exemplified by Tertullian's teaching on penance. What is the church to do with people who have committed public sin? Are they at this point outside of fellowship with the church? Does this imply that they are not saved and will go to hell if remaining in this state? What steps are required for them to be readmitted to the family? Does an "ordained" church leader have a determinative role in whether one is saved or not? Do leaders have the ability to impart forgiveness? If the answer to the two previous questions is no, then what is the purpose of church discipline? The reader is advised at this point to consider his/her biblical view of church discipline. Church discipline is taught in the New Testament.[21] We will see that how we apply church discipline says a lot about our view of repentance, forgiveness and salvation. The orthodox church, especially Rome, appears to have eventually veered far from biblical teaching on this question of penance. The relevant writing on the subject in Tertullian is *On Penance*. Here Tertullian describes long, drawn-out, humiliating public procedures required of a person who commits what later became defined as "mortal" sins (adultery, idolatry, murder, apostasy, fraud). In discussing whether sins committed subsequent to baptism may be forgiven, he calls baptism and penance two "planks" on which the sinner may be saved from shipwreck—language that he ultimately passed to the church.[22] In other words, he taught that this penance (defined as a set of actions performed in order to be reestablished as an accepted member of the church) was rquired for sins committed after baptism. Such teaching is not found in the New Testament. Public penance was allowed only once by Tertullian and his contemporaries. The duration of the acts of contrition was up to the bishop and in some cases it was until death. Martyrdom was one way the stain of sin could be removed, which may partially explain the attitude of some to death at the hands of persecutors.

A note about the word penance is in order. The Latin word is *paenitentia*. We get the English word penitentiary from this root. It has to do with punishment in order to achieve a justified position with another. For linguistic reasons, it is easy to confuse this with the biblical word repentance. The Greek word most often translated "repent" in English is *metanoia*. The word implies a change in mind and understanding. It implies a change of action as well, of course, but it has nothing to do with punishment or paying off a penalty.[23] It is unfortunate that the Latin versions of the Bible used *paenitentia* for the Greek word *metanoia* as the words have similar but not identical meanings, and the Latin word carried a stronger implication of the idea of penalty for a wrong rather than change of action and mind. Of course we get our English word repentance from the Latin *cognomen*. The use by the Latin translators represents what had become the practice in the church of requiring penance as a "second plank" in order to reach heaven.

We will say more on the role of penance, especially with regard to those who apostatized during the persecutions under Decius, Valerius and Diocletian. Ultimately, Tertullian shifted even farther from the biblical teaching on forgiveness for Christians. He rejected his own teaching. He moved to the Montanist position that restoration to the church was not possible for mortal sins, even upon public penance. "We do not forgive apostates; shall we forgive adulterers?" It may very well be this teaching for which he formally removed himself from the mainstream church and associated with the Montanists. Whether he changed his teaching in order to be with the Montanists or he joined them in order to teach the more rigorous doctrine he already believed is not known. In the short term, Tertullian's influence was somewhat limited. This may have been both because of his joining a schismatic group and because he wrote in Latin. The most influential writers of the third and fourth centuries were Greek both in language and thinking. In the end, Tertullian became key to Christian thinking, especially in the West, but only after his death. His influence on Cyprian and Augustine is profound.

The Alexandrian School

We now shift our study of important church fathers in the third century to Clement and Origen. They will, in a sense, represent the diametric opposite of Tertullian. Both were thoroughly steeped in Greek philosophy—especially Platonism, that branch of Greek philosophy that traced its origin to Plato. Both were decidedly Greek and "Eastern." Far from rejecting the conjoining of philosophy and Christian theology, they enthusiastically embraced it. Although Tertullian's influence in the long run was great, during the third century, Clement and Origen were more significant to developments than Tertullian.

By the third century, the governance of the church had evolved into geographic areas of influence whose power, over time, became more pronounced. In the third century the chief churches of importance were Jerusalem, Antioch, Rome and Alexandria. Later, these four plus Constantinople evolved into five patriarchates, each with a definite territory. We now turn our attention to Alexandria. Its large Jewish population may help to explain the early numerical growth of the church in this city at the head of the Nile River in Egypt. By the late second century, continuing well into the fourth, this most Greek of cities was the intellectual capital of Christianity. Alexandria was the home of the greatest library in the world. Alexandria, not Athens, was the center of Greek learning. It was also home to the first-century Jewish scholar and philosopher Philo. Philo sought to justify Judaism with Greek philosophy, especially Platonism. To do so, he developed an allegorical exegesis of the Old Testament. As explained previously, an allegorical interpretation involves beginning with the obvious historical meaning of the text and finding behind this text symbolical meanings in the objects or events with no clear indication in the text itself. For example, in his work *De Abrahamo* Philo said that the four kings Abraham met in Genesis 14 signify the four (Greek) passions—pleasure, desire, fear and grief, while the other five kings in the nine-king league in this story represent the five senses because they rule over us. A glance at the text in question will prove that there is no mention or even hint of the four passions or the five senses. Philo tried to demonstrate by such exegesis that Judaism has much in common with the philosophy of Plato. The hindsight of history tells us the similarity was principally between Greek philosophy and Philo, not Judaism.

One would think that important Christian interpreters would carefully avoid such speculative allegorizing. One would be wrong. In fact, thanks principally to the school of biblical study and theology at Alexandria, this became more or less the standard means of interpreting the Old Testament and to a lesser extent the New Testament. The motivation for this allegorical analysis of the Old Testament by Christian teachers such as Clement and Origen was virtually identical to that of Philo. Tertullian sought to do Christian apologetics by attacking pagan philosophy as Satanic. His argument for the reasonableness of Scripture came largely from fulfilled historical prophecy. The Alexandrine apologists/theologians chose on the contrary to embrace philosophy and show that Christianity has much in common with Pythagorus, Plato and Aristotle, yet that it is a further and better development of them.

There is another important point to bear in mind in understanding Alexandria, the church there and the famous Catachetical School of Alexandria in the period of its greatest influence from the third to the fifth centuries. Alexandria was perhaps the greatest center of Gnostic influence. In fact, there was even a Jewish Gnostic school there. Many of the Gnostic teachers who pulled disciples from the church and spread their heretical teaching across the Roman and Greek world originated in Alexandria. Examples include Valentinus, who was educated in Alexandria, as well as Basilides and Carpocrates. It is not by chance that the Nag Hammadi Library of Gnostic writings was discovered in near a monastery in Egypt. This collection of twelve codices is an Egyptian Coptic translation of a number of originally Greek Gnostic works of the Sethian and Valentinian schools. Clement and Origin were not Gnostics, but they were not totally averse to using some arguments that show affinity with the Gnostic thinking prevalent in Alexandria. A possible example is Origen's controversial belief in pre-incarnate souls.

Gnosticism is not the only religio-philosophical movement to find a welcome home in Alexandria. This center of Greek philosophy was home to Plotinus and the philosophical school he founded, which is known as Neoplatonism. Plotinus reached maturity studying in Alexandria. We can detect the Alexandrine fathers expressing their theology in terms that, if they are not influenced by Platonists or Neoplatonists, at a minimum use terminology familiar to this philosophical school. We will expand on Plotinus and Neoplotinism later.

Reflecting its nature as a center of learning, the church in Alexandria seems to have differed from other churches in the third century. It continued to be governed by a group of twelve elders who elected their chief elder/bishop. Here teachers maintained a stronger influence and independence in a place where the monarchical bishop had not taken root. The evidence supports the idea that the Catechetical School in Alexandria was a separate entity—not governed by the church there.

Clement of Alexandria

All truth is God's truth, wherever it may be found.

—Clement of Alexandria

Our first Alexandrine father is a good example of the tendency to adapt Christian theology and teaching to Greek philosophical thinking. Clement of Alexandria was born in the early 150s AD to a well-to-do non-Christian family who gave him a strong classical education. He lived until about AD 215. Relatively little is known of his personal life, but from his free and extensive quotes, we know he was very widely read in the Greek poets and philosophers of every stripe. Arguably, his most important contribution to Christian history is as the teacher of the prolific Origen. However, Clement was an important and original writer and thinker in his own right. After his conversion to Christianity, Clement traveled in Greece, Italy and Palestine, finally ending up in Alexandria. At first, he taught at his own private school. Later he began to teach at the famous Catechetical School sponsored by the church in Alexandria, eventually becoming the head of the school. He became a partner to the head of the school, Pantaenus, eventually succeeding him to become the head of this influential Christian center of scholarship.

Clement wrote extensively on Christian theology. Much of his work has been lost or is known only from fragments or from being mentioned by others. Most influential are his trilogy of treatises known as *Protrepticus* (Exhortation to the Greeks), *Paedagogus* (Instructor) and, most famously, *Stromata* (Miscellanies). *Protrepticus* found foreshadows of Christian teaching in Greek philosophy. *Paedogogus* or *The Teacher* was the first treatment of Christianity as an ethical system. This would have greatly pleased those of a Greek mindset. Like the Stoics, Clement valued moderation as an approach to life, as well as the denial of the physical aspects of life in favor of attaining a kind of godlikeness as the Christian ideal. The *Stromata* or *Miscellanies* is what its title implies: a varied collection of thoughts on intellectual aspects of Christian teaching. Clement stressed the *logos* theology, extending the emphasis of Justin.

Tertullian was well acquainted with the philosophers—especially the Stoics—but he was skeptical of Christians using philosophy to explain or defend their beliefs. Origen had a very different perspective. He used philosophy to expound Christianity. He integrated Christian teaching and Greek philosophy as well as Greek literary forms to create a systematic theology. His was a "Christian" Gnosticism. For him, faith is the true expression of *gnosis*; a Christian knowledge that is much deeper than mere doctrinal truth, assented to based on scriptural authority. To Clement, such deeper understanding is obtainable using a philosophical approach to become the perfect Christian Gnostic. Clement's God was relatively distant from humans. He was serene, unemotional and dispassionate rather than compassionate. In this, he was more like the "god" of Plato than the biblical God. The Greeks could not conceive of God being affected by human activity or changing in any way. Clement is rather obviously influenced by this thinking. He consistently allegorized biblical descriptions of God's anger, jealousy and other passions. Like Justin, he claimed that much Greek philosophy was borrowed from Old Testament ideas. Here Clement agreed with the first-century Jew Philo as well. Clement famously declared "All truth is God's truth, wherever it may be found."

Apparently, at the turn of the third century, the church in Alexandria had begun to include a number of well-to-do Christians, which probably motivated Clement to write his *Who Is the Rich Man Who Is Saved?* This published sermon explained that in Mark 10:17–22 Jesus does not necessarily condemn the possession of wealth per se, but the ungodly use of such wealth.

To summarize, depending on our perspective, we can be encouraged by or warned by the work of Clement of Alexandria. He made Christianity more understandable (and probably more acceptable) to the intellectually minded Greek. He helped the young Christian church to begin thinking more carefully and systematically about its theology. While accepting Greek philosophical usages, he adapted them to a unique Christian perspective and condemned much in Greek thinking that was not biblical. Did he and Origen go too far in adapting Christian ideas to suit Stoic, Epicurean or Platonic sensibilities? Did the tail wag the dog, rather than the other way around? Probably yes. Perhaps we can gain useful insight into the relationship between the modern church and such intellectual movements as modernism and postmodernism. Who is influencing whom? Like the church, we can "plunder the Egyptians" (Exodus 12:33, 36), gaining helpful ideas from psychology, business management practices and the like, but we should be cautious about the church being plundered spiritually by the very "Egyptian" wealth we are attempting to plunder. When does applying therapies created by non-Christian psychologists in Christian counseling or postmodern analysis to explain Christian teaching cross the line? A historical view of the back-and-forth relationship between Clement and Origen and the pagan philosophers can be helpful for us in thinking about our equivalent issues.

Origen of Alexandria (and Caesarea)

As mentioned above, some see the chief importance of Clement of Alexandria in his role as teacher of Origen. It bears noting in this regard that there is some debate over to what extent Origen was an actual pupil of Clement and to what extent the influence was less direct. Origen was the most influential Christian author between Paul and Augustine. He was a zealous Christian, a pioneer in biblical interpretation, a deep thinker and a prolific writer.

Origen was born in a Christian home in Alexandria about 185. Eusebius tells us[24] that his father Leonides was beheaded in the persecution of Septimus Severus in 203. The young Origen earnestly sought to join his father in martyrdom, and, again according to Eusebius, was only saved from this fate by his mother hiding his clothes so that he could not leave their house. Prevented from giving up his life, he encouraged his father not to consider his family in resisting his persecutors. Our picture of Origen as a zealous Christian is cemented by his youthfully foolish decision to apply Jesus' teaching about eunuchs in Matthew 19:12 quite literally to himself. As Eusebius reports,[25] Origen made himself a eunuch in a fit of youthful enthusiasm, out of a sincere desire to be able to teach both men and women. He foolishly believed that he could keep his self-mutilation secret. His rash act, secret for a time, was later revealed and used against him by his enemies who sought to censure Origen.

According to Eusebius,[26] Origen was a student of Clement of Alexandria "while yet a boy." When Clement fled the city in the persecution of Septimus Severus, Origen was accepted as head of the Catechetical School at the tender age of eighteen. He soon became the most well known teacher in Christendom, being invited to Palestine and even to Antioch, where he spoke with Julia, the mother of the emperor Alexander Severus. As his student Gregory Thaumaturgus enthusiastically described Origen's teaching in Alexandria, it included an eclectic blend of dialectics, natural philosophy, geometry, astronomy, philosophy (of course!), ethics, theology and scriptural studies. According to Eusebius.[27]

Origen teaching students in his catechetical school.

Ambrose, the influential bishop of Alexandria, supported the work of Origen, providing seven secretaries to write down his words, as well as an equal number of copyists. It was the influence of Origen that won Ambrose from the teaching of Valentinus to orthodox Christianity. After 232 Origen was forced to leave Alexandria by the local bishop, Demetrius. Whether this move was inspired by jealousy on the part of the bishop, by a desire to increase the power of the bishopric in Alexandria, or by concerns about the orthodoxy of this most controversial of teachers is not clear. Origen was enthusiastically received in Caesarea, where he had often taught previously.

Origen was easily the greatest Bible commentator up to his time. To assist his studies of the Hebrew Old Testament, he produced a *hexapla*—a parallel Old Testament with one column each for the Hebrew text, a Greek Transliteration (Hebrew words written using Greek letters), the Septuagint and three other Greek translations of the Hebrew. Imagine the work required to put this together! His commentaries on nearly every Old Testament book included hundreds of volumes. Bear in mind, however, that Origen was the chief Christian proponent of the allegorical hermeneutic. He sought to determine the "spiritual" meaning behind the literal text of the Old Testament, which allowed him to justify much of Greek philosophical thinking with the Bible. His division of the biblical meaning between the historical/literal/material and the pneumatic/spiritual/allegorical meaning corresponds to the Neoplatonist view of the division of the world between the lower physical reality and the higher spiritual reality.

Origen outlined an Old Testament canon that included the standard thirty-nine books of the Protestant canon, adding 1 and 2 Maccabees. About the New Testament, he mentioned all twenty-seven of the accepted Christian canon. He said that Matthew was originally written in "Hebrew" (presumably Aramaic), and that Mark wrote as requested by Peter. He argued that Paul did not write Hebrews because the Greek was too elegant to have come from the apostle's pen. He said, "But who it was who really wrote the epistle, God only knows." He noted, without adding his own opinion, that there was some dispute in his day over the inclusion of 2 Peter, as well as 2 and 3 John.

Near the end of an almost unimaginably prolific career in which he produced at least eight hundred manuscripts, Origen was imprisoned and tortured during the persecution begun by Decius. From what we know of him, we can easily imagine Origen's happiness at being allowed to suffer for Jesus in this way. Although he was not martyred at this time, it is likely that the stress of his treatment led to his death soon thereafter.

Most important for us is the teaching and more specifically the theology of Origen, and to these we now turn. Origen's goal was "to provide Christians who raise intellectual problems with answers in accordance with Scripture, so that they do not go and seek them in great Gnostic sects."[28] Some of his most important works are as follows:

Contra Celsum (Against Celsus). An apologetic response to Celsus, the Greek philosopher and ardent enemy of the Christian church. Celsus had published his sarcastic attack on Christianity in his work *On the True Doctrine.* Origen's response to Celsus, more than perhaps any other, established the Jesus movement as being on an equal intellectual footing with that of pagan philosophy. Its enemies could no longer claim that Christianity was only for the ignorant and uneducated. Origen quotes Celsus line-by-line, providing a blistering counter argument to both his specific and his general charges against the church. Because of the detailed and convincing response to the intellectual challenge to Christian faith by a leading philosopher of his day, Origen became one of the most influential teachers in the Roman/Greek world, so that even pagan philosophers came to his school to study. Although he is perhaps less known than Justin as an apologist, this treatise is considered by most scholars to be the most thoroughly developed defense of Christianity in the early church. It includes familiar arguments such as evidence from the miracles of Jesus and from fulfilled prophecy. To this Origen adds arguments about the moral superiority of Christianity, the lives and deaths of Jesus and his apostles, and the followers' refusal to reap financial benefits from their service to humanity. For example, when Celsus attacked the claim of his followers that Jesus worked miracles by calling him a mere magician, Origen responds:

> There would indeed be a resemblance between them, if Jesus, like the dealers in magical arts, had performed his works only for show; but now there is not a single juggler who, by means of his proceedings, invites his spectators to reform their manners, or trains those to the fear of God who are amazed at what they see, nor who tries to persuade them so to live as men who are justified by God.[29]

De Principiis (On First Principles). This document was the first truly systematic Christian theology. Here Origen began with the rule of faith, delivered by the apostles and recorded in the inspired Scriptures. To Origen, the role of the theologian is to elicit more fully the underlying meaning of the text—to find the hidden meaning underlying the spoken word. He continued and extended the Logos idea of Justin and Clement. Origen described the Son as "generated" rather than "emitted" from the Father because this led to him being of the same substance. As a Platonist, the time distinction implied by the word generated was insignificant to Origen, but it later led to theological problems (Arianism for example). Origen put Jesus in a subordinate state to the Father, and the Spirit even more so. Origen began to use the words *ousia* (meaning substance or essence) and *hypostasis* (meaning nature, entity, existence) to describe the relationship between Father and Son, but in a much less technical sense. Origen used the words interchangeably. As we will see, these terms later were used to express the distinct concepts of the oneness of the godhead in the case of *ousia* and the individuality of the Father and the Son in the case of *hypostasis*.

Thus far, so good, but Origen's speculations went further. In *De Principiis* he took the position that there is a preexistence of human souls. It is hard to know for sure why he took this position, but we know he used it to explain passages such as Romans 9:13, "Jacob I loved, but Esau I hated." To the Platonist, and therefore to Origen, God cannot harbor such an emotion as hate. Rather than invoking the foreknowledge of God to explain the phrase "Esau I hated," he said that Esau entered his corporeal state having already sinned in his preexistent state. Jacob, on the other hand, must have been more righteous in his preexistent state, explaining God's favor toward him. This sounds suspiciously like the Eastern concept of karma. Indeed, Origen has been accused of believing in reincarnation, but there is no evidence for this.

Also of grave concern for his later detractors, Origen leaned strongly toward a kind of great hope of the ultimate salvation of all souls. Fairly or not, he has been accused of being a Universalist (one who believes in universal salvation). Origen claimed to have found justification for this view in 1 Corinthians 15:28: in Christ, "God may be all in all." More likely, he found this concept in Greek philosophy. If God will be all, then at the end of time "there will no longer be any distinction between good and evil, seeing evil nowhere exists; for God is all things and to Him no evil is near."[30]

On Prayer and Exhortation to Martyrdom. These and many other works of Origen show him to be not just a deep thinker, but a practical teacher, concerned with the everyday spirituality of the church. Origen was devoted to Christian modesty, service, charity, purity of life, pacifism and to keeping Scripture at the heart of all his teaching.

Ultimately, despite all he did to build up the Christian church through his teaching and writing, it was his speculative theology that led to the downfall of Origen in the eyes of the church leadership—especially in the West, but this was not to happen for well over one hundred years after his death. Many Christians became known as Origenists. They took his ideas to extremes to which Origen certainly would not have agreed. This will be a familiar pattern in the history of Christianity. For example, many today are more Calvinistic than John Calvin. Many are more Pelagian than Pelagius or more Nestorian than Nestorius. It is hard for us to be sure where the ideas of Origen end and those of later followers who took his name began, but there is no doubt that many took his theology as a starting point from which to make clearly heretical claims about the nature of God and of Jesus. Origen and his writings were anathematized by the Fifth Ecumenical Council in 553, including fifteen specific charges. Among the heretical beliefs charged to Origen were the preexistence of souls, apocatastasis (Universalism) and the denial of a real and lasting bodily resurrection. His suspect writings were destroyed or edited in a way so as to remove the offending teachings. This is one reason it is hard to know how accurate the charges against him truly were.

Was Origen a hero of the faith or was he a heretic? This seems like a distant and abstract question to us. We do not have to decide about how to treat a neighbor or a coworker who is a present-day Origenist. Or do we…? Perhaps the distance we have from Origen can be helpful for us to gain perspective on how we should feel today about believers with views we believe to be false. And what about Tertullian who joined with the Montanists? His mistake seems to be heteropraxy (biblically unauthorized practice) rather than Origen's heterodoxy (false teaching). Which is worse, false teaching or wrong practice? Presumably, we would not give the right hand of fellowship to an Arius, Valentinus or Marcion who denied Jesus, but what about Origen? If he lived in our community, with his immensely successful teaching ministry, would we disown him, or would we give him the hand of Christian fellowship and perhaps attend some of his classes? Perhaps in doing so, we might even be able to encourage him to reconsider his false idea about the preexistence of souls. There is a sense in which this question is academic for us, but in its being academic, maybe it can help us think about how to treat a Calvinist or an Arminian, a Pentecostal or one who denies the present-day ministry of miracles. One thing for sure, Origen was a sincere, devoted follower of Jesus. He fully acknowledged the inspiration, if not the inerrancy of the Scripture.

Does a particular heterodox teaching fall into the "essential" category? If so, then perhaps we will take the advice of Paul with regard to the Judaizers in Galatia: "As we have already said, so now I say again: If anybody is preaching to you a gospel other than what you accepted, let him be eternally condemned!" (Galatians 1:9). On the other hand, the incorrect teaching may be in the important (rather than essential) or even the unimportant category. I, for one, choose to think of Origen as a great if flawed Christian, but I take his mistakes and the ends to which they led when extrapolated by those who followed him as a warning to leave that which is a mystery as a mystery and not to make unwarranted speculation in areas in which God has not spoken clearly. At the end of Origen's life we are ending four decades of relative peace for the Christian church. With the advent of the horrendous persecutions under Decius, all this changed.

Cyprian of Carthage (200–258)

> Outside the church, there is no salvation.
>
> —Cyprian of Carthage

The last of the four great "fathers" of the church in the third century

121

we will look at is Cyprian. With the career of Cyprian, we return to the West. From what we have seen about the growing distinction between the Eastern and the Western church, we expect that this great church father was more concerned with the governance of the church than with philosophical/ theological ideas, and we will not be proved wrong in this expectation.

Cyprian came to Christianity relatively late in life. Born in 200, he was from a very prosperous pagan family in Carthage. His was the finest education the Roman Empire could offer. It is not insignificant to his story that he was Roman rather than Greek by language and disposition. All of his writings were in Latin, which magnified his influence in the West and, conversely, limited his effect on the church in the East. Carthage is the city that had given Tertullian to the church, and it was the future home of Augustine. The future bishop of Carthage was influenced by a priest named Caecilius. His baptism came at the mature age of forty-six. Perhaps because of his high civic standing, or perhaps because of his zeal for his newfound faith, or both, Cyprian had a meteoric rise to prominence in the church in Carthage. He distributed his wealth to the poor in the city at a difficult time for the church. This endeared him to the Christians there.

Two years after his conversion, in 248, Cyprian was ordained a priest and almost immediately after that he was made bishop over a church in Carthage as well as the local congregations. Almost immediately, Cyprian became embroiled in controversies over the role of the organized church which were to define his ten-year ministry as bishop of the important North African church. One of the reasons Cyprian was so influential was because of his impeccable Christian life and his great love for the church. His advice was so influential that Stephen, the bishop (perhaps pope, as we shall see) in Rome, felt threatened by Cyprian, to the point that he condemned the beloved bishop. Ultimately, Cyprian's view of church structure and the basis for its unity became the accepted view of Roman Catholic Christianity. Some trace the formation of Roman Catholicism and Christendom to Cyprian. He defined the role of bishop, making it central to church governance, creating the idea that the salvation of one's soul was based on one's relationship to the bishop. At the risk of exaggerating, we can view the Protestant Reformation as a rebellion against this concept of the episcopate (*episkopos* being the Greek word for bishop).

The event that brought the ministry of Cyprian to the forefront of the Western Church was the persecution under Decius. The Roman emperor began his vicious attack on the church in 250. The persecutions in North Africa were particularly intense. Reluctantly, Cyprian agreed to go into hiding in the African desert. If he had not, he would almost certainly have been arrested and executed, as Decius attempted to destroy the church by beheading it (i.e. by killing its leaders). The Roman bishop and many others met this fate in the Decian persecution. For a time it appeared that Decius was succeeding. A great number of Christians "lapsed," offering sacrifice to the Roman gods. This included many church leaders. Congregations left leaderless began to question their need for bishops to tell them what to do. Cyprian worked tirelessly from hiding in the desert to rally the church and the remaining bishops.

When the persecution lightened for a time, Cyprian returned to Carthage to resume his public ministry. This is when the issue that was to define his career came to the fore. What was the church to do with those who had lapsed and denied their faith under threat of death or imprisonment? This was no small issue, as a majority of the Christians had lapsed, either by offering the sacrifice or by acquiring a certificate of sacrifice one way or another. Were they to be accepted back in fellowship with the church? Some supported a strict policy of denying fellowship to the lapsed (*lapsi*) or demanded that they remain under a permanent church discipline. Perhaps God would choose to save them in the end, but there was no forgiveness for such willful sin within the church. The "rigorist" party at one time or another was represented by Tertullian, Hippolytus of Rome and Novatian. Novatian led a group of rigorists in Rome, producing a schism there. The rigorists ultimately evolved into what became known as the Novatians. Other church leaders were known as "laxists." They pronounced a general "amnesty" and forgiveness of those who had sinned, and individual "confessors" received their repentance and accepted them back into full fellowship. Cyprian took a middle ground. To those who had personally offered the sacrifice, forgiveness of the church was only offered at the moment of death. Others had managed to get certificates of sacrifice without actually publicly denying Jesus by paying a bribe or by sending a slave to make the sacrifice. This group was put under church discipline and only reconciled to full fellowship in the church after a time of repentance, under the authority of the local bishop, of course. In any case, Cyprian said that a synod of bishops should decide the issue so as to maintain the unity of the church. For him, the issue of church authority and unity was as important as the salvation of the individual *lapsi*.

During this time Cyprian feuded with Stephen. Other Roman bishops had suggested a prime role for the bishop in Rome, but Stephen was the first to try to vigorously impose his primacy in practical ways over churches in the West. For this reason, some call him the first "pope." His chief rival was Cyprian, who refused to acknowledge his subordination to Stephen.

Cyprian had another strong disagreement with Stephen over the issue of rebaptism.[31] The question was whether a baptism performed upon a repentant believer was valid if issued by a person who was outside the mainstream church. Stephen took the view that anyone baptized in the name of the Father, Son and Holy Spirit was saved, regardless of who had performed the baptism. Cyprian argued that only baptism within the established church led to salvation, and therefore required those baptized in a group such as the Novatians to be baptized within "the church," to include the laying on of hands of an ordained bishop in order to be saved. Here we see a steady move toward the idea of sacramentalism and the idea of an intercessory priesthood. Cyprian famously put it this way: "He can no longer have God for his father who has not the church for his mother."[32] Stephen responded with the argument that this had not been the teaching and tradition of the church. To this Cyprian responded, "Custom is the antiquity of error,"[33] and one "who does not possess the Holy Spirit cannot impart the Holy Spirit."[34]

We do not know where these controversies would have led if fully worked out between Cyprian and Stephen, because both were killed in a new wave of persecution. The Roman claim to primacy faded for a time with the death of Stephen. Stephen's view on baptism won out in the West, although Cyprian's teaching hung on in North Africa for a while, to be renewed in the Donatist movement of the fourth century. Ultimately, the position of Cyprian that salvation is only found and maintained within the church steadily won out in both the East and the West, but not his view on the efficacy of baptisms performed by heretics.

Stephen died in 256. When a new round of persecution broke out in Carthage under Valerian in 257, Cyprian was driven from Carthage again. After a time of banishment, he came back to Carthage where he was arrested and beheaded in 258. The inspiring martyrdom of Cyprian is recorded in the *Acts of Cyprian.* His friends plotted his escape into the desert, but the revered bishop, now fifty-eight years old, refused their help. Unlike six years previously, this time he was not to be denied the glory of martyrdom. According to the account we have, Cyprian willingly undressed and nobly allowed himself to be beheaded in front of both pagans and Christians.

We have a great volume of letters both from and to Cyprian. His two most important written works are *Concerning the Lapsed* and *On the Unity of the Church.* The first summarizes Cyprian's view on the controversy over those who had compromised their faith during the Decian persecution. His view preserved the ideal of the mercy and grace of God, but probably more importantly to Cyprian, it maintained the prerogative of the ordained bishop and the unity of the church under his leadership.

Cyprian's teaching on salvation is found in his epistles, but especially in *On the Unity of the Church.* To him, salvation was not an individual affair between a repentant person and their God. Salvation did not exist outside the corporeal body of Christ, as represented by his bishops. As Cyprian said:

> But it is manifest where and by whom remission of sins can be given; to wit, that which is given in baptism. For first of all the Lord gave that power to Peter, upon whom He built the Church, and whence He appointed and showed the source of unity—the power, namely, that whatsoever he loosed on earth should be loosed in heaven. And after the resurrection, also, He speaks to the apostles, saying, "As the Father hath sent me, even so I send you." Who when He has said this, He breathed on them, and saith unto them, "Receive ye the Holy Ghost: whosesoever sins ye remit, they are remitted unto them; and whosesoever sins ye retain, they are retained." Whence we perceive that only they who are set over the Church and established in the Gospel law, and in the ordinance of the Lord, are allowed to baptize and to give remission of sins; but that without, nothing can either be bound or loosed, where there is none who can either bind or loose anything.[35]

To Cyprian, as later with the Roman Church, salvation was a process begun at baptism, but maintained throughout one's life through sanctification within the church and by virtue of participation in its sacraments. This thought was to be developed further by Augustine. With Cyprian, more than any other person with the possible exception of Augustine, the church became "Catholic." Against Stephen, Cyprian viewed "the church" as residing in the great bishops, not a single bishop. The bishops were interdependent, and authoritative decision came through consensus of the bishops, not from a primal bishop in Rome. Ultimately, this became the view of the Eastern Orthodox church, whereas the West moved toward primacy under the Roman pope.

Cyprian moved in the direction of making baptism a "sacrament." In other words, it became an action which is affective by the power of the one performing the ritual, not necessarily affected by the faith of the one baptized. Cyprian advised the baptism of infants. His teaching on original sin was to be developed more fully by Augustine. According to Cyprian, infants have "contracted the contagion of the ancient death at its earliest birth." In baptism "are remitted not his own sins, but the sins of another." In other words, baptism of an infant removes the sin imparted to the child from Adam. Clearly this happened apart from faith on the part of the infant.

Justo Gonzalez summarizes Cyprian's and the Eastern church's eventual view as follows:

> The unity of the church is in its episcopate, of which all bishops share as if it were a common property. This unity is not something to be added to truth, but is rather an essential part of Christian truth, so that where there is no unity there is also no truth. Apart from this unity there is no salvation. Apart from it there is no baptism, or Eucharist, or true martyrdom. However, this unity does not consist in being subject to a "bishop of bishops," but in the common faith, love, and communion of all bishops among themselves.[36]

How are we to view Cyprian? He was a man of apparently impeccable Christian character. Certainly his conversion seems to be genuine. His wide influence over the church in his own time was based largely on his charitable treatment of his friends and his enemies, on his generosity to the poor, on his humility and his unambiguous devotion to Jesus and to the church. He was a uniter rather than a divider of the church. Yet his legacy is a strongly hierarchical structure based, not on the priesthood of all believers, but on the authority of a very small segment of the church—men, some of whom at a future time were to have extremely dubious spiritual credentials. Biblically, where the Holy Spirit is, there is Christ. With Cyprian, where the bishop is, there is Christ. Cyprian did not begin the trend toward penance and works in order to receive forgiveness of the church, but certainly his legacy moved the church in the direction of the elaborate system of penance we will see developed in the Medieval Church. Arguably, Cyprian's policies saved the day for the church at the time—threatened with the possibility of breaking up and perhaps even of being destroyed. Certainly we can see sincerity in Cyprian's policies. But do the ends justify the means? The future history of the church in the West was to make that a dubious proposition.

Everett Ferguson describes four stages in the development of thinking about the nature of the church,[37] which can be helpful.

1. All members are saints—reflected in the New Testament. Montanism involved an effort to reclaim this view.

2. The clergy must be saints. The Novatianists and then more explicitly the Donatists represented this position.

3. The church embraced "saints" (martyrs and confessors) and "sinners." This view was taking shape in the mainstream of the third-century church [Stephen for example], and in the fourth century found expression in the distinction of monks from ordinary church members.

4. The sanctity of the church belongs not to individuals, but to the sacraments of the church.

This fourth stage was hinted at by Cyprian and was fully realized in Augustine.

The story of Cyprian gives us a good opportunity to use church history in order to help us reflect on our own personal view of salvation. Is salvation found only in the church as Cyprian taught? If so, what definition of the word "church" are we using in this context, the church universal or a local church? Those of us who do not accept the Roman tradition probably do not take as strong a view as Cyprian, but perhaps we are used to the idea of church "membership." Does one have to be a member of a church to be saved? Is the concept of membership even biblical? If not, then as an expedient for the local church is defining membership a good idea? Is submission and obedience to a church leadership a prerequisite to remaining saved once one is baptized? "Obey your leaders and submit to their authority. They keep watch over you as men who must give an account. Obey them so that their work will be a joy, not a burden, for that would be of no advantage to you" (Hebrews 13:17). How are we to apply this principle?

And what should be the policy of the local church toward those who have lapsed? Would we give the right hand of fellowship to those who have publicly denied Jesus and offered sacrifice to the twenty-first-century equivalent of an idol (assuming they are prepared to repent)? Is it the responsibility of the local church leadership to maintain standards of discipleship and to enforce such standards by identifying those who are "members" and those who are not? If we are no longer a member of a particular church, or if heaven forbid, we were disfellowshipped, does this have any eternal implications? If a member of our fellowship has been disciplined according to 1 Corinthians 5, and they repent, should we take them back? What about if they are repeat offenders? Cyprian and his compatriots allowed for only one opportunity to make penance and be received back into the fellowship of the church.

As noted earlier, today's religious context is radically different from that of Cyprian. It is hard for us to conceive of this, but in the third century the thought of having two bishops in the same city seemed unimaginable. Many of us live in a culture that very strongly emphasizes the importance and value of the individual rather than the group. For us, there are dozens and in larger cities hundreds of different "bishops" in our immediate neighborhood, if we take the different denominations and separate fellowships to be equivalent to a separate authoritative bishop. A "lapsed" member of a church that takes a strong stand on discipleship can simply go next door and get a fresh start.

What made sense to Cyprian has a completely different meaning in our context.

It is not my intention to provide answers to these intriguing questions, only to raise them. Who is saved? Does it matter at which church one is baptized and the belief that holds sway where the person is baptized? Is a doctrine of rebaptism biblical? Does ungodly behavior within a former fellowship affect our decision to accept someone as a member of our local church? Should it? Let us spend some time thinking about these important questions and let us turn our historical eyes to Cyprian in order to help us reach some conclusions.

The Church in the Second Half of the Third Century

It is convenient to separate church history in the third and early fourth centuries into two stages. From the persecution under Caesar Septimus Severus in 202–204 there was a time of relative peace, growth and consolidation in the church until the time of the persecutions under the rulers Decius and Valerian in 250–252 and 257–258. This was the period when the great church fathers Tertullian, Clement, Origen and Cyprian helped to mature the church. By 250 the church had become somewhat complacent. This fact was revealed during the troubles brought about by the persecution and the fallout within the church. The period from 258 until the persecution under Diocletian was another time of relative safety and growth for the church. The policy of Cyprian helped the church to avoid major schism and to continue to resist the dangerous theologies of Patripassianism or Modalism and Dynamic Monarchianism (see below). To this period in church history we will now turn.

Theological Controversies

In the third century Gnosticism gradually faded as a major threat to the church. Unfortunately, this did not bring theological controversies to an end. Whereas the extreme forms of Gnosticism were rather obviously heretical, the theological arguments of the late third century involved concepts of the deity that might seem to us subtleties over which it is not worth dividing the church. It is fairly easy for us to get lost in all the definitions and distinctions. The reader will have to pay careful attention to separate it all! This tendency for the church to argue over fine points of theology was to be a growing problem in the church for the next two hundred years.

Important Heterodox Theological Movements in the Early Church

Movement	Time Period	Definition	Major Figures
Gnosticism	1st–3rd century	God of OT and physical things in general are evil; Jesus is a spiritual emanation.	Marcion, Basilides, Valentinian
Docetism Adoptionism	2nd Century	Jesus only appeared to be a physical being. He was adopted as God's son at his baptism and left before the crucifixion.	Cerinthus
Ebionite	1st and 2nd Centuries	Jesus was a great Rabbi and nothing more. He was a mere man.	
Modalism Patripasianism Sabellianism	3rd Century	The Father, Son and Holy Spirit are three "modes" of one God. Rejects trinitarian language.	Praxeas, Sabellius
Monarchiansim	3rd Century	Jesus: from man to God	Paul of Samosata
Arianism	4th and 5th Centuries	Jesus is not God. He is the first and greatest creation of God.	Arius, Eusebius
Nestorianism	5th Century and beyond	Christ is two separate persons and has two natures: one human and changeable and the other divine.	Nestor
Monophysitism Eutychianism	5th Century and beyond	Christ as a single divine nature. His humanity is minimized.	Dioscorus, Eutyches

Two theological schools of thought were proposed and more or less rejected during the third century. The first that we will discuss is known as **Patripassianism** or **Modalism**. The Modalist viewed the Father, the Son and the Holy Spirit as three modes of activity—as three forms of revelation of the one God. The Modalist viewed God as revealing himself in more than one way, depending on the time and situation. There were not three distinct entities. God could act as Father, as Son or as Holy Spirit. The Son cannot literally speak to the Father unless he was talking to himself. Jesus had to go to the Father in order to send the Holy Spirit because Jesus is, in a sense, the Holy Spirit. This was true monotheism and in stark contrast to the Tertullian or the Nicene "trinity." Modalists certainly were not trinitarians. To its opponents it was known as Patripassianism, which means the Father suffered. This sarcastic label stemmed from a concern, motivated by Greek philosophy, over the question of God suffering. It was very difficult for people immersed in Greek thinking to imagine God suffering. The gospels clearly show Jesus suffering on the cross. If the Son is merely a "mode" of God then the Father suffered on the cross. How was a person who has not yet completely thrown off the Greek worldview to deal with this difficulty? Whether or not the Father suffered while Jesus was on the cross is something for us to debate, but to most Greeks, this was not possible.

Tertullian opposed modalism in his treatise *Against Praxeas*. If we take Tertullian at his word, Praxeas "says that the Father Himself came down into the Virgin, was Himself born of her, Himself suffered, indeed was Himself Jesus Christ."[38] Tertullian ironically noted concerning Praxeas, "By this Praxeas did a twofold service for the devil at Rome: he drove away prophecy, and he brought in heresy; he put to flight the Paraclete and he crucified the Father.[39] Here Tertullian is upset with Praxeas, both for opposing Montanus (who he is calling the Paraclete) and his prophecies and for supporting Modalism.

By far the most influential modalist was Sabellius. In fact, his influence was so great that Patripassianism came to be known in the East as Sabellianism. Sabellius was active in Rome about 220. To him, God revealed himself at various times as Father, Son or Spirit; certainly as no two of these simultaneously. Sabellius was excommunicated by Sixtus, the bishop of Rome in 220. The church was moved to more carefully define the trinity at least in part as a response to the ideas of Sabellius.

The second theological proposal that was labeled as heretical in the third century is known as **Monarchianism** or **Dynamic Monarchianism** (so called because Modalism is sometimes called Modalist Monarchianism). This view is closely associated with the charismatic Christian teacher Paul of Samosata.

It is akin to the second-century adoptionism. Paul taught that because of his righteous life, the power (Greek: *dynamis*) of God came upon the human Jesus. Before this, Jesus was a man and not God. In other words, according to Monarchainism, Jesus was man-become-God. Paul became bishop in Antioch in 260. A synod was called in Antioch in 268 to deal with this heterodox teaching.[40] The synod deposed Paul, but because he had local political support, he refused to leave his position as bishop. When his political supporter, Queen Zenobia of Palmyra was deposed by the emperor Aurelian in 272, the Christians brought their case before Aurelian who finally deposed Paul. This is the first recorded case of a Roman emperor interceding in a Christian church issue. Paul was accused by his detractors of maintaining a private bodyguard, sitting on a high throne in worship services and of replacing psalms addressed to Jesus with hymns to himself sung by a choir of women. Eusebius accused Paul of "pomp and haughtiness of his heart."[41] How valid these charges were is hard to judge, but we can infer that Paul may have applied his Monarchian view of Jesus, in some sense, to himself. With the deposition of Paul of Samosata and the negative image associated with him, Monarchianism as a theology faded from view.

Asceticism

Asceticism did not become a powerful movement within Christianity until the fourth century. The great impetus at that time toward asceticism was worldliness that had crept into the church. The church in the third century was still relatively vigorous in its standards of purity and godliness. Of course, Tertullian had many sympathies with ascetic thinking, admonishing the church to live a very simple life, separate from many of the influences of the world. During the persecutions of Decius and Valerius, it became commonplace for Christians to flee into the desert in North Africa, but such journeys were generally temporary. The first influential ascetic in Christianity began his life in the desert as a hermit in the third century. This great ascetic Christian was Anthony of Egypt, also known as Anthony of the Desert or Anthony the Anchorite. Most of what we know about Anthony comes from his biographer Athanasia of Alexandria, who wrote in 360. In about 285, at the age of 34, Anthony headed out into the desert west of Alexandria. This was the beginning of a career as a hermit and the head of a loosely-knit group of fellow ascetics that stretched until his death in 356 at the ripe old age of 105! We will have more to say about Anthony in the next chapter.

Christian Life

Many of the developments of church life in the third and early fourth centuries can be seen as extrapolations of trends begun in the second. Worship became considerably more standardized. Participation of the members who were not clergy in the worship was reduced greatly. The clergy/laity divide gradually became more like a chasm. Some sort of a church calendar began to take shape. Veneration of saints and martyrs took on a life of its own as members would meet to pray in graveyards to honor the dead. While we can see these trends as a departure from apostolic Christianity, there is much to admire in the life of the church of this period. All the evidence we have points to a church that had powerful and convicting love for one another. Their Jesus-imitating service to the needs of one another and to those outside the fellowship still served as a fantastic magnet to the nonbelievers. This was still generally a very vigorous Christianity, despite any disturbing trends we can point out. Growth of the church, although uneven in its rate, was overall still quite spectacular, to the point that the Roman government could no longer ignore this sect. As we have seen, soon it would become the second most influential institution in the Roman world—second only to the Roman government and its associated pagan religion.

Why? Why did this young Christian movement continue to grow against all odds and, in arguably the most significant social and religious revolution in human history, why did it eventually completely replace its competitors—the Mystery Religions, Eastern dualist religions such as Manichaeism, and most powerful of all, the Greek pagan philosophies such as Stoicism, Epicureanism and Neoplatonism? The list below summarized the principle causes of this unprecedented triumph of the Church.

1. Early on it was the incomparable zeal and personal conviction of those who had personally known Jesus of Nazareth and those directly influenced by these witnesses.

2. Add to this the powerful truth-claims related to fulfilled prophecies, miracles and the resurrection.

As the immediacy of the events faded and as these influences naturally were reduced somewhat as well, why did the church continue its exponential growth?

3. Because of the obvious and inescapable moral/ethical superiority of the adherents to this growing Christian movement.

4. Because, after Origen, Christian theology was seen as intellectually on par with the Stoicism and Neoplatonism if its day, but with much

to offer to the common person that these Greek philosophies did not offer.

5. Having been established as a movement with intellectual credentials, the church offered meaning, purpose and dignity for both poor and rich, for both the intellectual and the uneducated. Perhaps most significantly of all, it offered the same meaning and purpose and nearly the same dignity for both male and female—something that the Mystery religions and the "true philosophy" absolutely did not offer. Many of the influential church members in the first three centuries were female and this is no accident.

6. Because it is the truth and God was behind this movement.

There is no doubt that the purity and the incomparable self-sacrifice of the followers of Jesus in the first centuries was a significant factor in their growth. Much of what the church did was what the Stoics and Epicureans had been preaching in their ethics all along. The difference between Greek philosophy and Christianity is that the former had relatively little impact on the lives of the masses, whereas even the strongest critics of the Jesus movement could not deny that the Christians practiced not only what they preached, but what the philosophers preached as well. The philosophers felt that an honorable and ethical life was attainable only for the educated few, not for the uneducated masses. The church proved this expectation to be wrong. The Roman philosopher/physician Galen pointed out this striking feature of the Christian church. He said that their teaching of "rewards and punishments in a future life" led to a lifestyle "not inferior to that of genuine philosophers." To Galen, this fact was especially notable in the disciples' "restraint in cohabitation," "self-control in matters of food and drink," "keen pursuit of [social] justice" and "contempt of death." What a great testimony the lives of these early Christians provided! As early as the second century, Ignatius had to admonish the churches against using too much of church funds to purchase the freedom of slaves.

A good example of incomparable Christian behavior and its effects on pagans is provided by the events surrounding the great plague that struck Egypt in the 250s. Eusebius tells us, quoting from Dionysius of Alexandria that:

> Most of our brethren, by their exceeding great love and brotherly affection, not sparing themselves, and adhering to one another, were constantly superintending the sick, ministering to their wants without fear and without cessation, and healing them in Christ, have departed most sweetly with them.[42]

He reports that elders and deacons joined in the work, many sacrificing their lives in order to care for the sick, both among the Christians and the pagans. They risked their lives to give a decent burial to all alike.

> Among the heathen it was the direct reverse. They both repelled those who began to be sick, and avoided their dearest friends. They would cast them out into the roads half dead, or throw them when dead without burial.[43]

Although many Christians died in this manner, in the long run the church in Alexandria actually grew faster than before, both because the disciples had a greater survival rate because of the care received and because of the wonderful example of the Christian lifestyle to the heathen.

Worship

As hinted above, the worship of the church continued to evolve to include pagan influences. Language was borrowed from Roman ritual cultic sacrificial practices. Ministers/presbyters began to be called priests. It is not hard to see why this borrowing from pagan (or perhaps Jewish) ideas tended to erode the biblical teaching of the priesthood of all believers (1 Peter 2:9). By the fifth century, as we will see, the evolution of a neo-pagan priestly cult within Christianity was nearly complete. Church buildings were called temples by Christian writers in the third century. Even more alarmingly, the table at which the communion items were prepared became known as an altar, as if a sacrifice were being offered every week, rather than a remembrance of the death of Jesus.

In the third century, the great honor given to the martyrs in the second century began to evolve into a cult of martyrs. We know from Tertullian that by this time, Christians were already taking part in funeral processions, borrowed from pagan practices. Groups of disciples began to gather to worship in Christian cemeteries and catacombs in order to honor fallen Christians. It is a common myth that the early Christians spent time in the catacombs in order to escape persecutions or to worship in secret. The evidence tells a different story. Christians visited the catacombs for reasons of their own, in order to observe the cult of the saints.[44] Evidence for this is that the practice continued for several centuries after the persecution of the church had ceased. Of course, Tertullian strongly opposed such pagan influence. His opposition was eventually ineffective! This trend increased after the persecutions of Decius (249–251) and Valerius (253–260), during which thousands of Christians lost their lives, adding to the list of martyrs.

Cyprian was the first we know of who called the Lord's Supper a sacrifice in the name and memory of the martyrs. The church began to call the day of death of the famous martyrs their "birthday," (i.e. their birth to immortality). It became common practice to commemorate the day of death of these martyrs. In the third century the commemoration of martyrs was largely a local matter. This practice gradually expanded into an elaborate martyrology and a church calendar full of saints' days. By the end of the third century we begin to find inscriptions in Christian funerary sites such as "Peter and Paul, pray for us all." Christians began to pray to or through the departed martyrs. The biblical teaching that "there is one God and one mediator between God and men, the man Christ Jesus" (1 Timothy 2:5) began to lose force with these innovations. The idea of the cultic practice was for the worshipper to ask for the fallen one to intercede for them before the throne of God. Here we see a well-developed cultic veneration which was to see a further evolution in future centuries into what we find in the modern Eastern Orthodox and Roman Catholic churches. All this comports well with Greek and Roman practice, with its reliance on long-dead heroes. Supplicants traveled great distances to seek help by touching or praying to the relics of fallen heroes. Roman cultic hero worship included the sharing of a meal in memory of the fallen for the sake of the living.

In the third century a well-established system of penance began to emerge. It is important to note that penance is not the same as repentance. Biblically, repentance is a radical change of mind that leads to a change of action (2 Corinthians 7:8–11). The system of penance was built by church fathers such as Cyprian in order to deal with the public aspect of restoring those who had sinned. It was especially associated with the question of the *lapsi*—those who compromised during the persecutions of Galerius and Diocletian. When one who had lapsed into sin came to the bishop in order to be restored to the fellowship, a procedure for public confession, a tradition of specific acts and even a more or less set timeframe before readmittance to full fellowship was established. The penitents were ordered to wear mourning clothes, to observe weeping and fasting for a set time, to perform vigils, to bring alms, to prostrate themselves before the church and to receive the laying on of hands of the bishop. It is easy to see why the church leaders felt this was a useful expedient in order to protect the purity of Christian conviction and holiness within the church. Perhaps if the practice had been limited in time and scope it might have been more helpful than hurtful to the church. Unfortunately it did not turn out that way. It is also not hard to detect an evolution away from pure New Testament practice here. Generally, the penitent was allowed only one such penance. A second opportunity was not offered. It seems fair to ask for the biblical warrant for allowing exactly one opportunity to repent and renew one's faith within the fellowship. The Novation and Donatist church schisms were largely based on questions related to penance and church discipline.

It is one of the more unfortunate facts of Christian history that when the Greek New Testament was translated into the Latin, the Greek word for repentance, *metanoia* (literally change of mind), was translated into a Latin word that came from this church practice of penance, *paenitentia*. By the Middle Ages, repentance/penance had evolved in the West into a series of outward acts which could eliminate the effects of sin. How far a divergence from biblical teaching this represents!

Art and Culture

In the third century a uniquely Christian art emerged which used the typical Roman style. The first evidence we have for "Christian" art comes from the Roman catacombs about AD 200. It is likely that the primitive church refrained from religious art, not principally because they were too busy or too poor, but by conscious choice. We do not have direct, specific New Testament statements either for or against the use of art, sculpture or music in Christian worship, but we can speculate that, as the church avoided the musical instruments of pagan worship, they also chose not to make artistic representations of religious themes. We cannot rule out the possibility that prohibitions against the use of instruments and the visual arts in worship traces back to the apostles. All we can say about this is that such advice cannot be found in the New Testament documents and we do not have strong evidence of such a prohibition even among the early church fathers. A lack of evidence one way or another makes for a weak argument. In any case, as we argued above, to use silence in the Scripture on a particular question as prescriptive for Christian worship today is generally not justified. Another possible reason the early Christians avoided the use of images was influence from Jewish thinking. Because of the Ten Commandments, the Jews did not make sculpture or even two-dimensional depictions of humans at all. Still another possible contributing explanation for the lack of Christian art is the relative poverty of the Christians and the transitory nature of their meeting places.

Early Christian art consisted largely of symbolic images. In the early third century Clement of Alexandria listed images that were appropriate for disciples to use in their personal seal rings. These included the dove, fish, ship, lyre, anchor and fisherman. Use of idolatrous images, weapons and wine cups were prohibited for obvious reasons. Our earliest examples of clearly Christian art are found in Rome, associated with cemeteries and their underground equivalent, the catacombs. Early on, scenes from both the Old and New Testament are found. Favorites included scenes from Jonah, which carried an association with Christian baptism, as well as its symbolism of the resurrection of Jesus. A common New Testament theme was the raising of Lazarus, which is an obvious choice for funerary art. Also found are depictions of baptisms, the Eucharist and the love feast.

As already mentioned, the earliest clearly identified Christian place of worship thus far is one in a city in Syria, Dura Europos on the Euphrates River. This house church included a baptistery with paintings of the Good Shepherd, the woman at the well, the healing of the paralytic at the Pool of Siloam, Jesus and Peter walking on water and others. It may be a significant indication of the practice of the church at that time that there was no painting in the actual worship/assembly room. Perhaps one intention of these paintings was to communicate the gospel stories to the largely illiterate congregation. We know this was a primary intention of Medieval art in the basilicas. In the third century churches began to purchase and use larger buildings as meeting places. Large, elaborate basilicas for worship were not built until the time of Constantine.

Pagan Philosophy and Religion in the Third and Early Fourth Centuries

Two significant religious move-ments arose during the third century. Both were to have a significant effect on the course of Christian thought and church history, and the second of the two was influenced, in turn, by Christian ideas.

The first of these we will consider is known to modern scholars as Neoplatonism. This movement can be seen as a revival but also an extension of the philosophy of Plato. The figure most strongly related to the formation

Bust of Plotinus

137

of this new and vigorous philosophical movement was Plotinus. Plotinus was born about AD 205. Much of his career was spent in Alexandria. His biographer, Porphyry, tells us that Plotinus rejected all the philosophies of his day, including the Epicureans, Neopythagoreans and Stoics. Finally he heard a philosopher named Ammonius Saccas who was part of a new school that eventually became known as the Neoplatonists. After teaching for twelve years in Alexandria, Plotinus attempted travel to Persia and India to learn from Eastern philosophers. Later he journeyed to Rome where he had a large following and became very influential on many senators and even the emperor Gallienus. Scholars speculate that it was the influence of Plotinus on Gallienus that led to the end of the persecutions of the church in the 250s. Plotinus preached tolerance of other philosophies. Here in Rome he took on as his student the very influential Porphyry, who wrote the most important anti-Christian polemic in the third century.

The chief writing of Plotinus is found in his *Enneads*, which were collected and edited by Porphyry after his death in 270. The philosophy of Plotinus had much in common with that of the Platonic school. He spiritualized the world, seeing it as governed by a sort of universal soul, painting the physical creation as an emanation of this universal godlike soul. To Plotinus, as to the Christian theologian Gregory of Nyssa in the fourth century, evil was a lack of good—the result of being pulled toward the physical and away from the spiritual. Evil is related to good as darkness is to light. The former is the lack of the latter. We will see the influence of Plotinus on Augustine in this thinking. The cosmology of Plotinus involved a supreme and totally transcendent "One" who was completely removed from physical reality. This "One" had no distinction, no discernable qualities, no emotions and was unaffected by human lives. The "God" of Neoplatonism had no thought or self-contemplating intelligence. It simply was. The One was the source of the world, but did not will its creation. Plotinus denied the biblical picture of creation *ex nihilo* (out of nothing). Rather his universe is pantheistic. Knowledge (*nous*), the universal soul and nature are emanations of the One. The influence of Plotinus is seen in Gregory of Nyssa and Augustine. It continued all the way to the 16th century, being found in the theologian Bruno and the scientist Kepler.

Unlike Plotinus, who did not criticize Christianity as far as we know, his most important student, Porphyry (c. 232–c. 305), took it upon himself to mount a strong if mainly intellectual critique of the Jesus movement. He argued that the Genesis creation account does not make sense because it has night and day appearing before the heavenly objects. He attempted to undermine the inspiration of the book of Daniel by claiming that it was written after the persecutions of Antiochus Epiphanes (167–164 BC), which it is supposed to prophesy. Both criticisms are quite easily shown to be invalid.[45] It is hard to assess how successful Porphyry was at turning people from the faith at the time. His was a reasoned rather than an emotional attack on biblical Christianity—one which took to task Christian theology and did not attack the person of Jesus Christ. He is a forerunner of much of the critique of biblical inspiration today. There is nothing new under the sun.

Whereas Neoplatonism was chiefly a philosophy and not a religion, Manichaeism had aspects of both. The founder of this religion was Mani (216–276), also known in the West as Manes. His was an eclectic belief system— an apparent attempt to form a unified world religion. Mani was Persian. Consequently, the chief aspect of his religious system was a stark dualism reminiscent of Zoroastrianism, the native religion of Persia. Manichaeism's worldview had a more or less equal battle between good and evil, light and dark. Unlike Plotinus, for whom darkness is the absence of light, according to Manes evil is real and is in conflict with good in this dualistic system. Mani combined aspects of Gnosticism, of Buddhist thinking, ideas from the Jewish/Christian Elkesaite sect (a group in Parthia/Persia similar to the Ebionites) and even orthodox Christianity in his religious stew. Modern skeptical scholars have attempted to paint the biblical Jesus as borrowed from other religions, including Manichaeism, but certainly the borrowing was in the other direction. For example, his followers claimed that Mani was crucified, but with none of the convincing evidence we have available for the crucifixion and resurrection of Jesus. The elect members of this sect lived ascetic lives, abstaining from sex, from eating meat and even from most kinds of work. The Christian view is that the physical creation is good—very good (Genesis 1:25). As with so many man-made religions, Manichaeism viewed creation as evil, which explains Mani's emphasis on asceticism. The cosmology of Manichaeism is complex, showing affinities with Eastern cosmologies. This fact will be important to us later.

Mani's followers were aggressive in their evangelism. The religion spread from India in the East all the way to Rome in the West. In the early fourth century, the influence of Manichaeism was sufficient to warrant comment by Eusebius. He refers to that "madman" Manes.[46] He tells us that Mani claimed to be the Paraclete of John 16:7–11, and that he purposefully chose twelve chief disciples in imitation of the ministry of Jesus. One of Manichaeism's most famous converts was Augustine. We will see that through this conversion and his subsequent conversion to Christianity, Mani's influence crept into Christendom, even to modern times.

The Growing Division Between East and West

One of the themes of the first millennium of Christian history is the gradual drifting away of the Eastern from the Western church, culminating in the final official division between the Roman and Byzantine churches in 1054. Obviously, this division was not the result of a single event. In fact, one can see the seeds of this separation already in the third century. As mentioned earlier, within a generation of the resurrection of Jesus, the church had become principally Greek in language and culture. Even in the Latin West, important bishops such as Irenaeus were Greek in every way. By the third century this was no longer the case. The language of the church in Carthage and Rome was Latin. Eventually, whether a Christian teacher or theologian came to have a wide influence locally depended largely on the language they used in their writing. Tertullian had great influence in the West and very little in the East. With Origen it was the opposite. Who influenced whom? Did the West influence the theology of Tertullian or did Tertullian influence the thinking in the Western church? Both, but one can make a stronger case for the former.

Language was a factor, but not the biggest one which distinguished the church in Gaul, Spain, Italy and Africa from that in Asia Minor, Palestine, Egypt and Mesopotamia. The Roman spirit was concerned with law, with government, with practical matters in the here and now. The Greek mindset was much more other-worldly and esoteric. The Western church at a very early date tended to be more hierarchical. We have already noted that Alexandria, in the East, resisted the monarchical bishop well into the fourth century. Where the West focused on doctrine, the East focused on theology. The West emphasized the humanity of Jesus; the East (with important exceptions) emphasized his deity. The Eastern church was concerned with experiencing Jesus and with spiritual transformation. Western Christendom emphasized sacrament and works. As we will see, in the East, the church was content to be an arm of the state, whereas in the West the church became the state.

These trends are clearly illustrated by looking at the concerns of Cyprian and Tertullian versus Clement of Alexandria and Origen. Cyprian attempted to create a stable church government, where Origen sought détente with Greek philosophy. One of the most obvious aspects of the growing separation between East and West was the rise to preeminence of the church in Rome, even in the third century. Already in the beginning of the third century, the church in Rome was trying to assert its ascendant role over the entire Christian church. The Roman bishops mainly concerned themselves with church politics and pastoral issues, leaving the Eastern churches such as Antioch, Jerusalem and Alexandria and later Constantinople to fight the divisive theological battles that began in the late third century. Its ability to stay above the fray only increased the influence of Rome in the long run. The earliest creedal statement we have, known as the Old Roman Symbol, originated in Rome. Formal ordination of priests, first mentioned by Hippolytus in his *Apostolic Tradition* about AD 215, began in Rome as well. Roman bishops had already been tracing their authority back to Peter and Paul by the third century, claiming apostolic authority. The bishops of Rome attempted to claim a kind of universal authority over all the churches as early as Victor in the 190s. As already mentioned, Stephen, bishop of Rome in the time of Cyprian, made even stronger claims of Roman supremacy. However, it was not until after the time of Constantine that this claim was taken seriously in the West, and nothing remotely like the papacy existed during the third and early fourth centuries.

Schisms in the Late Third and Early Fourth Centuries

Novatianism

Two of the three schisms we will consider at this point were the direct result of anti-Christian persecutions and their aftermath. Both raised important questions of church discipline, standards of commitment and the meaning of discipleship to Jesus. The first of these is associated with Novatian. He and his schism have already been mentioned briefly because of his connection to Cyprian.

Novatian was an elder/presbyter in Rome in the period immediately following the persecutions under Decius and Valerian. He was a "rigorist" with regard to fellowship. He taught that once a Christian committed a sin that caused him or her to leave the fellowship of the church, there was no forgiveness—there was no way to be readmitted to the body of Christ. The context of this controversy is those who had compromised with the Roman Empire during the persecution. Novatian refused to readmit those who had denied Jesus. The "laxists" in Rome supported the immediate restoration of those who had lapsed. In Carthage, Cyprian proposed a middle ground, requiring a procedure of penance, overseen by the local bishop. In the midst of this controversy a new bishop was elected in Rome. Cornelius took the moderate position. Rather than support his new bishop, Novatian began a schism by having himself appointed bishop of Rome by a number of the neighboring bishops who took the same rigorist position on Christian fellowship. Eusebius does not mince words about this divider of the church:

Novatian, indeed, and those who so arrogantly united with him, and those that had determined to adopt the uncharitable and most inhuman opinion of the man, these that considered among those that were alienated from the church; but that brethren who had incurred a calamity should be treated and healed with the remedies of repentance [penance].[47]

It raises questions of the role of the local church leadership in setting standards of commitment for members of the fellowship and how these standards are to be applied or enforced. It is helpful for us to ask ourselves what stand we would have taken over the Novatian controversy—whether we would have supported the more strict Novatians or the more forgiving attitude of Cyprian.

Our situation today is really quite different from the third century. Those disciplined by the church in the third century literally had nowhere else to go within Christianity. Today, if a member is caught up in sin and is asked to leave the fellowship, there are an unlimited number of options, including "Christian" groups with a very low standard of commitment. Does this change the game for us compared to the early church?

Most of us probably would not have sided with Novatian. We understand biblically that church discipline is intended to warn the church, but also to bring the one disciplined back into fellowship with the body. 2 Corinthians 2:6–8 is surely relevant here. Concerning one who had been disciplined by the church, Paul said:

The punishment inflicted on him by the majority is sufficient for him. Now instead, you ought to forgive and comfort him, so that he will not be overwhelmed by excessive sorrow. I urge you, therefore, to reaffirm your love for him.

Should there be a process in place for such a restoration? Perhaps, but it seems that the system of penance instituted by the church and enforced by Cyprian is not in line with the spirit expressed by Paul. In any case, if there is not an astounding love within the fellowship, God's intention for the process of discipline and restoration will not work. Perhaps we need to start there.

Donatism

What has the emperor to do with the church?

—Donatus of Carthage

If we were following strict chronology, we would cover the Arian heresy next. However, the Donatist schism, which occurred almost sixty years after that of Novatianism, has enough in common with the former that we will consider this first. Like Novatianism, the problem with Donatus was over the question of discipleship and church discipline. This time the threat to church unity was greater and more lasting. The intervening years had changed the political climate within the church, with dramatic implications.

The situation behind the Donatists is a bit complicated. Actually, it is quite complicated. The context is the period immediately following the persecutions of Diocletian at Carthage in North Africa. A certain Caecilian was elected by presbyters of the local church to succeed Mensurius in 311. A wealthy and pious woman in Carthage named Lucilla had feuded with Mensurius. She had observed the practice of kissing the bone of a martyr before the taking of communion. As shocking as this might seem to us, we can see the sincerity of devotion of this woman, especially at a time immediately after great numbers of Christians had been executed under Diocletian. Mensurius forbade the practice of kissing the bones of the martyrs, probably both out of concern for an unchristian veneration of the saints and because this was a matter of authority of the bishop. Many pious saints, including Lucilla, were receiving advice from confessors, not the bishop. Confessors were a class of devoted Christians, many of whom were living ascetic lives in the desert, to whom Christians would go for instruction. These hermits and other holy men represented a parallel kind of authority in the church. Here we can see that a strong, centralized hierarchy in the church, which had been formed to prevent division in the church, was acting to create division. We ought to be careful of the seeds we sow.

When those in agreement with Mensurius appointed Caesilian, a schism ensued. To complicate matters, during the extreme persecution under Diocletian when church leaders fled to the desert, Mensurius had entrusted church possessions to wealthy members of the church. When Constantine ruled that the confiscated church property was to be returned, a political question arose. Which group would be given the property? Constantine's government was called into this issue.

This raised still further problems. In North Africa there were three distinct ethnic groups. The Latins were the wealthy, aristocratic class. Mensurius and Caesilian were from this class of wealthy outsiders. Another ethnic group in North Africa was the Punics. When the Romans conquered Africa and Numidia in the Punic wars, this ethnic group was forced to serve them, as they were the former rulers of North Africa at the time of the Carthaginian

Empire. The Punics were the small landowners and the farmers in Africa and Numidia.[48] A third ethnic group was the Berbers. These were the true "natives" of the area. They tended to live in the steppes and the desert, on the outskirts of civilization. A clear majority of the Christians in North Africa at the time were from the latter two groups. They had come to Christianity at a time when the Roman Empire was persecuting the church. Now the tables were turned. The power of the state was to align with the "church" against what the Punics and Berbers perceived to be their own interests.

Constantine entrusted to the bishop of Rome the decision of which group received the property—the rigorist, mostly Punic and Berber churches, or the laxist, mostly Latin churches. It is not hard to guess which faction was favored. The bishop in Rome gave the property to the minority Latin "laxists." Whether the decision was in support of political allies or because it represented a more Christlike gracious attitude to those who have fallen into sin may be hard to separate.

Here is where the issue of church authority and discipline entered the equation, leading to a long-lasting schism. The appointment of Mensurius had proceeded without the customary input of the Numidian bishops, who would have represented the Punic or Berber element in the church. One of those who had supported Mensurius was Felix, bishop of Aptunga. Felix was among the *traditori* (the root of our word traitor, literally those who handed over). The *traditori* were infamous because they had handed the Christian Scripture over to be burned during the persecution of Diocletian. To the Numidian bishops, Felix had denied the faith and was no longer qualified to participate in the appointment of a bishop. During the Novatian schism the question was the readmittance of the common member to the fellowship. With the Donatist schism, the question was the readmission of a *lapsist* to an ordained leadership position within the church. Whether their opposition was due to a sincere commitment to Christian lifestyle or an excuse to rebel against the outsider—the Latin leadership—is hard to determine from our distant perspective. In any case, the Numidian bishops selected an alternative bishop of Carthage by the name of Majorinus. When Majorinus died in 313, he was succeeded by Donatus, after whom this group came to be known.

The question of the joining of church and state entered into this division as well. This was relatively new for the church in the early fourth century. With hindsight we can see the sinister potential to this juxtaposition. In 313 Constantine extended to the Christian clergy two grants: The priests and bishops of the Church were to be given financial support from the state and were to be exempt from the duty of collecting taxes for the government. Were the Donatist clergy to receive these grants? Constantine called for a synod[49] of bishops in Arles in Gaul (France) in 314 to decide this question. Many believe that the first church council called by a head of state was the one in Nicaea in 325. Not true. Church historians do not normally list the synod in Arles among the great councils. Perhaps there is some justification for this because the questions decided at Arles were of a more narrow scope than at the later synods, and participation only included Western bishops. In a pair of decisions that will seem confusing to us, the bishops at Arles decided to bar the traditores from the clergy, but to uphold the validity of the ordinations performed by the lapsed clergy. In effect, they had decided against the Donatists. The question of whether the validity of an ordination comes from the authority and holiness of the one who lays on hands or from the authority of the church in the abstract will be a major issue for the church, coming to a head with Augustine.

In 316 Constantine decided definitively against the Donatist sect. He began a government-sponsored persecution of these Christians in 320. Not surprisingly, this hardened the position of the Donatists. Donatus famously said, "What has the emperor to do with the church?"[50] To this we might respond, "Good question." The Donatist churches did not die out. The bulk of the Punic and Berber Christians stood with this group. In fact, they became the majority of the Christians in Numidia and perhaps North Africa in general. They had a missionary zeal that was largely absent in the orthodox church, planting rival churches and building places of assembly which often were more impressive than their Catholic counterparts.

We will leave the Donatist problem for a while, as the controversy with this sect was a chief pillar around which the career of Augustine was defined almost one hundred years later. However, before we move on, this division raises a number of issues that are clearly relevant to the church today.

Which was the true Church after the schism, the Donatists or the orthodox Catholic Church? Perhaps both were. The theological differences were not major. If we favor a more hard-line view of the Christian lifestyle, we might go with the Donatists. On the other hand, the New Testament clearly teaches the possibility of grace and restoration of a repentant one who has fallen into sin. Remember, though, that this is a question, not about membership but about the spiritual authority of a bishop. To make the question more complicated, the rigorist versus laxist issue may well have been a foil for a fight about who has authority over whom. Does a local church have to submit to the authority of a distant hierarchy? Biblically, what is the relationship between one church with its local leaders and another church? Is there a biblical answer, or does expediency determine what is best? Does "the Church" as an abstract entity have authority over a local leadership? In the primitive church cooperation between churches seemed to be the model, but this was not to be the trend as time passed. Clearly these questions are relevant for us today. Many Christian denominations use the hierarchical model, with a central authority to hire and fire local leaders. Others have a congregational model. One advantage of looking at this in a historical context is that we can see where the choices being made in the early fourth century led in the long run and perhaps learn from what we see.

What should be the relationship between the Christian church and the government? Doesn't money from the state always come with strings attached? Should the church in the fourth century have accepted that which was offered to it by Constantine? Would we have done the same in our modern context? Should church leaders be held to a higher standard of Christian conduct and commitment than the other members? Can a leader who has denied the faith ever be renewed to major leadership roles in the church? The Bible teaches (1 Timothy 3:2) that the elder/overseer should be above reproach. True, but at what point does grace apply? Were the Donatists right, then, in their opposition to the church in Rome on the question of ordination? The Donatist question can cast light on how we handle controversies today. Both the Roman bishop Miltiades and Donatus defended their positions based on theological concerns, but was this really what was going on? To quote from renowned church historian Everett Ferguson, "How theological concerns are intertwined with personal and social concerns is often difficult to disentangle, and this is particularly the case with Donatism."[51] All of us will do well to remember this maxim. We think in complete sincerity that we take such and such position for theological or biblical reasons, but often the reality is more complicated.

Arianism

There was once when the Son was not.

—Arius of Alexandria

The last major theological division that we will consider in this chapter is the one begun by Arius. Whereas the division that occurred in the Western church surrounding Donatus involved questions of church government, the problems raised by Arius in the Eastern church were about philosophical/theological issues. From what we already know about the growing cultural division between East and West, this distinction is not a surprise at all. The Arian heresy will carry us to the Council of Nicaea and bring to a close our study of primitive Christianity before it became Christendom. The story brings us back to Alexandria. Arius' background is obscure. It has been claimed that he came from North Africa, in Libya. Whatever his place of birth, he studied theology in Antioch at the catechetical school there before coming to Alexandria. We will be hearing quite a bit about the division between theological ideas emanating from the schools in Antioch and Alexandria. All along, going back to Clement and Origen, teachers in Alexandria had stressed the divinity of Jesus over and above his humanity. Those in Antioch also claimed Origen as their theological father, but they emphasized much more strongly the humanity of Jesus and his submission to the father. Add to the mix the strong influence on Christian thinkers of the Greek idea that God cannot change and that he is very distant from humanity—impassible, unaffected by human emotions. Paul of Samosata (already mentioned in connection with the adoptionist heresy) and Lucian of Antioch, the tutor of Arius, represent this train of thought. While in Antioch, Arius became friends with Eusebius of Nicomedia (not to be confused with Eusebius of Caesarea who wrote *Ecclesiastical History*, with whom he sharply disagreed on theology), who was later to become his strongest ally.

Arius arrived in Alexandria in 311 where he was anointed as a priest. Here he began to sharply disagree with the theology of the reigning bishop, Alexander of Alexandria. Alexander, a modest and humble man by all accounts, emphasized the ineffable and unchanging nature of Jesus, typical of an Alexandrine Christian. Viewing things with his Antiochene sensibility, Arius saw Alexander as teaching the Sabellian/Modalist heresy, making the Father, Son and Spirit different modes of one person, not three separate persons.

It appears that the younger Arius was quite a charismatic speaker. Eventually he inspired the common people to parade through Alexandria, chanting and holding up signs with the slogan "There was (once) when the Son was not." One is reminded of the charismatic Absalom creating a popular following and rebelling against David in Jerusalem (2 Samuel 14-18). Because we do not have any of Arius' writings extant except for quotations from his enemies, we should be cautious about characterizing him from the writings of his critics, but it seems that Arius was an ambitious man who was willing to appeal to the crowd. Quite possibly he swung all the way to the conclusion that Jesus was a created being at least in part to distinguish himself from his rival Alexander, whom he hoped to replace as bishop in Alexandria. In any case, he eventually became hardened in his position. To Arius and his followers Jesus was a creature, and not equal to God. Arius taught at the school in Alexandria, delivered public speeches and wrote letters to neighboring churches, all to undermine Alexander and his theology. Soon this conflict broke out into a theological war between the followers of Alexander and Arius.

Alexander appealed to other bishops in the Eastern Mediterranean, calling a synod in Alexandria. Before this could occur, Arius aroused what can best be called a mob, marching, chanting slogans, singing songs. A riot occurred between the followers of the two camps, right in front of the basilica in Alexandria. What an embarrassment to Christianity! Finally the synod met in 318. Alexander accused Arius of reducing Jesus to less than God. He charged Arius with teaching that Jesus could have fallen like Satan. He accused him of teaching a more sophisticated version of adoptionism, a teaching which had already been pronounced heretical. The synod condemned the teaching of Arius, pronouncing it heresy, and removed Arius from the presbytery.

If we can trust the accuracy of those who quoted the words of Arius, the charges seem to have been warranted. For example, Arius described the relationship between Father and Son as follows:

> And Christ is not true God,...even he was made God.... The Son does not know the Father exactly, nor does the Logos see the Father perfectly,... for he is not the true and only Logos of the Father, but by a name alone he is called Logos and Sophia [ie. Wisdom] and by grace is called Son and Power.[52]

In the end, both groups claimed that salvation was at stake, essentially wanting to disfellowship (anathematize) the other group. Arius fled to the side of his friend Eusebius of Nicomedia, from where he continued a campaign to convince bishops who had not attended the synod in Alexandria to his cause. We will see that his campaign was not without success. The ceaseless battle over the teaching of Arius was what motivated Constantine to call the Council of Nicaea.

Looking back at the Arian heresy through the lens of history, we can imagine what might have happened if Christian charity had prevailed. What if Arius and Alexander had been willing to simply sit down and talk together, with the aim to protect, not their pride and their position, but the church of which they were shepherds. Perhaps they could have resolved their differences sufficiently to be able to work together, even if they did not totally agree. Perhaps they could have avoided destroying the faith of so many. Eventually, Arius moved so far that the church had no choice but to declare his teaching heresy. If Jesus is not God then we are not saved through his death on the cross. The teaching of Arius is that of the Jehovah's Witness group today. To lower Jesus to a creation is to make him a sort of a demigod. It is to teach a different Jesus from the one in the Bible. This is indeed a salvation issue.

Persecutions Come to an End: Constantine and the Edict of Milan

We now turn to the career of one of the giant figures in the history of Christianity: Constantine "the Great" (AD 272–337). To some, Constantine is the hero who saved Christianity. To others he inadvertently but almost singlehandedly destroyed the integrity of the Christian movement. The truth lies somewhere in between. One thing we can say for sure, the history of Christianity can be divided into pre- and post-Constantine. This division is not an arbitrary one. After Constantine, nothing would be the same again. There is no doubt that we can gain many insights into how to do (or perhaps how not to do) Christianity from the events surrounding the life of this enigmatic man.

Constantine

In order to place Constantine into our historical narrative, let us go back just a bit. We have already seen that Diocletian started a new and vicious persecution against the church in 303. He published a series of edicts commanding the destruction of all Christian churches, the turning over and burning of Christian Scriptures and the arrest, torture and execution of Christian leaders if they would not confess allegiance to the Roman gods. In 305, possibly for health reasons, Diocletian divided the Roman Empire into four geographical regions, with Constantius and Galerius to rule as Augusti—essentially as co-emperors, and with Severus and Maximin as Caesars, which was one step below the Augusti. Galerius controlled the East, Severus ruled Italy and Constantius was over Gaul, Germany and Britain. Constantius was the father of Constantine "the Great." He was a Neoplatonist. As with most from this Greek philosophical school, he believed in religious toleration. Combine this with the fact that his wife Helena was a devout Christian, and we can easily see why Constantius, of the four rulers, was the most tolerant of the Christian church. He appears to have enforced Diocletian's edicts against the church without zeal, trying his best to minimize their impact. For all practical purposes, Christianity was tolerated in Gaul. Eusebius said of Constantius:

He had no share in the hostility raised against us but even preserved and protected those pious persons under him free from harm and slander. Neither did he demolish the churches nor devise any other mischief against us, and at length he enjoyed a most happy and blessed death. He was the only one who, at his death, did peaceably and gloriously leave the government to his own son as his successor.... His son, Constantine, therefore...resolved to tread in the footsteps of his father.[53]

Constantius died in 306. The young Constantine, at the age of 34, took military and administrative control of Gaul, Britain and the German frontier, pronouncing himself Augustus. The situation in the empire was relatively static for a few years while Constantine stabilized his power in the North. He stayed out of problems in Italy, which led to Maxentius taking Italy

from Severus and promoting himself to Caesar. In 311, Gallienus, the zealous persecutor of the church in the East, was succeeded by Licinius.

Scholars generally agree that the turning point in the life and career of Constantine occurred in 312. He entered battle with his troops against Maxentius, now the Augustus who controlled Rome and the Italian peninsula. In what is known as the Battle of Milvian

Chi Rho symbol adapted by Constantine's troops (chi rho being the first two letters of the Greek word Christ)

Bridge, the considerably smaller army of Constantine routed the troops of Maxentius. The battle occurred at a bridge that crosses the Tiber, giving the victorious army free access to Rome. We have conflicting accounts of a mystical experience that Constantine had at the time of the battle. Constantine said he saw a vision of the Christian Chi Rho symbol in a dream in which he was told to conquer in the name of Jesus Christ. It is possible that the interpretation Constantine gave to his dream was influenced by his Christian adviser, Hosius, bishop of Cordoba in Spain. Eusebius, unabashed fan of Constantine, gives a more romantic version of the story, having Constantine seeing his vision of the Christian symbol in the sky above the battle. In any case, there is no doubt that the victory at Milvian Bridge was momentous. Constantine became master of the Roman West. From this point, he moved decidedly to support and even to promote the Christian movement.

Constantine did not become a Christian at this time, but he committed himself to a pro-Christian policy. The most common view is that he delayed baptism until near his death twenty-five years later. It is believed that he was baptized by Eusebius of Nicomedia in 337. While some point to the Battle of Milvian Bridge as the key turning point for church history, others mention the Edict of Milan that was published in 313. Constantine met with Licinius, emperor of the East in Milan. They published a joint official document that was promulgated throughout the empire. It gave full and free rights to "Christians and all others."

Head of the Colossus of Constantine

More than one copy of the edict sent by Licinius to rulers in the East has been recovered, so we have access to the text. The edict of Milan not only gave freedom of religion to the entire Roman Empire, it also represented a treaty of peace, giving stability to a delicate balance of power between East and West, Licinius and Constantine.

From this point, Constantine began a gradual, irreversible process of Christianization of the empire. He was strongly encouraged in this by his ever-active mother Helena. We have already seen that he intervened, albeit reluctantly, in the Council of Arles in 314, which renounced the Donatist sect and that he offered to help support the Christian clergy and grant them freedom from the duty of taxation. Christian soldiers began to enter the Roman army. Remember that before this time, bishops had been virtually unanimous in teaching against Christians serving in the military.

In the meantime, Licinius launched a sort of last-gasp persecution of the church in the eastern empire in 320. This was no minor persecution, as we know from Eusebius. The persecution created political problems for Constantine, as it put pressure on him from his Christian allies to intervene militarily, perhaps when he was not yet ready. Finally, in 324, the two met in battle at Adrianople, in Thrace, at the border of modern Greece and Turkey. Licinius self-consciously represented the old, pagan Rome, while Constantine saw himself as the head of a Christian army. The result was the defeat of Licinius. He retreated, appointing Martius Martinianus Caesar, but Constantine continued marching east, defeating the pagan army at the Hellespont and Chrysopolis. In 325, Constantine took the throne of a united

Roman Empire.

How will we analyze the effect of Constantine's conversion, real or not, on Christianity? It is hard to overstate the long-term effect of the toleration of Christianity. Constantine went much further than toleration. He positively supported the orthodox Catholic Church, even intervening in church political and theological disputes. At the time of the Edict of Toleration, the Christian church was a decided minority in the Roman empire, even if it was the largest religious group in the empire. With Constantine, Christianity became more popular. Thousands flooded into the church. Most of those baptized were not repentant disciples of Jesus. Even before 313, worldliness was a major issue in the church, but beginning with the toleration, an increasing proportion did not possess a Christian character. With financial and political support from Constantine, encouraged by his mother, large Christian basilicas were built in the cities of the empire. Without the purifying power of persecution, the level of commitment to the pure Christian gospel was diluted. The change in church culture was not necessarily sudden, but the inexorable trend toward accepting pagan practices, in the end, virtually destroyed the unique Christian character of the church.

We should not overstate the amount of change that actually happened during Constantine's life. It is the inexorable trend that is the key to understanding the impact of the toleration and support of the church. In fact, Constantine did not completely turn his back on the pagan culture of Rome. He was, by nature, a unifier of diverse people. As far as we know, he maintained his position as the symbolic head of the Roman cult—as Pontifex Maximus—throughout his career. Pagans did not all suddenly embrace the state-supported Christian Church. During the fourth century there was even a renaissance of Neoplatonic thought, and the dualist Manichaean sect made great gains. When the cross first appeared on Roman coins in 314, the image of *Sol Invictus* and *Mars Conservator* was also on the money.

Although Constantine did not break decisively with paganism, he was uncomfortable with Rome, the Senate and its pagan association. For this reason, he decided to establish a new capital at the gateway to the East: Byzantium, on the Straits of Bosporus, which separate Europe from Asia. His new city took the name Constantinople. Constantine embarked on a massive building program. The emperor certainly was not the first Roman emperor to create a legacy through the building of monuments. What made Constantine different is that his monumental projects were church buildings. Christian churches up to that time had been modest affairs, but this was radically changed under the first Christian emperor. His basilicas were built in the Roman style for reception halls, courtrooms and marketplaces, on a grand scale. Still-famous basilicas were constructed under his orders, including St. Paul's and St. Peter's outside Rome (later the site of the Vatican) and St. John Lateran in Rome. Influenced by his mother Helena, Constantine had basilicas built at pilgrimage sites such as the Church of the Nativity in Bethlehem and the Church of the Holy Sepulchre at the supposed site of Jesus' tomb.

What should be the relationship between a Christian emperor and the clergy? The church struggled to discover what kind of relationship it should have with a political ruler who was supportive of their cause. In fact, one could make an excellent case that a Christian empire is a contradiction in terms. The truism that absolute power corrupts absolutely has merit. Constantine is a case in point. While he thought of himself as a sort of bishop of bishops (his son Constantius actually took this title for himself), and while he felt competent to intervene in theological questions, Constantine behaved in ways that are blatantly unchristian. It is believed that Constantine had both his son Crispus and his wife Fausta murdered for political reasons. It did not take long for the inescapable problems of a "Christian" emperor holding ultimate political power to emerge.

Eusebius of Caesarea

Reaction at the time to the toleration and the support of the emperor varied from a cautious optimism to a conviction that the arrival of Christendom under Constantine was God's providence, marking the coming of a new golden age and signaling the advent of the end of the world. Eusebius said of the triumph of Constantine and his support of the church, "This was not done by any mere human agency." He invoked "the evident superintendence of divine Providence"[54] to explain the rise of Constantine over his rivals. What we do not hear from church leaders at the time is warnings that toleration could indirectly lead to the destruction of the holy nature of the Christian church. They did not have what we have, which is the benefit of hindsight. Here, again, is evidence that a study of church history can be instructive.

Eusebius of Caesarea was in the second category. He was an unapologetic enthusiast for Constantine. We call him Eusebius of Caesarea to distinguish him from Eusebius of Nicomedia who was from the opposite party in the Arian controversy at the time and was actually a more influential figure during his life time than our Eusebius of Caesarea. One can argue that Eusebius of Caesarea is not a major figure in the history of Christianity if compared with Irenaeus, Cyprian or Augustine. To some extent this is true, but, as we will see, Eusebius was present at all the key events of his time. His importance to our story is sealed by his position as the first systematic historian of the primitive church.

Eusebius was born about 264, near the end of the reign of Emperor Gallienus (250–266). Having survived the persecutions at the beginning of the fourth century, he lived until 339. He said of himself that as a youth he lived in Palestine.[55] He also said that it was in Palestine in 296 that he saw the future Emperor Constantine while he was traveling with Diocletian. The future historian of the Church was appointed as presbyter (priest) by his mentor Pamphilus. Pamphilus was an eminent Bible scholar and an enthusiastic supporter of Origen of Alexandria. Later, Eusebius' enthusiasm for Origen was used against him, as Origen was posthumously declared a heretic for his views on the divinity of Jesus. Eusebius suffered under the persecution of Diocletian. He was arrested at that time but later released unharmed. His enemies later used his relatively light treatment by the Romans against him, even charging that he offered sacrifice to the Roman god. Almost certainly this was a spurious charge.

Eusebius was appointed bishop of Caesarea in 313 (and thus the label Eusebius of Caesarea), at the time that the peace of Constantine came to the church. He immediately began his career as a writer, producing a Christian apology against paganism (*Preparation for the Gospel*) and a defense of the truth of the Christian message through fulfilled prophecy (*Demonstration of the Gospel*). He wrote several commentaries, a parallel of the Gospels and a geographical and historical sketch of the Bible.

Eusebius wrote his famous *Ecclesiastical History* some time between 320 and the accession of Constantine to the throne of the entire Roman Empire and the Council of Nicaea in 325. The events of his history end with what was, for Eusebius, the crowning event of his life, when the Christian emperor took the throne of the empire. Eusebius was generally a careful historian. He rarely failed to mention his sources, which were usually earlier Christian writers. His reliability decreases somewhat as one moves to earlier periods in the church. For example, his stories of the martyrdoms of the apostles may include some unreliable tradition. We cannot say for sure that these stories are apocryphal, as he is sometimes the only source we have. While Eusebius is generally reliable, he certainly did not hesitate to allow his biases to enter into his history. At times he treats those with whom he did not agree in a rather obviously unbalanced way. He also probably gave to himself an exaggerated importance in the events that transpired, even claiming that he had written the source document from which the Nicene Creed was drafted. Eusebius wrote a detailed report of the proceedings of the Council of Nicaea (see below), which are an invaluable source for understanding this important event. Later in his life, he produced two significant works on the relationship between theology and political thinking, *Life of Constantine* and *Praise of Constantine*. Here he foreshadowed the ideas of Augustine with regard to church and state.

Eusebius was not only a writer. He took an active role in the theological issues of his day—especially the Arian controversy. Although trained as an avid Origenist, his energy was devoted to bringing peace through compromise between the warring parties. In fact, his seemingly sincere effort to find a compromise position between Athanasius, bishop of Alexandria and Eusebius of Nicomedia on the Arian question was to cause problems for our Eusebius.

As the first systematic church historian, the importance of Eusebius is clear. In his own words, "…as the first of those who have entered the subject, we are attempting a trackless and unbeaten path."[56] This is not an exaggeration. There are countless details in early church history that we would not have without Eusebius recording quotations from his contemporaries and those who came before him.

The biggest weakness of Eusebius was his overly enthusiastic view of the role of Constantine in the history of Christianity. This clearly colored his historical perspective. We should bear in mind that some time after he finished writing *Ecclesiastical History* Constantine became his patron—essentially paying his salary. A fairly balanced view of Eusebius is provided by Michael J. Hollerich:

> Eusebius has been an inviting target for students of the Constantinian era. At one time or another they have characterized him as a political propagandist, a good courtier, the shrewd and worldly adviser of the Emperor Constantine, the great publicist of the first Christian emperor, the first in a long succession of ecclesiastical politicians, the herald of Byzantinism, a political theologian, a political metaphysician, and a caesaropapist. It is obvious that these are not, in the main, neutral descriptions. Much traditional scholarship, sometimes with barely suppressed disdain, has regarded Eusebius as one who risked his orthodoxy and perhaps his character because of his zeal for the Constantinian establishment.... The standard assessment has exaggerated the importance of political themes and political motives in Eusebius's life and writings and has failed to do justice to him as a churchman and a scholar.[57]

The Council of Nicaea and the Arian Controversy

Our story now takes us to the East. Political controversies in the church were generally worked out in the Latin West, while theological controversies, for the most part, were fought in the Greek East. The story of the Council of Nicaea will bring to a close the present chapter. It will mark for us in easily-defined terms many of the transitions in Christianity as it passed from its formative, apostolic and post-apostolic early history to the time of Christendom and a very different kind of Christian church from that established by the apostles.

The first general council was called by Constantine, with the express purpose of settling the issue of Arianism. Constantine arranged for the synod to gather at the small city of Nicaea, near the eastern shores of the Sea of Marmara, about fifty miles southeast of the future Constantinople. This was the temporary headquarters of his Eastern government while Constantinople was being built.

Many have grossly distorted what happened at Nicaea, even inventing wild stories that the Council removed books from the canon, made major revisions of the accepted text of the New Testament, removing references to reincarnation, inventing the idea for the first time that Jesus was deity and many other completely unfounded myths. Such was the thesis of *The DaVinci Code* by Dan Brown, a rather poor book from a scholarly perspective, even if a really good read. Fortunately for us, we have two different summaries of the proceedings, both from eyewitnesses. For this reason, such claims can be laid to rest, at least for those willing to let the evidence decide what they accept as true.

In fact, the actual decisions of the 250-plus bishops[58] who assembled at Nicaea were not particularly revolutionary. Although an important new word was added to the theological dictionary at this meeting, as we will see, the major result of the meeting was to produce a creed that was a compromise between extreme positions and that did not propose a radical new theology at all.

Nicaea is perhaps the most famous meeting of Christian minds in history. Its importance is not so much that the decisions promulgated there were revolutionary. It marks a very important signpost in the history of Christianity more because of the precedents it set for the future than the new ideas that were discussed. First of all, this synod of bishops was the first truly ecumenical (universal) meeting of church leaders since the Jerusalem Council, recorded in Acts 15. Second, it was the first one at which anathemas were published.[59] In other words, it was the first church council after the New Testament whose decisions and condemnations were generally accepted as binding on all Christians everywhere.

Up until this Council there was no agreed-upon means to determine big questions of doctrine or practice across the entire Christian church other than use of the Scripture. Of course, most Bible-believing Christians think this is exactly where such questions should be answered. Period. Over one hundred years before, Irenaeus had invoked apostolic tradition as a means to defend against heresy, but with the Arian controversy the apostolic tradition in this case was not sufficiently clear for a decisive determination. The problem that the Catholic Church faced was that in the controversy with those who supported the Arian position, both sides were able to present what appeared to be a perfectly reasonable defense of their position using the Scriptures. Arguments of this sort tended to end in a tie, or at best an indecisive conclusion. The game-changing precedent taken at Nicaea was to solve the question by publishing a consensus anathema. Where an argument could not be won by using Scripture, it could be settled by disfellowshipping and marking as doomed to hell those who held to a particular position (unless, of course, they were willing to repent and come back into the fold).

Most of us cringe at this precedent. We would argue that the cure was far worse than the disease. If a group of Christian leaders, no matter how wise and spiritual, are able to determine for all time the truth of a position by majority vote, clearly the authority of the Scripture is in serious danger. The history of church councils after Nicea gives credence to this concern. However, if we argue for choosing an expedient path—one which accomplishes the desired task efficiently—then the precedent set at Nicaea was a good one. What do we conclude from this? We should be cautious that expedient solutions to practical problems can be harmful to obeying the truth of the Bible in the long run.

The second dramatic precedent set at the first Council of Nicaea was the issuing of a Creed that was intended to be used as the grounds for determining who is and who is not a Christian. Up until this time, creeds had been a very common device within the church. There had been a number of different creeds that were generally associated with the great centers of Christianity such as Rome, Alexandria and Antioch. These were generally used as baptismal confessions in order to ensure that a new convert was introduced to the church having accepted the basic gospel truths. As such, they rarely if ever had been the cause of divisions within Christianity. This was to change radically after 325. The famed Nicene Creed was accepted as truly binding only somewhat gradually after the Council, but inexorably, it came to be a tool to determine orthodoxy. Either one accepted and was willing to state this creed publicly, or one was established to be not a Christian, at least by the Catholic Church.

We could mention a third quite significant precedent set at Nicaea, which is that a church council was called by a sitting emperor of a political state, Constantine. The emperor sat on a raised throne, presiding over the gathering, with his chief spiritual advisor, Hosius, at his side. This was clearly a very dramatic turning point in the relationship between the Christian church and the state. The problem with claiming this precedent is that technically, Nicaea was *not* the first example of a head of a political state calling for a church conference. The first council called by Constantine, although not as broad in the questions it addressed and certainly not ecumenical, was the one to decide the issue of Donatism in 314.

The immediate background to this, the first truly ecumenical Council, is the Arian controversy, with its stark disagreement over the nature of Jesus. Is he equal to God? Is he subordinate to God? Is he in fact God, or is he a powerful first creation of God? Is he just another aspect of God? This was not a brand-new discussion in the Christian church, but in Alexandria the debate between the bishop Alexander and his charismatic priest Arius and his supporters rose to a fever pitch. We have already seen that Arius and his teaching were condemned at a synod in Alexandria in 318. Arius was excommunicated. Unfortunately, this did not settle the question. Arius was strongly supported by the influential Eusebius of Nicomedia, who attempted to overthrow his condemnation. A relatively small synod in Antioch in 325 condemned the Christological view of Eusebius of Caesarea because he would not strongly condemn Arius. Constantine was always one to seek peace and unity where his subjects tended toward divisiveness. He made the fateful choice to intervene. It was his personal decision to call the great meeting of bishops in his royal palace at Nicaea in 325. He even offered to provide financial support and security to those attending.

In the end, the bishops who gathered were predominantly Greek. Only five of the bishops who signed the agreements at Nicaea have been definitely identified as being from the West. Two of these were representatives of the Roman bishop. One was Hosius, the chief Christian adviser to Constantine. In any case, for sheer numbers of bishops the turnout was impressive. Although the delegation from the Latin churches was small, this was the first synod in the East to include bishops from Rome. Despite the sparse representation from the West, it was seen in its time as a universal council. Eusebius describes the range of bishops who attended with great enthusiasm.

The most distinguished ministers of God met together from every part of Europe, Asian and Africa. The sacred edifice, as if enlarged by the pleasure of God, enclosed at the same time within its walls, both Syrians and Cilicians, Phoenicians, Arabians and inhabitants of Palestine; Egyptians, Thebeans, and Lybians, with others arriving from Mesopotamia. A bishop from Persia was also present. Nor was the Scythian absent from this assembly. Pontus, also, and Galatia, Pamphylia and Cappadocia, Asia and Phrygia furnished representatives from their most able divines. Thracians too, Macedonians, Achaians and Epirotes and those who resided at a vast distance beyond them, were convened.[60]

Eusebius also mentioned Hosius from Spain and the presbyters from Rome. Constantine did not just call the bishops to gather, Eusebius tells us that he actually presided over this gathering.

The great majority at the Nicene Council favored the view of Alexander, at least in the sense that they favored his view over the supporters of the Arian position. However, the range of thinking, even of those who opposed Arius and Eusebius of Nicomedia, was rather broad, and this had to be taken into account in order to reach some sort of consensus. Although Modalism had already been condemned, there were bishops such as Eustathius of Antioch who leaned toward this extreme, seeing the Son as merely a "mode" of God. Alexander of Alexandria, Hosius and the Roman contingent represented a second view. Although they were not Modalists, they saw the Son as equal to the Father and the Arian position as heretical. Therefore, to them it was something that must be completely eliminated from the Church. A third group, represented by Eusebius of Caesarea, was influenced by Origen. They saw Jesus as God, but they took a rather strong subordinationist view, seeing Jesus as deity, but in a subordinate position to the Father. This group was willing to accommodate the Arian position. Then, of course, there was the small minority who supported the Arian Christology.

The supporters of Arius committed a strategic blunder at the conference. Their leader Eusebius of Nicomedia stood before the bishops and read from a prepared statement which was a clear and blatant denial of the deity of Jesus. Many of the bishops at the meeting who were not fully cognizant of the issue at hand were shocked. Some literally covered their ears, shouting for the blasphemy to be stopped. One grabbed the document out of Eusebius' hands and stomped on it in front of the gathering. Probably at this point, the ultimate result was already decided. Arianism was to be condemned.

The compromise position between the other three factions at the synod congealed around the Greek *homoousios* to describe the Son's relationship to the Father. This word has been translated as consubstantial. In fact, the

Latin translation is *consubstantialis*. The decision was to describe the Son as being of the same substance as the Father. Clearly, this favored the position of Alexander over that of Eusebius of Caesarea. The evidence is that he was lukewarm at best about the insertion of this word into the Nicene Creed. In fact, its insertion was to create a backlash in the years that followed the Council. The backlash was intensified because the use of consubstantial, if taken in a more physical sense, could be used to support Modalism. A group eventually arose which preferred to use the word *homoiousios* (note the slight change in spelling from *homoousios*) to describe Jesus. This word means of a similar substance. It pictured Jesus as deity, but as decidedly subordinate to the Father and not exactly the same substance. Initially, this was the position of Eusebius of Caesarea. Looking back through the lens of time, it is hard to imagine, but the insertion of a single letter was to create a battle that raged for generations. As is the nature of human beings, both camps defined their view, not so much according to biblical thinking, but in opposition to those in the other camp. But we are getting ahead of ourselves.

The use of the word *homoousios* to describe the deity of Jesus may seem a small thing to us, but at the time it represented a watershed. For the first time, a nonbiblical word was used in a creed—one which was eventually to become a universal creed of the orthodox church. This is definitely not a small thing. Even today, some theologians will debate the wisdom of the choice at Nicaea to use this word, but the verdict of history is mostly favorable to the decision to describe the Son as being of the same substance as the Father. Most reading this book will probably agree with the concept, even if they are generally opposed to the use of creeds as a test of faith.

Who came up with this idea? To historians of Christian theology this question is similar to a historian of America asking, "Who was the chief mind behind the writing of the American Declaration of Independence?" The answer is that we do not know. Eusebius gave unreserved credit to Constantine himself for proposing the use of *homoousios* in what became known as the Nicene Creed. Given his obsequious relationship with Constantine, Eusebius' statement should be taken with a grain of salt. Others have proposed that Hosius, Eustathius or Alexander came up with this idea. What we know for sure is that this word was anathema to those in the Arian camp, and this is very likely one motivation for choosing it. An irony of the life and teaching of Arius is that the most significant long-term result of his teaching was that it forced the church to more carefully define the meaning of both the humanity and the divinity of Jesus, and to do so in a direction the exact opposite of what he proposed. This is an example of perhaps the most oft-repeated pattern in church history. What we are is defined more by what we oppose than what we support.

The Nicene Creed[61]

We believe in one God, the Father All-sovereign, maker of all things visible and invisible;

And in one Lord Jesus Christ, the Son of God, begotten of the Father, only-begotten, that is, of the substance of the Father, God of God, Light of Light, true God of true God, begotten, not made, of one substance [*homoousios*] with the Father, through whom all things were made, things in heaven and things on the earth; who for us men and for our salvation came down and was made flesh, and became man, suffered, and rose on the third day, ascended into the heavens, and is coming to judge the living and the dead;

And in the Holy Spirit.

And those who say "There was when he was not,"
And "Before he was begotten he was not,"
And that "He came into being from what-is-not,"
Or those who allege that the Son of God is "of another substance or essence,[62] "or "created," or "changeable," or "alterable,"
These the catholic and apostolic church anathematizes.

A few items in this, the first universal creed of the Catholic Church, jump out immediately. First, it is obvious that the principal intent of the Council was to define the relationship of the Son to the Father. More than ninety percent of the content focuses on the place of the Son within the trinity. Second, virtually nothing was said about the Holy Spirit. Concern about this issue was delayed for a number of years. Some have speculated that a pendulum swing against Montanism was the reason discussion of the Holy Spirit was avoided at Nicaea. In other words, the bishops feared a revival of this charismatic movement. A third thing to notice is that the creed is in two parts. First is a traditional "creed"—a statement of faith. Second is a series of anathemas. Those who grew up in liturgical churches reciting the Nicene Creed are only familiar with the first part. The anathemas are no longer read in such churches. These anathemas were clearly intended to remove the ideas of Arius and Eusebius of Nicomedia from the orthodox church. These were exactly the catchphrases used by Arius to define his position. Lastly, although the term "begotten" is biblical, the word translated as "not made" is not. As with the use of the word *homoousios*, the framers decided to use an unbiblical word here in order to nail down a specific plank in the platform against the Arian view that Jesus was created by the Father.

The fact that the Council of Nicaea was able to reach a consensus is remarkable. Likely, this was achieved in large part because of the influence of Constantine. He called the synod for this very reason. We can imagine participants like Eusebius of Caesarea holding their noses when they signed it. Ironically, in later years Eusebius became in important defender of the Nicene statement of the faith. As far as we know, only two of the 250 bishops refused to sign the published decision of the synod. Both were from Libya. It is likely they chose not to sign the agreement more out of a desire to express their independence (typical of the North Africans) and out of friendship with Arius than from theological conviction.

The creed and associated anathemas were not the only achievement of the Nicene Council. The bishops decided on a common date for the celebration of Easter. Twenty laws or "canons" were approved. These were not doctrinal in nature. They were policy statements about how church affairs were to be organized. For example, it was decided that eunuchs could be ordained as priests as long as their castration had not been a matter of choice on their part. A modern reader can best understand the distinction between creed and canon in this: About the creed they said, "We believe," but about the canons they said, "We decide." The bishops also agreed on a common strategy for dealing with Novatians, former followers of Paul of Samosata and others who wanted to return to the Catholic fellowship.

How should we view the Council of Nicaea almost seventeen centuries after it took place? One way of viewing it is that the bishops in attendance succeeded in defining the godhead in a way that protected the mystery. In other words, they opposed unbiblical views of deity in a way that preserved the natural wonder and mystery about the relationship between Father and Son. They did not overly define the nature of the relationship between Father and Son, but did so sufficiently to rule out what today nearly all of us would see as truly unacceptable theology. In this sense, the council was a success. However, to the extent that the decisions of the bishops represented a concession to the authority of a worldly prince and the use of a nonbiblical creed as a condition of fellowship, some might see it as a disaster. In any case, in the immediate event it was seen as a success by Constantine and most of the bishops. Unfortunately, the peace over the issue of Arianism was short-lived. In fact, within fifty years Arian theology threatened to overwhelm the Catholic Church. But this story will have to wait for our next episode—the story of the post-Nicene church.

Summary

Many momentous events in Christian history transpired during the third and early fourth centuries. The greatest persecutions of the church were followed by the diametric opposite—full toleration and even state support for the Christian church within the Roman Empire. Christianity spread outside the Roman sphere of influence, to Ethiopia, Armenia and the Persian/Sassanid Empire to the East. The first hundred years of the era marked what may be the greatest flowering of the true Christian spirit, while the last generation marked a transition toward the acceptance of Christendom—the joining at the hip of the Church and the state. This was to be a nearly unmitigated disaster for the Church in the long run. In a sense, the following chapters are the story of the results of this dramatic change and attempts to correct the mistakes that ensued.

CHAPTER NOTES: _____

1. Tertullian, *Against the Jews*, VII.
2. For example, Harnack, *The Mission and Expansion of Christianity*, Vol. II p. 144.
3. Kenneth Scott Latourette, *The First Five Centuries*, Vol. 1 (New York: Harper and Row, 1970), p. 105.
4. Tertullian, *Ad Scapulum*, IV.
5. Eusebius, *Ecclesiastical History*, VI.34.1.
6. Ibid., VI.41.9–14.
7. Cyprian, *Epistle*, 81.
8. Eusebius, *Ecclesiastical History*, VIII.1.2, 5.
9. Ibid. VIII.2–4.
10. Eusebius, *Martyrs of Palestine and Ecclesiastical History*, VIII, Lactantius, De Mortibus Persecutorum.
11. Eusebius, *Ecclesiastical History*, VIII.2, 7.
12. Eusebius, *Ecclesiastical History*, VIII.11.
13. Tertullian, *Apology*, 50.
14. Tertullian, *Apology*, 18.
15. Tertullian, *Prescription Against Heretics*, 7.
16. Tertullian, *Against Praxeas*, 1, taken from the translation by Dr. Holmes on Christian Classics Ethereal Library, www.ccel.org.

17. Tertullian, *Against Praxeas*, 12.
18. Ibid. 2.
19. Ibid. 8.
20. Ibid. 30.
21. Relevant passages are 1 Corinthians 5:1–13, Titus 3:9–11 and Matthew 18:15–20.
22. Tertullian, *On Penance*, 12.
23. A thorough treatment of the biblical meaning and practice of metanoia, including a distinction with penance, is found in Edward J. Anton, *Repentance: A Cosmic Shift of Mind and Heart* (Waltham, MA: DPI Books, 2005).
24. Eusebius, *Ecclesiastical History*, VI.1.1.
25. Ibid. VI.8.
26. Eusebius, *Ecclesiastical History*, VI.5.1.
27. Ibid. VI.23.1.
28. Henri Crouzel, *Origen*, translated by A. S. Worrall (San Francisco: Harper and Row, 1989), p. 14.
29. Origen, *Against Celsus*, 68.
30. Origin, *De Principiis*, 3.6.
31. Eusebius *Ecclesiastical History*, VII.3.1, 5.4–5.
32. Cyprian, *On the Unity of the Church*, 7.6.
33. Cyprian, *Epistle*, 70.2–3.
34. Cyprian, *Epistle*, 74.7.
35. Cyprian, Epistle, 71, *To Jubaianus, Concerning the Baptism of Heretics*, 7, taken from *The Anti-Nicene Fathers: Translations of the Writings of the Fathers Down to A. D. 325*, ed. Alexander Roberts and James Donaldson (Grand Rapids, MI: Eerdmans, 1988).
36. Justo Gonzalez, *A History of Christian Thought*, volume 1, *From the Beginnings to the Council of Chalcedon* (Nashville: Abingdon, 1992), p. 245.
37. Everett Ferguson, *Church History, Volume One*, (Grand Rapids, MI: Zondervan, 2005), p. 148.
38. Tertullian, *Against Praxeas*, 1.
39. Ibid.
40. Eusebius, *Ecclesiastical History*, VII.27.1–2
41. Ibid. VII.31.8.
42. Eusebius, *Ecclesiastical History*, VII.22.1–10
43. Ibid.
44. Although this is a correct statement, it is worth noting that generally the word saint was used of all departed Christians in the third century, not of particularly "holy" martyrs in the third century. The practice of denoting particularly holy fallen Christians as a list of "saints," separate from the mass of believers, began in the fifth century.
45. See John Oakes, *Is There a God*, (Spring, TX: IPI Books, 2006) p. 110 for the first and John Oakes, *Daniel, Prophet to the Nations*, (Spring, TX: IPI Books, 2008) especially pp. 46–49 for the second.
46. Eusebius, *Ecclesiastical History*, VII.31.1–2.

47. Eusebius, *Ecclesiastical History*, VI.43.3–22.

48. Numidia is the area of North Africa immediately to the west of Carthage. Today it would roughly be equivalent to Algeria, whereas Carthage and its surrounding territory, known as Africa at the time, could be thought of as roughly equivalent to Tunisia today.

49. Synod is the Greek word which was used for an authoritative gathering of church bishops. It became the traditional label for these events in the Eastern church. The word for such meetings in the West was Council. This became the traditional word for these authoritative assemblies in the Latin church.

50. Taken as a quote from an opponent to the group: Optatus, *Against the Donatists*, 3.3.

51. Everett Ferguson, *Church History Volume One: From Christ to Pre-Reformation* (Grand Rapids, MI: Zondervan, 2005).

52. A quote of Arian writing from Robert C. Gregg and Dennis E. Groh, *Early Arianism: A View of Salvation* (Philadelphia: Fortress Press, 1981), p. 8.

53. Eusebius, *Ecclesiastical History*, VIII.13.13–14.

54. Eusebius, *Ecclesiastical History*, VIII.16.2.

55. Eusebius, *Life of Constantine*, XIX.

56. Eusebius, *Ecclesiastical History*, I.1.3.

57. Michael J. Hollerich, *Church History*, Vol. 59, taken from Wikipedia on Eusebius, 1990.

58. This is a conservative number from Eusebius. Athanasius, who attended, gave the number of bishops attending the council as 318. Eustathius of Antioch, an active participant, estimated the number to be 270, but admitted he did not make a careful count.

59. The word is a direct transliteration of the Greek *anathema*, which means literally set apart or dedicated to. It came to have the meaning of one set apart for evil from the established, orthodox church. The one anathematized was excommunicated and assumed by the Catholic Church to be condemned to hell.

60. Eusebius, *Life of Constantine*, L.3.7.

61. The Creed given here is not exactly the same as what is commonly known as the Niconc Creed today. The reason is that the Creed used in Catholic, Orthodox and Protestant churches today was actually produced by the Council of Constantinople in 381. This will be covered in the next chapter. Technically, what is now known as the Nicene Creed ought to be called the Niceno-Constantinopolitan Creed. For obvious reasons, most drop the unwieldy longer name.

62. Here the word translated as essence is the Greek word *hypostasis*, another word basically meaning substance. Significantly it is used here interchangeably with *homoousios*. Later on, these words will be distinguished by the church.

CHAPTER FOUR
NICEA TO CHALCEDON: AUGUSTINE OF HIPPO AND THE EMERGENCE OF CHRISTENDOM
AD 326–451

Our next chapter in the history of Christianity begins with a Church council having just finished (Nicaea, 325), it ends with a Church council (Chalcedon, 451), and it can be divided into a first and second half by a third key Church council (Constantinople, 381). It is the period when Christology was fought over and settled, at least as far as the orthodox Catholic Church was concerned. It is a period dominated by one personality—Augustine of Hippo. He emerged as the preeminent influence over the church during this phase in the history of Christianity. The period begins with Christendom as a working idea but with only a tenuous toehold in reality. It ends with Christendom triumphant. By 451, church joined to and enforced by the State had become the accepted and lasting reality. The time period we are studying begins with a confident and renewed Roman power under Constantine, supporting the Nicene confession. It ends with the western Roman Empire fallen to the barbarian armies, under Arian leadership and with the eastern Roman Empire at Constantinople under siege.

The period from Nicaea to Chalcedon is unique in the history of Christianity in the way unity was maintained. In the first century, the unity of the church was maintained by the teaching of the apostles and the legacy of Jesus Christ himself. In the second century, the unity of the body of Christ was continued principally through the influence of the church fathers who maintained the spirit of the apostles and those who had known them. In the period leading up to Nicaea, the relational and doctrinal unity of the church began to be challenged as the church became quite spread out and as the Latin West and the Greek East diverged. For the time period in question in our present chapter, the unity of the Christian church was maintained principally by the consensus arrived at in Church councils. For better or for worse, it appeared that the churches had found a mechanism through which to remain connected, both relationally and doctrinally. After Chalcedon, as the western Roman Empire disintegrated, the means of maintaining a unified fellowship gradually shifted. The unifying power behind Christendom moved from the councils to a more autocratic power system. Rather than a semi-democratic consensus of bishops, unity was maintained principally at two centers of authority. In the former Latin world there was the Roman church, headed by the Pope. In the East there was the church in Constantinople, headed by its patriarch. But that is the subject of a future chapter. During the time between Nicaea and Chalcedon, the papacy had not yet emerged as the principal means of governing the church, despite the emerging claims of the bishops in Rome.

The Continued Spread of Christianity

During the fourth and early fifth centuries Christianity spread geographically as well as growing numerically. The quality of many of the conversions was suspect, but the faith of those who pushed belief in Jesus beyond where it had reached previously is inspiring. Missionary work during this time was not generally sponsored by a particular individual church. There was no missionary society or general church organization designed to spread the gospel. The faith was carried to new areas and peoples by courageous individuals. In the fifth century, this work was done increasingly by monks who had been trained in monasteries.

The Church of the East

We have already seen that the Christian faith spread to the East, into Armenia and Georgia in the third century. The gospel was carried into the political realm of Persia more slowly than the Roman world because the Sassanid emperors sponsored the state religion, Zoroastrianism. Already in the second century, Christianity was found in Syriac-speaking parts of the Roman Empire. The New Testament was translated into Syriac as early as the second century. In the early fifth century, an improved version of the Syriac known as the Peshitta was produced, possibly by Rabbula, bishop of Edessa from 411–435. A literary tradition grew in the Syriac language where there had been very little previously. The tradition grew up around the Syriac Christian culture.

Slowly, despite strong persecution under the Sassanid emperors, this Syriac form of Christianity spread into Persia proper, especially in Mesopotamia. Ironically, when Christianity became the accepted religion in the Roman Empire in the fourth century brought on increased persecution of the church in Persian-held areas. Before this, the Christians in the Roman Empire had been a group of persecuted outsiders. For this reason they were at least somewhat welcomed in Persian realms as potential rivals to Roman power. Suddenly with Constantine's rise to power, to be a Christian meant one was thought of as a likely ally of Persia's hated enemy, Rome. In fact, church leaders from Roman-controlled areas began to intervene on behalf of their brothers in Sassanid Persia. It is not surprising that when Constantine proclaimed himself the protector of the Christian Church, including those in the East, this did not produce a favorable reaction in Persia! A vicious persecution of the church broke out in 339 under Sassanid Emperor Sapor II, who ruled Persia from 310–379. The emperor demanded that the patriarch oversee the collection of a double tax of all Christian believers. Mar Shimun, the patriarch of Seleucia-Ctesiphon refused and he, five bishops and one hundred priests were summarily executed on Good Friday, 344.[1] This persecution continued intermittently for forty years, claiming the two successors to Mar Shimun. It may well have produced more martyrs than those under Decius and Diocletian combined. Sozomen, a Christian historian in the fifth century, reported that the published list of martyrs in Persia reached 16,000.[2] The total number, including those not recorded by name, was much greater than this figure. Interestingly, it appears that the proportion of those who apostasized in Persia was much lower than had been the case in the Roman Empire in the previous persecutions. The church of the East was apparently quite vigorous in its faith. This vigor continued even as the church in the West grew in numbers but declined radically in quality of faith for the average member.

Another unique aspect of what is now commonly known as the Church of the East was its greater emphasis on missionary evangelism. The Syriac-speaking people were a minority both in the Roman and Persian areas where they lived. They tended to be traders and merchants. Not unlike the Jews in Europe and around the Mediterranean during the Middle Ages, these people were often relatively wealthy. They spread the Christian faith wherever they went. Although the faith spread phenomenally widely, it never became the majority anywhere in the East and probably was not even a large minority.

Hard evidence is more difficult to obtain for the spread of Christianity to the East than in the West. There is probably some truth to the story of a certain Saba who, in the first half of the fifth century, converted from Zoroastrianism to Christianity due to the influence of his Christian nurse.[3] After his baptism, he distributed his significant wealth to the poor and joined a monastery. Later, he became a missionary, converting a Zoroastrian priest and an entire city to the faith. He even evangelized, with some success, among the Kurds.

Probably during the fourth but definitely during the fifth century,

Christianity spread to Central Asia. The churches in the cities of Merv (in present-day Turkmenistan) and Herat (in present-day Afghanistan) had their own bishops by 420. Almost certainly Christianity had entered the Indian subcontinent by the fifth century, although the details are uncertain. As early as the Council of Nicaea, a bishop John "the Persian" titled himself bishop "of all Persia and Great India." We should not take too much from this, however, because it is not clear what geographical area is referred to as India in this title. Some have conjectured that the persecutions of Sapor II forced elements of the Syriac-speaking Christians to what we now call Pakistan and India. In the 350s AD Roman Emperor Constantius sent "Theophilus the Indian" on a mission to Southern Arabia and to "other parts of India." This is both evidence for the spread of Christianity and of the possibility that "India" at this time might have referred to southern Arabia rather than the Indian subcontinent.

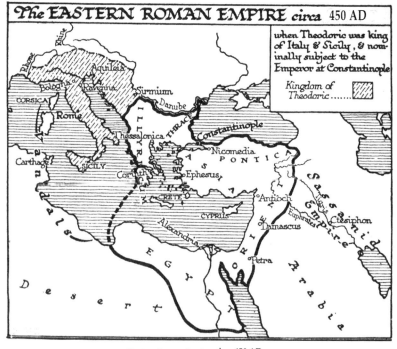

Eastern Roman Empire, circa 450 AD

Somewhat more solid evidence for the existence of Christianity in India is provided by Cosmas Indicopleustes, the historian and Nestorian Christian.[4] He traveled extensively in the East in the sixth century. Cosmas reported finding Christians and a presiding bishop in Taprobana (thought to be the island of Ceylon), as well as in Male "where pepper grows" and Kallina, where there was a bishop. Most likely Male and Kallina were on the West Coast of India.[5]

After the reign of Sapor II the Sassanid rulers were more tolerant of Christianity, although persecutions continued. A number of Persian nobles were converted to the faith. In 410 a local Syriac council was held which created an independent group of churches under the bishop in the Sassanid capital of Seleucia-Ctesiphon. The patriarch of the East was known as the *Catholicos*. A second persecution broke out in Persia in 420–422 that led to a synod of Eastern bishops in 424. This group declared its independence from Greek and Roman bishops. This was a politically astute move because it made it possible for the Sassanid rulers to tolerate the church within their realms and at the same time maintain enmity to Rome. This is a key moment in the history of Christianity. From this point onward, the Church of the East set an independent course, both politically and theologically. Eventually it became the home of Nestorian Christianity. We will see the genesis of this movement toward the end of the present chapter.

Asceticism and monasticism were major elements in the Church of the East, almost from its inception. The first monasteries in Persia were built somewhere between 330 and 340. The fact that the Christians suffered severe persecutions in Persia for well over a century after toleration had come to the church in the Roman Empire played a major role here. It is a commonplace of Christian history that when the church is strongly persecuted, one tendency is for its members to withdraw from the world. The ethnic minority Christians withdrew from rather than joining in the local culture. The tendency to withdraw from the world, combined with the fact that the Church of the East insisted on using Syriac rather than Persian in its liturgy, limited the acceptance of the Christian faith. This and the fact that the Catholicos of the East was largely cut off from the orthodox Church provides an explanation of the virtual disappearance of the church in Persia and further to the East under the Muslim onslaught beginning in the seventh century.

Other Christian Missions

The most dramatic geographic spread of Christianity in the fourth and early fifth centuries was in the East, but steady growth occurred elsewhere. The gospel found its way into Arabia from at least two directions. Missionaries entered the southwest of the Arabian peninsula from Abyssinia/Ethiopia.

Others came from Syriac churches in Mesopotamia. As mentioned above, Theophilus was sent by Constantius on a mission in the 350s to Arabia. He worked among the Himrayites, in present-day Yemen in Southwest Arabia. Philostratus reports the conversion of a Himrayite king and the construction of three churches at this time. Later the churches in Yemen were closely associated with the Ethiopian church, headquartered in Axum, on the Western side of the Red Sea in present-day Eritrea. Frumentius was a missionary in Axum in the early fourth century. He was appointed bishop of Axum by Athanasius of Alexandria. Frumentius was able to convert the Axumite king Ezana before the year 350. Evidence for this is provided by the fact that the coins minted during the reign of Ezana were changed from pagan to Christian symbols. Eventually, the Axumite kingdom became the center of the monophysite Coptic form of Christianity, but that is a matter for a future chapter.

The growth of Christianity to the South was limited by the Sahara Desert, but its spread to the North and West continued, even if more slowly than in the East. No doubt, the gospel was spread to the Britons, the Irish, the Goths and others by numerous individual disciples whose names and sacrifices we do not know. Three individual evangelists of the time are worthy of our special attention. These are Martin of Tours; Ulfilas, apostle to the Goths and Patrick, evangelist of the Irish and the Scots. A common quality in the career of all three of these great men is that their missionary work was individual. There was no concerted effort to spread the faith to the outlying pagan tribes at this time when the Roman Empire was decaying.

It is regrettable that we have less detailed knowledge of the Church of the East. The reason for this lack of information is both because the language of the church was a less familiar Syriac and because our Christian heritage is primarily Western rather than Eastern-focused in general. Surely, if we had more information about Christianity in the East there would be many inspiring stories of faith under great pressure from the political and religious enemies of the Christian movement.

Martin of Tours (316–397)

Martin of Tours is the most well known of those who brought Christianity to Gaul (roughly France, Belgium and southwest Germany). He was born to pagan parents in 316 or 317. The son of an officer, Martin entered the army in his teens. While serving in the Roman army in Northern Gaul, Martin divided his cloak with a beggar on a cold winter day. According to the famous story, that night he dreamed that Jesus Christ was clothed with the half he had given the beggar, saying that it was he to whom Martin had given the cloak.

171

Martin was baptized at eighteen. Two years later he resigned from the army, saying, "I am a soldier of Christ. I cannot fight." He attached himself to the great Hilary, Bishop of Potiers (more on him below). He became the most ardent supporter of monasticism in Gaul and is credited with introducing asceticism in the West. Martin established a monastery near Tours in 372.

Martin was appointed bishop of Tours by acclamation of the disciples there. He paid great attention to evangelizing in the countryside. This was something that had been largely ignored in most of the places Christianity had penetrated. When the urban Roman culture fell apart in the fifth century, the work of bishop/monks such as Martin to bring the faith to the agrarian peoples proved to be decisive in the continuity of Christianity. Martin was not a great scholar, but was noted for his zeal, good nature and great courage. He was later credited with many miracles. Of course, it is difficult to judge such claims. From the fourth century on, claims of physical miracles, rather than victory in philosophical debates, was a major factor in the spread of the Christian faith. As the faith spread to the countryside and as the Roman system of education evaporated, claims of the miraculous increased. A profoundly superstitious mindset gradually overtook the church.

Ulfilas (310–381)

Our second evangelist of note is Ulfilas, prophet to the Goths. We know almost nothing of his youth. In fact, we really do not know all that much about the later life of this enigmatic man either. However, from what we know of his accomplishments, he must have led a truly spectacular life. The circumstances of his conversion are not clear, but most likely he spent considerable time in Constantinople and was baptized there. He was ordained bishop of "the Christians in Gothia" by Eusebius of Nicomedia some time around 340. Either because it was the prevailing faith at the Roman court, or because of the influence of Eusebius, or perhaps out of personal conviction, Ulfilas was an Arian. This fact was to have a profound effect as the Gothic brand of Christianity was spread throughout Gaul, Spain and Northern Africa by the invasions of the Goths and their relatives the Vandals. Under the tutelage of Ulfilas, the Goths became Arians.

Ulfilas returned to Gothia (present day Hungary and upper Romania) as a missionary. Apparently he had a great measure of success in his work. The Arian converts in Gothia were sufficient to get the attention of Athenaric, the king of the Goths. Ulfilas appealed to Rome for permission to move the Christian converts to Moesia (Romania and northern Bulgaria) to escape violent persecution by the pagan Gothic king. He worked in Moesia among Goths living within the Roman Empire for more than thirty years. His impressive list of accomplishments includes a translation of the Bible into his native Gothic. Up to that time, Gothic was not a written language, so Ulfilas invented his own alphabet, similar to the Greek, in order to produce his translation. Fragments of the Gothic Bible have been recovered, including the Codex Argenteus. Another important contribution of Ulfilas was to produce a creed for the Goths in their language. This "Creed of Ulfilas" was a mildly Arian confession which, again, had a great influence on the course of both political and church history for the next two hundred years.

Eventually a rival to the Gothic throne named Fritigern rose up. It is not clear if Ulfilas converted him to Christianity or whether the connection was indirect, coming from those influenced by Ulfilas. The sincerity of this conversion is suspect as well, but in any case, eventually Fritigern, allied with the Romans, defeated Athenaric. Within only a few years the mass of the Goths accepted "Christian" baptism. Some scholars speculate that the Arian form of Christianity was particularly acceptable to the Goths because of some similarities to their pagan beliefs, including a distant "All-Father," and subordinate deities who mediated between man and the All-Father. In any case, the Arian or Arian belief system of the tribes who later overran all of the western Roman Empire proved to be a significant factor, both religiously and politically. It made the Goths more resistant to being incorporated into the old Roman system, hastening the disintegration of Roman culture and urban life.

Patrick (389–461)

The last of our list of great missionaries of the period is Patrick, evangelist of Ireland and Scotland. The life of "Saint" Patrick is one of the most romantic stories in the history of Christianity. Fortunately, he left an autobiography for the first forty-five years of his life, so we have a lot of information about this model missionary.

Patrick was born in Britain at about the time it was being abandoned by the Roman legions. He was born into a Christian family, his grandfather on his father's side having been a priest and his father a deacon.[7] In his own words, he did not take his Christian faith very seriously. Patrick was taken as a slave to Ireland

St. Patrick stained glass window from Cathedral of Christ the Light, Oakland, CA.

as the result of a raid by "barbarian" Scots (as they were called at that time) at the age of about sixteen. He worked as a slave, tending flocks for six years during which time he says he came to a strong faith in God. According to Patrick, he had a vision at night telling him a ship was ready to take him home. He fled from his owner and was taken on by a captain. Unfortunately for Patrick, he was carried to Gaul rather than Britain. After much wandering, which included a possible trip to Italy, he ended up at a monastery at Lerins, off the coast of southern France. Patrick was a strong supporter of monasticism throughout his life. From his later writings we know that he had considerable education in the Bible during this time.

Finally, after many years, Patrick was restored to his family in Britain. According to Patrick, soon after rejoining his family, he had another vision. In the vision, "I saw a man coming, as it were, from Ireland." The man carried a number of letters in his hand. One of them had the heading "The Voice of the Irish." Then he heard a group of Irish voices crying out to him, "Come and walk with us once more." Patrick was faithful to this vision. He took the gospel beyond the farthest boundaries of the Roman Empire in the West. Patrick certainly was not the first or the only missionary to the Irish people but he was by far the most successful. Palladius was sent to the island by Celestine I, bishop of Rome, as bishop to the Irish in 431. However, Patrick's mission was unique at the time, as he focused on converting pagans from the ancient Druidic religion, rather than on only ministering to Christians already on the island. His knowledge of the local Gaelic which was gained while he was a slave was a big help in reaching the common people. Patrick reports that he baptized thousands. Patrick's missionary work brought him before kings. It inspired much persecution from the druidic priests. He was always in danger of arrest, torture or death. By all accounts Patrick was courageous, humble, patient, persuasive, inspiring and an effective leader.

The Irish church came to have many unique characteristics under the influence of Patrick. Of course, it suffered from the weight of thousands of questionable conversions, but despite this, it had a vitality that most churches lacked in mainland Europe. Its structure was not as hierarchical or centralized. The churches in Ireland were not organized into dioceses. Monasticism was a major element in Ireland from the beginning. The leadership was composed largely of monks. Although Patrick was ministering beyond the farthest frontiers of Roman influence, he brought the use of a pure kind of Latin and a strong emphasis on education to the Irish church. During the Middle Ages, the Irish church became a source of spiritual energy, learning and culture to the ravaged areas of mainland Europe. It is ironic that the strongest remnant of Roman culture, education and Christian spirituality in the early Middle Ages was found outside the former empire.

Nicaea to Ephesus

It is time to return to the story of the evolution of Christian theology where we left it: at the end of the Council of Nicaea, in 325. The Arian controversy did not die with the Council of Nicaea or with the publication of the Nicene Creed. In fact, the publishing of the Nicene decision actually served as a launching pad for the Arian heresy that was condemned at the Synod. Even if Nicaea had ended the discussion of the deity of Jesus within the mainstream church, other questions remained. To most of us, whether we are a fan of creeds or not, the Nicene Creed would appear to give sufficient definition to the nature of the trinity. However, very important matters of Christology remained undefined by the orthodox church in 325. To the Eastern Christians, familiar with philosophical subtleties, the remaining questions were easy to discern. If Jesus is of the same substance with the father, then in what sense could he also be human? Was he divine first, then human? Or might it have been the reverse? This is a question, not about the trinity but about Christ—in other words it is a question of Christology. We (i.e. modern, Western believers) would probably be satisfied to say that this is a mystery, and to some extent we would be right. It should be left as a mystery. However, we owe a debt of gratitude to the Christian theologians in the fourth and fifth centuries who helped to define the implications of the combined humanity and deity of Jesus of Nazareth in a satisfactory way. We will see that the process by which this was worked out by the church during the time of the great Church councils was messy to the point of embarrassment.

As the bishops headed home from Nicaea, the peace obtained by the compromise was already doomed to an early end. In the East, the number who leaned more closely to the Arian position and who were uncomfortable with the use of *homoousios* may even have been the majority. Those who favored the thinking of Arius without openly identifying with his now-officially heretical theology are referred to by scholars as moderate Arians. They were willing to describe Jesus as being of a similar substance, but not of the identical substance with the Father. They felt that the use of *homoousios* inserted an implied Modalism (Father, Son and Spirit are different modes of a singular God) into the Creed. Avowed Sabellianists/Modalists such as Ancelus of Ancyra touted the creed as supportive of their view, making it very difficult for moderates to support the Nicene decisions.

Another synod was called in 335 in Tyre, ostensibly to more carefully define the results of Nicaea. By this time, Alexander was dead. Eusebius of Nicomedia and the new bishop of Alexandria, Athanasius, represented the competing views of God at Tyre. This was not a general council, as Western bishops were not represented. The result probably would have been different if they had taken part. The decision of the council was to reverse the Nicene anathemas. Arius was restored to the faith (although he died before this decision was carried out), and Athanasius was condemned. He fled into the desert, not for the last time. Soon after, in 339, Eusebius of Nicomedia was appointed bishop of Constantinople. This was a position that gave him great influence over the imperial court, which he astutely used to the advantage of the pro-Arian party.

Athanasius

He indeed assumed humanity that we might become God.

—Athanasius of Alexandria

Let us take a moment to look at Athanasius, the chief proponent of the Nicene position for the next fifty years of our story. Athanasius of Alexandria was born in 293. He was trained in Alexandria under Alexander, rising to be his secretary and chief assistant at the Council of Nicaea. He played a major role in the proceedings of the Council. When Alexander died in 328, Athanasius was the logical choice to succeed to the bishopric of Alexandria, a position he held until his death in 373.

Alexander was tenacious, to say the least. He was like a bull dog. He has been called "the saint of stubbornness." Once he became sure of a particular position, he fought for that idea regardless of the personal consequences. He was exiled from his position as bishop of Alexandria no less than five times by four different emperors. The first time he fled to the desert in exile was in 335. Constantine had switched sides, favoring Arius. Arius demanded he be reinstated in Alexandria. Knowing Athanasius, we can predict his reaction. As a result, Athanasius was exiled to Trier, on the opposite end of the Roman Empire. During his travels, he contacted many Western bishops, gaining much support for his Nicene position. He also wrote a biography, *The Life of Anthony*, and began to spread enthusiasm for monasticism in the West.

Sixteen of his forty-five years as patriarch of Alexandria were spent in exile. Still, Athanasius never backed down as the public figure most widely seen as the defender of the Nicene faith. During his several periods of exile, he wrote extensively. He is most noted for his polemics against the Arians, *Apology Against the Arians, Four Orations Against the Arians* and *History of the Arians*. During his second exile, he was placed under indictment by the pro-Arian emperor Constantius II, with the order that he be executed if he attempted to return to his "See" (i.e. the flock over whom he was bishop) in Alexandria. When he returned from his second exile in 346, he was received with joy by the Egyptians as a national hero, only to be exiled again in 350 by Constantius.

Another important work of Athanasius was his *On the Incarnation*. This was his work on soteriology (the doctrine of salvation). He argued that our salvation was sealed by Jesus' incarnation. Over time the East emphasized the incarnation as the chief means of salvation. God becoming flesh allows us, who are of the flesh, to come to God. Athanasius' doctrine of salvation stressed deification. Because of Christ's incarnation, he is united with all who are in him, bringing truth and knowledge of God in place of human ignorance, and bringing eternal life instead of death to those who participate in this process. To the Greek to be deified meant to become immortal. In the Christian context deification came to mean a process by which we become more like God through the influence of Jesus in our life. Athanasius put this in a rather striking way: "He indeed assumed humanity that we might become God."[8] This statement sounds shocking to us. It may very well be that Athanasius went too far here. However, Athanasius did not mean by this that we literally become God or a god as Joseph Smith (founder of Mormonism) taught, but that we begin to acquire godlikeness because in the Son, God acquired humanness. For those trying to understand Eastern Orthodoxy even today, this idea of deification should be born in mind. To the East, salvation is a process of change—deification—in this life.

The Western view of soteriology stressed the crucifixion rather than the incarnation. Anyone who studied in a Catholic school is well aware of the Roman emphasis on the crucifixion. We are saved by God's death on a cross rather than by God's becoming flesh. Eastern ideas of salvation stressed our salvation now, through the incarnation, whereas Western ideas of salvation stressed our future salvation through the death of Jesus. The Bible mentions both our present salvation (1 Peter 2:2) and our future salvation (Hebrews 6:11, Galatians 5:5), allowing for both interpretations. Biblically, we are saved "already, but not yet." The East/West dichotomy is not biblical as there is some truth in both ideas. Besides, the thing missing from both views of salvation was the importance of the resurrection of Jesus for our salvation (Romans 6:5–10, 1 Peter 3:21). We do not find theologians in the third through fifth centuries mentioning the importance of the resurrection in our salvation.

Those of us with a Western Christian mindset probably have more to learn from the East than from the West, given our biased upbringing.

Homoousios, Homoiousios and Homoios

Constantine died in 337 after a long and relatively successful rule of the Roman Empire. In what seems a contradiction, this emperor who so ardently stressed the unity of the Roman Empire at almost any cost, failed to leave a plan for his own succession that could maintain the unity of the empire. Constantine II received the area Constantine had inherited from his father in 306—Gaul, Spain and Britain. His brother Constans ruled over Africa, Italy and Illyricum (the Western Balkans). Constantius II received Greece, Moesia and the East, including Egypt. In 340 the situation simplified somewhat when Constans defeated Constantine II in battle and took over all of the West. In 350, Constans was assassinated, giving the West to Constantius II as well. Finally, in 353, Constantius defeated a usurper Magnetius who had taken control of part of the West after an uprising over Constantius' persecution of pagans. From this date he took control of the entire Roman Empire. Constantius was a supporter of the Arian or at least the semi-Arian position. Generally the imperial camp supported Arianism, whereas the clerics tended to support the Nicene position.

Constantius took a harder anti-pagan line than his father Constantine, ordering that "superstition cease and that the folly of sacrifices be abolished."[9] This decree led to the overturning of pagan altars by Christians in many areas, which, in turn, caused violent uprisings against the Christian rulers. Constantius ordered the statue of the Roman pagan god Victory removed from the Senate in Rome. This statue had been placed there by Augustus after the battle of Actium. With a brief interlude during the reign of Julian (see below) the successors of Constantine gradually took a harder stance against paganism. However, at this point there was not a general persecution of pagans in Rome. In fact, we will see a brief flowering of paganism in the late fourth century.

Having briefly reviewed the political situation in the Empire, let us return to the theological battles. In the controversies that ensued in the East, generally the moderate Arians looked to the emperors for political support, while the Nicene position represented the West and at times the majority of bishops. The entire controversy can be seen as an ecclesiastical/imperial battle, although this would be a great oversimplification.

The theological controversies in the fourth century have been pictured as a battle between the orthodox/Nicene and the Arian description of Jesus. The reality is more subtle. What is pictured as an argument over the position of Arius and his successors is really a struggle of the entire church to define its position on where Jesus fits in the deity. If Jesus is of the same substance as the Father (*homoousios*), in exactly what sense is he the same as the Father? If I were to make a small statue "of the same substance" as that from which Michelangelo made his David, does that mean I used the same type of marble, or does that mean I used the same actual piece of marble (requiring that I take a chunk out of the original)? After Nicaea, some began to propose the use of the word *homoiousios* (of a similar substance) to represent the former idea while others continued to insist on the use of *homoousios* (of the same substance) to represent the second idea in this Michelangelian illustration. To compound what can be seen as a nitpicky splitting of hairs, still others, those of a far-reaching semi-Arian or strict Arian view, preferred to use the term homoios, making the Son similar to the Father.

Four Views of the Relationship Between Father and Son

Homoousios	Jesus is of the same substance as the Father.
Homoiousios	Jesus is of a similar substance as the Father.
Homoios	Jesus is similar to the Father (semi-Arian or Arian).
Anomios	Jesus is unlike the Father (a radical Arian position).

As the church struggled over these definitions, the Nicene position was at a decided disadvantage. Ironically, part of this bias was the result of its victory at Nicaea. The worst thing a presidential candidate can do for his or her approval rating is to win the election. From that point, the opposition has the advantage of pointing out all the reasons the one in power should not be there, without having to provide a strong argument for its own position. In fact, the Nicene position only gained the advantage when Julian "the Apostate" tried to reassert paganism during his brief rule of Rome. Suddenly on the outside, the Nicene position looked much more attractive.

A long and, for us, confusing series of smaller councils ensued between 340 and 360, most supported by Constantius.[10] Athanasius, the chief public supporter of the Nicene position, was repeatedly attacked and condemned, whereas the *homoeans* gained strength. A larger council of eastern bishops was held in 360 at Nice in Thrace that created a semi-Arian creed. The creed used the word *homoios*; the Son is similar to the Father. This creed was agreed to in principle at a council of western bishops at Ariminum in the West, also in 360. It became known as the Creed of Ariminum, and all bishops in the East and West agreed, in principle, to a semi-Arian creed. Famously, at this point Jerome complained, "The whole world groaned and was astonished to find itself Arian."[11] The Creed of Ariminum was to become the defining one among the Goths for the next three centuries when they were converted by Ulfilas. These barbarian converts became Arian as a result.

Julian "the Apostate"

These impious Galileans not only feed their own poor, but ours also.

—Julian "The Apostate"

The rule of Julian was a short one, but it was to prove decisive in determining the direction of theological discussion in the Christian church for a considerable time. Constantius II died in 361, leaving the throne to his cousin Julian. The future emperor was raised as a Christian but trained in the classics. His tutor and guardian from the age of seven was Eusebius of Nicomedia. His background, then, was Arian. According to his own writings, Julian became a secret pagan at about the age of twenty, in 352. He did not publicly declare his convictions at the time, for obvious reasons. Why he rejected Christianity is not clear, but given that his cousin Constantius, supposedly a Christian, had murdered his entire family except for himself and his half-brother Gallus, we have more than sufficient reason. The hypocrisy of supposed believers is one of the best tools of the enemies of Christianity. Julian studied Neoplatonism and became an enthusiastic supporter of this philosophy. He is sometimes known as Julian "the Philosopher." He was also initiated into the Eleusinian Mystery religion and Mithraism. Shortly after Constantius' death in November 361, on December 11, 361, Julian entered his capital at Constantinople. He announced his rejection of Christianity and revoked the privileges of the "Galileans." He supported the Eleusinian Mysteries and other pagan religions. Christians were forbidden to teach pagan literature, which effectively shut them out of the educational system in the empire. True to his Neoplatonist ideal, he did not persecute Christianity. However, he put the blame for the Roman Empire's disasters and defeats on the Church. He wrote a polemic *Against the Galileans*, in which he denounced his former religion, borrowing much from Porphyry. His was a conservative reaction to the Christianization of the empire—a desire to return to the glory days of pagan Rome. Julian declared a general toleration of all religions. He decreed the return of exiled dissident Christian bishops, including Athanasius. Probably he hoped to destabilize the Church by this act. It turned out that his policy had the opposite effect. He also proposed that the Jewish temple in Jerusalem be rebuilt.

Julian is famous for his unintended compliment to the Christian church. He said of the Church:

These impious Galileans not only feed their own poor, but ours also; welcoming them into their agapae (love feasts), they attract them, as children are attracted with cakes.[12]

While the pagan priests neglect the poor, the hated Galileans devote themselves to works of charity, and by a display of false compassion have established and given effect to their pernicious errors. See their love-feasts, and their tables spread for the indigent. Such practice is common among them, and causes a contempt for our gods.[13]

Julian paid indirect and unintended compliments to Christians by demanding that pagan priests organize their work in order to offer Christian-style charity, to care for the dead and to live exemplary, moral lives.

We can always debate the positives and negatives of the reign of particular rulers in the past. Arguably, despite his vehement opposition to Christianity and his support of the old pagan beliefs, Julian probably did the church a favor in the long run. His opposition served to unite the pro-Nicene party and brought about a resurgence of orthodox teachers, helping to propel the careers of John Chrysostom and Gregory Nazianzus, who publicly vilified Julian. In any case his program of re-paganization was cut off prematurely. In a move to shore up the support of the army in the East, Julian set off on a campaign against the Sassanid Persians in March 363. He was wounded in battle near Mesopotamia and died in June 363, having ruled for only nineteen months. He was succeeded by Jovian and soon after by Valentinian I, both of whom were Christians, but were fairly tolerant of pagan religion.

The Cappadocian Fathers

From all that has been said, it is clear that there was a lot of confusion and infighting in the Christian church within the Roman Empire in the thirty years following the death of Constantine. It was at this crucial point that the Cappadocian fathers took the reins and created a solution to the satisfaction of all but the most ardent of the Arians. Cappadocia is a region in northern Asia Minor (modern Turkey), on the Black Sea. It became the source of the greatest theologians, Christian teachers and orators of the second half of the fourth century.

The need of the time was to find a middle ground between Arianism on one side and Sabellianism on the other—between rejecting the deity of Jesus and thinking of him as merely an aspect of the Father. With hindsight, we can see that the use of *homoousios*, though proper, was too vague, and a new vocabulary was needed to explain in what sense Jesus was identical to the Father and in what sense he was distinct from the Father. The solution advanced by the Cappadocian fathers and Athanasius starting in 361 and published at the

Council of Constantinople of 381 involved the careful use of another Greek word: *hypostasis*.

The definitions and uses to which the two Greek words *homoousios* and *hypostasis* were used by the Eastern church in defining Christology is likely to strain the patience of most of us with regard to the fine points of a language with which we are not familiar. However, the reader will need to have some faith here. It will be worth the effort, as this was the basis for the final formation of a Christian theology that we have inherited and which successfully defined and defended Christianity in its long battles with false theologies. What can be very confusing for us is that both the words *ousios* and *hypostasis* can be translated as substance. *Ousios* carries the connotation of substance in a broader and more abstract sense. It means the substance of a thing as in its fundamental nature. *Hypostasis* can also be translated as substance, but its distinction from the former word is that it can have a meaning of the essence of a particular thing or of a particular example of a thing. The solution of Basil and the two Gregorys (see below) was to describe the relationship between the Father and the Son as *homoousios* but with three *hypostases*. This could be translated as the Father and the Son are related to one another as one substance and three substances. That would be confusing in English! The implied meaning given to the formula by the Cappadocian fathers was the Father, Son and Spirit are one substance, but three persons. This formula, if accepted, would considerably narrow the field of acceptable Christian theology. It absolutely and for all time ruled out Arianism and Jesus as a created being, because Jesus is of the same substance as the father, but at the same time, it absolutely and for all time ruled out Sabellianism because the Father, Son (and later the Holy Spirit) are three *hypostases*—three substances/persons as to their individual nature.

It is to the story of these Christian teachers we will turn next, but before we do so, let us overthrow a misconception. It is a common thought today that all this discussion of one nature and three persons was and still is mere philosophizing and rationalizing away what should be left as a mystery. It is of no relevance for the common Christian and has no practical implications whatsoever. This thinking is misguided. First of all, the idea that these were mere ivory tower discussions of an elite clergy, out of touch with the common Christian and his concerns, is simply not true. Gregory of Nyssa tells us that at the time of the second ecumenical council in Constantinople, the Trinitarian controversy was all the rage among regular folks. He said, "If you ask for change, someone philosophizes to you on the Begotten and the Unbegotten. If you ask the price of bread, you are told, 'The Father is greater and the Son inferior.' If you ask, 'Is the bath ready,' someone answers 'The Son was created from nothing.'"[14] It is very hard to imagine such a conversation on the street today, but Gregory reports that the common believer was extremely interested in the issues we are considering.

How practical is the question of the relationship between the members of the trinity is debatable, but let us put to bed the idea that Athanasius, Basil and others were trying to rationalize away what should be left a mystery. The exact opposite is the case. Their desire, as seen both from their words and from the facts of the matter, was to protect the mystery. Sabellianism and Arianism were attempts to simplify and to demystify the deity—to make it more palatable to human reason. The teachers who were ultimately anathematized by the early church were trying to make Jesus more logical. Logically, Jesus is either less than the Father and created by him or he is a mere aspect of the Father. However, logic has nothing to do with biblical truth. We can be grateful to these men who created a hedge around the mystery of the deity in the fourth and fifth centuries.

Basil of Caesarea (330–379)

The first of our Cappadocian fathers is Basil "the Great." He was born in one of the many Caesareas in the Roman world—this one in Cappadocia. His spiritual pedigree was impressive. One of his grandfathers was martyred during the persecutions of Diocletian. His grandmother, Macrina, was a well-known Christian woman who had studied under the famous teacher Gregory Thaumaturgus, who was himself a student of Origen. His sister, also called Macrina, became a very influential nun. His brother was the future Gregory of Nyssa.

Basil had a strong classical education. He befriended both the future Gregory of Nazianzus and the emperor Julian "the Apostate" while in school in Athens. For a while, the future orator, theologian and church administrator worked as both a lawyer and a teacher of rhetoric. At the age of twenty-five, upon hearing the preaching of the charismatic Eustathius of Sebaste, he had a spiritual awakening.

> I had wasted so much time on follies and spent nearly all of my youth in vain labors, and devotion to the teachings of a wisdom that God has made foolish. Suddenly, I awoke as out of a deep sleep. I beheld the wonderful light of the gospel truth, and I recognized the nothingness of the wisdom of the princes of this world.[15]

Basil was baptized in 357, gave all his possessions to the poor, and never looked back. He was a man of tireless energy and a vast array of interests. He was an ascetic and a great supporter of the monastic life, although he never became a monk. He, along with Pachomius, is known as the Father of Eastern Monasticism. It was not Basil's nature to withdraw from public life for long, however. Basil and Gregory of Nazianzus fought for orthodoxy in Cappadocia. In a series of public debates with the best known Arian rhetoricians, with agents of Arian Emperor Valens overseeing the event, Basil was triumphant. This victory may have determined the direction of his career as a church bishop and administrator. Initially, Basil was a strong supporter of homoiousianism, taking a middle ground between the Nicene position of Athanasius and Arianism. Later on, he switched to supporting the Nicene position. His goal all along was to unite the two factions. He, along with the other Cappadocian fathers, working with Athanasius, created the *homoousios/hypostasis* theology.

On the death of Eusebius (a second Eusebius of Caesarea, not the historian) of Caesarea in 370, Basil took the position of bishop of Caesarea, making him also exarch of Pontus and metropolitan over a number of bishops. He began innumerable works for the poor, publicly rebuked government officials for corruption, and oversaw the building of a complex later known as the Basiliad, including a poorhouse, a hospice and a hospital. With all this work, he also was a prolific writer. Over three hundred letters are extant, along with many works, including his *Refutation of the Apology of the Impious Eunomius*. This was written against the teaching of Eunomius of Cyzicus who took an extreme anomian (the Son is not similar to the Father) Arian position, as well as his *On the Holy Spirit*, in which he was one of the first to begin to discuss the place of the Holy Spirit in the deity. Basil used a wonderful analogy to describe how the Holy Spirit can come from the Father without being less than the Father or created by the Father. His analogy for the Father, Son and Holy Spirit was the sun, its light and its warmth. Although the sun generates light and heat, it cannot exist apart from the light and the heat. The light (Son) and heat (Holy Spirit) are generated by the sun, but they do not come into existence after the sun. Indeed, there is no separate existence of the three, even though they can be perceived as different. Of course, no analogy taken from human experience can adequately explain the godhead, but this is perhaps the best one that has been used.

Basil also published a number of liturgical works. He had a large role in creating what is now the liturgy of the Greek-speaking Eastern Orthodox Church. Under his influence, Christian worship became more and more formalized, with a written liturgy being repeated for the daily and weekly worship, rather than spontaneous or memorized prayers. Genuine Christian worship lost out in this process, at least in the long run, as the participation of the individual worshipper was lessened. Despite this weakness, Eastern Christianity has a stronger legacy of spiritual worship than Roman Christianity, and Basil's work can be given some credit for this.

Some may not see his work to create a liturgy as a positive development, but his influence on biblical hermeneutics can be seen as a definite positive. Along with the other Cappadocian fathers, Basil argued against the allegorical interpretation of the Scriptures that had been standard fare almost from the beginning. He, along with the school of Antioch, opposed the free allegorizing of the Alexandrian school.

> I know the laws of allegory, though less by myself than from the works of others. There are those, truly, who do not admit the common sense of the Scriptures, for whom water is not water, but some other nature, who see in a plant, in a fish, what their fancy wishes, who change the nature of reptiles and of wild beasts to suit their allegories, like the interpreters of dreams who explain visions in sleep to make them serve their own end.[16]

The Cappadocian fathers favored taking the Bible literally where it was clearly intended to be taken literally, especially in such historical books as Genesis, the Kings and the Chronicles. Unlike Origen, Clement and the theological school in Alexandria, they interpreted historical passages historically. As Basil pointed out above, allegorical interpretation leaves one free to interpret passages of Scripture almost any way one wants to, allowing the interpreter to make the Scriptures serve their own end. A free, allegorical use of the Scripture allows both sincere orthodox Christians and heretics to support their beliefs using questionable hermeneutics. Thank you to Basil and his Cappadocian friends for restoring good methods of Bible study.

Gregory of Nazianzus (329–389)

> What was not assumed was not healed, but that which is united with his Godhead is also saved.
>
> —Gregory of Nazianzus

Gregory was a lifelong friend of Basil. Their careers have much in common. He was born to wealthy Christian parents in Arianzum in Cappadocia, near Nazianzus. His father was bishop of Nazianzus. Like Basil, he was trained in Scripture and rhetoric. Also like Basil, he was strongly attracted to asceticism. He was baptized in 358, after which he spent a year with Basil in contemplation, helping him to compile a summary of Origen's works and working with him to create monastic rules.

Unlike his friend, however, he loathed the life of active service, preferring the life of a hermit. Despite his protests, Gregory was ordained as a presbyter/priest in Nazianzus by his father in 361. He called his father's action "an act of tyranny."[17] Several times in his life he tried to flee from his duties as priest or bishop to the wilderness, to lead a life of contemplation. "Quiet and freedom from affairs is more precious than the splendors of a busy life."[18]

As already mentioned, he and Basil battled successfully with the Arian rhetoricians in Caesarea. In order to strengthen his position against the Arians in Cappadocia by numerical superiority of bishops, Basil appointed Gregory bishop of the tiny city of Sasima in 372. Gregory refused to serve in the "utterly dreadful, pokey little hole; a paltry horse-stop on the main road…devoid of water, vegetation or the company of gentlemen."[19] In 372, he worked in Nazianzus to help his sick father. When his father died, he refused to be appointed bishop of Nazianzus. He donated most of his inheritance to the poor. Soon afterward he retired to an ascetic life for three years.

A turning point in the life of Gregory was the death of Valens, the last Arian emperor of the East, in 378. When Theodosius I took the throne, the door was opened to pro-Nicene theology in Constantinople. Probably against his instincts, Gregory was convinced to move to Constantinople to shepherd a small group of pro-Nicene Christians. It was here that Gregory was thrown into an absolutely crucial moment in the development of Christian theology. Basil had died without seeing his (and Athanasius' and the other Cappadocians') proposed solution to the trinitarian controversies put in place. Gregory's sermons in Constantinople were wildly popular. His Arian enemies decided to take decisive action against him. On Easter, 379, a mob of Arian supporters burst into a church service, wounding Gregory and killing another bishop. Soon after this embarrassing incident, Peter, the bishop of Alexandria, tried to get Gregory deposed. This represents the decades-long jealousy between the Antiochene and Alexandrine schools in Constantinople. Finally, in 380, Theodosius arrived in Constantinople, determined to oust the Arian bishops from the capitol. He appointed Gregory of Nazianzus as archbishop of Constantinople. When Theodosius called the second ecumenical Council in Constantinople in 381, Gregory was in a place to put forward the one substance, three person (*homoousios*, three *hypostases*) doctrine of the trinity. Theodosius asked him to preside over the Council. He also supported the teaching that the Holy Spirit, like the Son, is God.

We will see more on the Council of Constantinople later. What is clear is that, unlike Basil, Gregory was uncomfortable with such a position of authority. He humbly asked to be relieved of his office of bishop of Constantinople during the Council in 381:

> Let me be as the Prophet Jonah! I was responsible for the storm, but I would sacrifice myself for the salvation of the ship. Seize me and throw me.... I was not happy when I ascended the throne, and gladly would I descend it.[20]

Gregory returned to Nazianzus, resuming the role (if not the title) of bishop for a time, finally fleeing to a life of solitude for the last five years of his life.

One more important theological contribution of Gregory of Nazianzus bears mention. In describing the role of the Holy Spirit in the trinity, he is the first one to use the idea of the Holy Spirit *proceeding* from the Father. In his theology, the Father is unbegotten, the Son is the only *begotten* and the Spirit *proceeds* from the Father.

> The Holy Spirit is truly Spirit, coming forth from the Father indeed, but not after the manner of the Son, for it is not by generation but by procession, since I must coin a word for the sake of clearness.[21]

Eventually, this was to become standard wording in orthodox Christianity. Gregory preached that the trinity is and ought to remain a mystery. He also, like Athanasius and Basil, taught the idea of deification—that we can acquire more and more of the nature of God through imitation of the incarnate Son.

Gregory of Nyssa (335–394)

As much could be said of Gregory of Nyssa as has already been said of Basil and Gregory of Nazianzus. However, he had enough in common with the other two that only a couple of comments will be made here about the third of the Cappadocian fathers. Gregory was the brother of Basil. Like Gregory of Nazianzus, he preferred the monastic life, but was convinced by Basil, partially for political reasons, to take the bishopric of Nyssa.

Gregory of Nyssa's theology was similar to that of Basil and his fellow Gregory. Of the three, he was the most accomplished in philosophy. One thing added by the Nyssan Gregory was the idea that God is infinite. Origen had argued that God must be finite because only the finite can be knowable. Gregory of Nyssa countered this, arguing that if God is limited, then there is something greater than God. Therefore he must be infinite. This argument was probably borrowed directly from Neoplatonism. He stressed *theosis* or divinization (deification). We have already seen that deification was and still is a major emphasis of Eastern Christianity. Western theologians have accused Gregory of Nyssa of teaching *apokastasis*, or universalism. Probably this is an exaggeration, but Gregory's optimistic theology may have moved too far in the direction of implying all men will be saved. He was not challenged on this front during his lifetime. The role of Gregory of Nyssa in the Council of Constantinople was crucial. He delivered the opening address to the assembled bishops. He, along with Nazianzus, with the full support of Theodosius I, pushed through the one essence, three persons theological formula.

John "Chrysostom" (347–407)

John Chrysostom, "the Golden-Tongued," is chiefly known for his eloquent and powerful preaching. Like Basil, he came from a Christian household. He was born in Antioch. His father died when he was quite young. His mother, Anthusa, though only twenty years of age, renounced marriage and devoted herself to raising her son, providing a strong education in both the Scripture and classic, pagan rhetoric. The combination was to prove fruitful, as John became the most famous orator of the early church. John was baptized at eighteen. Like the Cappadocian fathers, he was drawn to asceticism. He spent two years living in an isolated mountain cave, standing continually, hardly sleeping. Apparently this ruined his health, but fortunately it did not ruin his voice. Appointed as a presbyter in 386, he became chief preacher in the church in Antioch.

John's strength was as an expository preacher. Chrysostom is not his last name, but his nickname, meaning Golden Mouth. His method was to choose a biblical passage, give the meaning of the scripture and then to make practical applications. Like Basil, he sought the plain meaning of the text and avoided allegorizing. His themes were Christian morality, helping the poor and avoiding the abuse of power and wealth.

John's prominence in the church was increased when he was called to be archbishop in Constantinople in 398. He refused to take part in lavish events in which bishops before him had participated. His zeal for the church led him to an act we would see as negative. In 401 he led a mob that destroyed the temple in Ephesus to "Artemis of the Ephesians." Christian zeal led to the destruction of one of the seven ancient wonders of the world. In denouncing the excesses of the rich and the extravagant dress of women, John's golden tongue got him in trouble with Eudoxia, the wife of Arcadius, Emperor of the East.

She demanded he be deposed. About Eudoxia he said, "Once more Herodia demands the head of John on a platter." Add to that the ire of Theophilus (who did not deserve the name[22]), the bishop of Alexandria, who resented a leader of the Antiochene school taking the leadership in Constantinople. John's attempts at reform earned him popular support, but not the support of the worldly bishops. They created a clique that had the golden-tongued preacher exiled from Constantinople in 403, despite riots in support of John by the common people who loved this humble preacher. Thirty-six bishops met in Calchedon, in the "Synod of the Oak" to depose him from office. He refused to stop performing his function as bishop. While in the middle of baptizing a group of catachumens, he was carried off. The baptismal was stained with blood. He died in exile in 407.

Most famous of John Chrysostom's writings are his sermons. Hundreds have survived. His preaching was biblical and practical. He railed against Christians becoming involved in pagan entertainments. One of his complaints to his congregants still rings true today.

> If you ask who is Amos or Obadiah, how many apostles there were or prophets, they stand mute; but if you ask them about the horses or the drivers, they answer with more solemnity than sophists or rhetors.[23]

The modern church could use more preachers like John the Golden Tongued! Like Basil, John was influential in Christian liturgy. Today his *Divine Liturgy of St. John Chrysostom* is the standard liturgy recited at the communion service in the Eastern Orthodox Church.

The First Council of Constantinople (381)

The reign of Theodosius I "the Great" (379–395) turned Christian history in a decidedly different direction. Up until his reign, the imperial court had been favorable toward Arian or semi-Arian theology. It would have seemed quite likely before he took the throne that an Arian creed might become the accepted one throughout Christendom. Indeed, a semi-Arian creed had already been promulgated at Ariminum in 360 with the support of Constantius, although it was not accepted everywhere. It is interesting to wonder what the future would have looked like if the entire church within the Roman Empire had become Arian in the late fourth century. Would true Christianity have survived on the fringes as a persecuted minority or might it have been reestablished at another time and place? Perhaps the true Christian church might have been more vigorous in the long run if it had remained a persecuted minority. It is human nature to hope for prosperity for the church, but at times adversity rather than outward success strengthens the church in the long run.

In any case, the political situation changed dramatically with Theodosius. Before he came to power, pagan sacrifice had been outlawed, but most of the rites, observances, temples and priests of paganism had been allowed. Many pagans still held high office in the Roman government. Theodosius and his successors Arcadius and Honorius gradually increased the severity of their proscriptions against pagan worship. Theodosius encouraged the destruction of many pagan temples or their diversion to Christian use. At times, monks oversaw the destruction of the temples. The emperor demanded that pagans be excluded from civil offices and the military. What a turnaround from less than a century before! Still, Theodosius did not actively persecute the pagan religions. It was only after 451 that pagans were ordered to attend Christian churches for instruction and to be baptized. By that time, the "Christian" churches the pagans were ordered to join had been paganized to a shocking extent.

Theodosius pursued an active policy of unifying Christianity under Nicene theology. His most significant act in that regard was to call for what became known as the second ecumenical Council at Constantinople in 381. Approximately 150 bishops attended this Council. Only considerably later was it listed as one of the general synods. Unlike Nicaea, we do not have a detailed description of the proceedings of this Council. Even the creed published at Constantinople has a somewhat dubious history in that it seems to have been contained in its entirety in a letter by Epiphanius written before the Council met.

The Council began by reaffirming the legitimacy of the Council of Nicaea, including the Nicene Creed. Having done this, the synod produced an amplified creed that incorporated some of the theology of Athanasius and the Cappadocian fathers. This creed is sometimes given the unwieldy label the Niceno-Constantinopolitan Creed. This, by the way, is the "Nicene Creed" recited in liturgical churches today, not the one produced at Nicaea.

The Nicene/Constantinople Creed

We believe in one God the Father Almighty, maker of heaven and earth and of all things visible and invisible;

And in one Lord Jesus Christ, the only-begotten Son of God, begotten from the Father before all ages, light from light, true God from true God, begotten, not made, of one substance with the Father, through Whom all things came into existence, Who, because of us men and for our salvation came down from heaven, and was incarnate from the Holy Spirit and the Virgin Mary and became man, and was crucified for us under Pontius Pilate, and suffered and was buried, and rose again on the third day according to the Scriptures and ascended to heaven, and sits on the right hand of the Father, and will come again with glory to judge the living and dead, of Whose kingdom there will be no end;

And in the Holy Spirit, the Lord and life-giver, Who proceeds from the Father, Who, with the Father and the Son is together worshipped and together glorified, Who spoke through the prophets;

In one holy Catholic and apostolic Church. We confess one baptism for the remission of sins; we look forward to the resurrection of the dead in the life of the world to come. Amen.

Theodosius published a decree that this creed was binding on all Christian clerics in the Roman Empire. Ultimately, it became the principal doctrinal statement of Christendom for all creedal churches. A couple of features should be noted here. First, it specifies that the Holy Spirit proceeds from the Father. This creed sealed the church's view of the nature of the personhood of the Father, Son and Spirit: that the Father is unbegotten, the Son is begotten from the Father and the Holy Spirit proceeds from the Father. Second, it no longer included the anathemas in the Nicene Creed. Perhaps somewhat surprisingly, the creed does not specify the consubstantiality (*homoousios*) of the trinity or its three person (*hypostasis*) nature, but both of these are implied. At a second synod at Constantinople in 382 (at which Western bishops could not attend), a decision was promulgated that made the Cappadocian theology definite.

According to this faith there is one Godhead, Power and Substance (ousia) of the Father and the Son and the Holy Spirit; the dignity being equal, and the majesty being equal in three perfect essences (hypostases) and three perfect persons.[24]

The Nicene/Constantinopolitan Creed was to prove extremely successful. It was more successful than the creed from Nicaea because it pleased the moderate wings on both sides of the controversy. It definitely ruled out any kind of Sabellianism in a way that was satisfactory to those who wanted to stress the separate natures of the Father, the Son and the Holy Spirit. It also definitively ruled out every kind of Arianism to the satisfaction of those who wanted to stress the unity of the Godhead. The clearer Nicene/Constantinopolitan Creed was able to unite the different factions in a way the more vague Nicene Creed never could. It became a tool that, in the end, completely defeated the Arian wing of Christianity, at least until a certain Charles Taze Russell (founder of the Jehovah's Witness sect) came onto the scene.

Although the creed published at Constantinople does not contain any anathemas, the Council did publish a number of separate condemnations. It specifically anathematized the Eunomians (a radical neo-Arian group), Pneumatomachians (also called the Macedonians, a group that denied the deity of the Holy Spirit), Sabellians and Apollinarians. We will talk about Apollinarius in our discussion of Christology below. Another important decision of the Council was to publish a canon establishing the archbishop of Constantinople on a near-equal authority to the archbishop of Rome, "because Constantinople is the New Rome." This decision was a foreshadowing of a conflict and later a division that has persisted to the present day.

Aftermath of Constantinople I: Christological Controversies

We are about to shift our focus back to the West and to the biggest actor in our play—Augustine, but first we must set the stage somewhat for the Christological controversies of the late fourth and early fifth centuries which were to lead to the third and fourth ecumenical councils at Ephesus (431) and Chalcedon (451).

Constantinople I more or less settled the question of the nature of God, at least as far as the bishops were concerned. However, the consensus decisions at this synod did not address the key question of Christology. If Jesus is of one substance with the Father, and if the Father is unchanging, then how could it be that the begotten Son took on human flesh? The question of the humanness of Jesus was definitely not settled at Constantinople. A wide range of views on this question still existed within the churches and among the bishops. Those influenced by the Alexandrine school were more interested in speculative philosophical questions. Neoplatonism still had a very strong influence in Alexandria and among those trained there. Because to them, the Father was distant, unchanging and was not at all subject to human emotions, they tended to minimize the humanness of Jesus to as great an extent as possible within orthodox theology.

The opposite end of the orthodox spectrum was represented by the School at Antioch and those influenced by them. They were more interested in the humanness of Jesus and in personal Christian experience. Their Jesus was one who could relate to the human condition and could reconcile man to God as a high priest who was familiar with suffering. This little description can be applied to the Eastern Orthodox churches even today.

We have already seen in our discussion of the theological battles over the nature of God that human logic seems to demand that a believer choose one side or the other. Logically, either God is one and Jesus is simply a manifestation of that God with no individual personhood, or Jesus is in a subordinate position to the one God and is of a lesser, demigod status. Human reason demands a choice, yet the church was able to produce a creed at Constantinople that did not concede to human reason, leaving the exact details of the trinity as an unfathomable mystery.

The situation with Christology was similar. Logically, Jesus is either deity—distant and unchanging, unaffected by the vicissitudes of human emotions—or he is human, with all that implies. One rational way to deal with this dichotomy is to minimize the humanness of Jesus or to explain it away. This is what the Alexandrines tended to do. Another reasonable solution (by human reasoning, anyway) is to focus on the humanness of Jesus and find a way to rationalize away his deity. This is the direction in which the Antiochenes leaned in their theology. The problem is that biblically, either rational solution is problematic. As Paul said, "Greeks look for wisdom," but "God made foolish the wisdom of the world" (1 Corinthians 1:20–22). Human logic will never be able to analyze God. Again, a solution that embraced both natures of Jesus, leaving the apparent rational difficulties as a mystery, was required. In a nutshell, this is what was accomplished at Ephesus and Chalcedon. However, the road that led to Chalcedon was long and very messy. Actually, that is an understatement. It was a horrible, embarrassing, scandalous mess. Hopefully, the church you are a part of can work out conflicts over theology or doctrine in a much more Christian way than the church in the fifth century did! We will go part way down that road now, exit off the road for a while, and come back to finish our journey to Chalcedon at the end of the chapter.

Both Antioch and Alexandria sought to control the church in Constantinople, the "new Rome." They used political subterfuge, lobbying and at times mob violence to enforce their particular point of view and their favorite candidates in Constantinople. It is tempting to label Alexandria as the "bad guy" in these conflicts, but this would be an unfair simplification. We have already seen that Basil, somewhat cynically, appointed the two Gregorys as bishops of relatively minor cities, at least in part in order to increase the number of appointed bishops in his sphere of influence. We have also seen Gregory of Nazianzus step down as archbishop of Constantinople under pressure from

Alexandrine opponents. Add to the theological differences the different hermeneutics of the two schools. Alexandria stressed allegorical interpretation in order to make Christianity palatable to Greek philosophical sensitivities. Antioch stressed the literal/historical/grammatical sense of Scriptures. The greatest teacher in Antioch at the time was Theodore of Mopsuestia. As an example of his hermeneutics, he refused to interpret the Song of Solomon as an allegory of Christ's love for the church, but instead saw it as a love poem about human physical love. Naturally, Alexandria, which dominated the hermeneutics of the day, took it as an allegory. The debate about Song of Songs has not yet ended, as many evangelical teachers today agree with Alexandria.

Another distinction of the schools of thought was in their soteriology (theology of salvation). Alexandria stressed deification and our healing by identification with the divine nature of Jesus. Antioch did not reject deification. However, with their emphasis on the humanness of Jesus, they had a much stronger emphasis on free will and the human role in salvation. They saw an analogy in Jesus' humanness as he bent his will to that of the Father. We will see that this explains Pelagius' welcome in Jerusalem when he was driven from Rome.

Back to Christology. To the Alexandrine, the human aspect of the Son was minimized. It was a kind of a shell, a tool of his divine nature. The Son had a divine will, but no human will. This is the monophysite (one will) point of view. It is sometimes called Word/flesh Christology. In other words, the divine Word (*logos*) took on flesh without becoming flesh or being fully human. The Antiochine perspective is sometimes called Word/man Christology, emphasizing that the Word of God became man. Any terminology is limited in its ability to explain the positions, but Word/man vs. Word/flesh is helpful.

Apollinaris

This brings us to Apollinaris and Apollinarianism. Apollinaris was bishop of Laodicea until he was deposed at Constantinople. Although Laodicea is geographically closer to Antioch than to Alexandria, the Christology of Apollinaris did not reflect this fact. He accepted the Nicene theology, but in a way that was very Alexandrian. According to Apollinaris, in Jesus, the divine *Logos* took the place of the human soul and/or spirit. In other words, Jesus did not have a human soul or a human will, but only a divine spirit and will. His Christology is sometimes ungraciously referred to as God-in-a-bod. It appears almost identical to second-century Docetism, but Apollinaris vigorously refuted claims that he denied the real humanness of Jesus. Gregory of Nazianzus delivered the decisive argument against this heretical proposal: "What was not assumed was not healed, but that which is united with his Godhead is also saved."[25] In other words, if Jesus had no human soul, then he cannot bring healing to those with a human soul—us! Although Apollinarianism was anathematized in 381 at Constantinople, Christologies of a similar vein continued to be found in Alexandria and its allies.

Theodore of Mopsuestia (350–428)

> He is both Lord and the Son of David.
>
> —Theodore of Mopsuestia

For now, let us allow Theodore of Mopsuestia to represent the view of Christology in Antioch. Theodore was a good friend of John Chrysostom. In 392 he was appointed as bishop of Mopsuestia, in southeastern Turkey today. The concerns of Theodore were to defend the unchangeable nature of the *Logos*, to assert the reality of the human struggles of Jesus and to allow for his freedom of will. Jesus, as *Logos*, is true God, and does not change, but when Jesus "became flesh" he acquired another nature—a changeable human nature. This union was not a natural one. Jesus, in his assumed fully human nature, could experience suffering, could be tempted, and could experience doubt. It was the human nature in Jesus that could learn obedience from what he suffered (Hebrews 5:8). If not, then according to Theodore, Jesus could not fully identify with humans and therefore could not be a high priest, bringing salvation to humans. The way Theodore described the Son:

> He is not God alone nor man alone, but he is truly both by nature, that is to say God and man: God the Word who assumed and man who was assumed. The one who assumed is not the same as the one who was assumed, nor is the one who was assumed the same as the one who assumed, but the one who assumed is God while the one who was assumed is a man.... He is both Lord and the Son of David: Son of David because of his [human] nature, and Lord because of the honor that came to him.[26]

This is a dualistic Christology. Does Theodore go too far? We will see. Theodore was careful to stress the great intimacy of the human/divine union in Jesus, going so far as to use the term "one person." Those who followed his lead, most notably Nestorius, probably did go too far in creating a two-nature Jesus. Diodore of Tarsus, a predecessor of Theodore in the Antiochene tradition, spoke of "two sons"—the Son of God and the Son of David. For good reason, Theodore was careful not to use this terminology.

Antiochian and Alexandrian Theologians

Alexandrian Theologians	Antiochian Theologians
Athanasius (293–373)	Eustathius of Antioch (270–337)
Apollonaris of Laodicea (?–390)	Diodore of Tarsus (?–390)
Cyril of Alexandria (376–444)	Theodore of Mopsuestia (350–428)
Dioscorus (?–454)	Nestorius (386–451)
Eutyches (380–456)	Theodoret (393–457)

In 422, Theodore gave sanctuary to Pelagius when he had been expelled from Rome (more on him below), at which time he wrote *Against the Defenders of Original Sin*. It appears that he took the right side in this controversy as well. He showed Christian hospitality to one who had been refused it in Rome. Over one hundred years after his death, Theodore was declared a heretic. This unfortunate act was most likely not because of anything Theodore taught, but because of his association with Nestorius, who he probably did meet in 428, but whose Christology he most likely did not accept.

We are about to turn to Augustine, but perhaps it is time to do a little evaluation here. What are we learning from all this discussion of the trinity and Christology? These are not issues that most Christians struggle with today at all. A few thoughts in response to this come to mind. First of all, by viewing these battles from a distance, we can gain appreciation that it may not be as easy to establish a correct biblical view of Jesus or of the Holy Spirit from the Scriptures as we think. The Arians and the Sabellians had logic and many scriptures on their side. Perhaps our view of deity and of Jesus is formed more by the Christian tradition than we realize. This does not make the orthodox view wrong—not at all—but it might help us see the need to think more carefully about the biblical evidence for our view of Jesus. We might gain an appreciation for the work done by the Christian bishops in the fourth and fifth century, some of whom risked their lives and certainly their livelihoods to defend apostolic Christianity. Seeing the sincerity of Arius, Nestorius (see below) and others, perhaps we might even gain more sympathy for our Mormon and Jehovah's Witness friends, even as we recoil at their unbiblical view of the Father, the Son and the Holy Spirit.

With this brief introduction to Christological questions, it is finally time to turn our attention to our long-awaited central figure of the consular period of Church History, Augustine.

Augustine: The City of God

Man's free will avails him nothing, save to do evil.

Take away the word [sacrament], and the water is neither more nor less than water.

Men's evil wills are prepared by God and predestination. God, in his timeless wisdom had decided to prepare only the will of a few.

—Augustine

We now leave the East and philosophical foment over the nature of Jesus Christ to consider the life of Augustine. He is almost universally considered the most influential teacher, administrator and theologian of Christianity between Paul and Martin Luther. Although thoroughly trained in Eastern thinking—especially the Neoplatonism of Plotinus—the work of Augustine will be practical and legal. His concern will not be principally with abstract theology but the salvation of human souls within the Church universal. His thinking set the standard for Western Christendom, at times for the better and more often for the worse, for more than one thousand years. His work covered almost every important area of Christian practice and doctrine. He is the bridge: the last of the great Church fathers and the forerunner of Medieval Christianity. He did not create the idea of conjoining church and state, but he made it a matter of Christian dogma.

We know as much about Augustine as virtually any ancient person. This is in part because of his intimate, psychological autobiography *Confessions*. Augustine was the most prolific writer of ancient Christianity and possibly of the ancient world in general. Despite all this, his was the active life of a bishop in the second largest city in Roman Africa.

Augustine was born in 354 in Thagaste, a small city in the Roman province of Africa, in what is the far northeastern corner of Algeria today. He was born into a Catholic Christian family in an area where Donatist Christianity was predominant. His family was from the lower aristocracy in an out-of-the-way part of the empire. The chief influence throughout his life was his mother Monica. Monica was a dedicated Christian. Typical of her day, she was not above superstitious practices such as eating meals at the tombs of the dead.[27] The evidence is that Monica was a strong, and even a controlling personality. When her son left for Italy at the age of 28, he snuck out at night so as to not have to explain himself to his mother. His ploy did not work, as Monica, at an advanced age, followed him across the Mediterranean, all the way to Milan in Northern Italy out of concern for his soul. She went so far as to play a manipulative trick on her son in a successful attempt to force him to renounce the concubine with whom he had lived for fifteen years.

Augustine, in his *Confessions*, described the sins of his youth in lurid detail, although most of us would not think him unusually sinful. Looking back at his youth, from the eyes of one who was convinced of original sin, he saw himself as a sinner even as a baby. He had "thrown himself on the breast with a disturbing greed."[28] He had exploded with anger whenever he failed to communicate his wishes to his mother.

He mused, "I myself have seen a baby jealous: it was too young to speak, but it was livid with anger as it watched another baby at the breast."[29]

Augustine received a good but basic classical education, focusing on the Latin authors Ovid and Cicero. He did not learn Greek until well after reaching adulthood. In fact, he is the first important church father who did not know Greek. A young Augustine left the backwater of Thagaste at 17 years of age to further his education in Carthage. The innocent country kid was not ready for the temptations of the big city. He got caught up into sexual sin in Carthage and discovered the pleasures of the theatre as well. In Carthage, he took a concubine. He lived with her from the age of eighteen to thirty-three years. He gained a son Theodatus through this illicit relationship. Going from bad to worse, both from the perspective of his mother and of Augustine in his *Confessions*, he became an adherent to the Manichean sect at the age of twenty. When he came home in 375 after his conversion, his mother shut him out of the house.

The Manichees may have appealed to the rebellious youth Augustine because they claimed to be both an intellectual and a moral reformation of Christianity. Manichaeism is a dualistic religion. To its founder, Mani, evil was caused by God. He said that we have a good soul in us which is passive and an evil soul within us which is active. The Manichean must learn to suppress the evil soul and bring out the good soul in himself. There is good evidence that this dualistic perspective informed Augustine's thinking throughout his Christian life. He had a very negative view of the physical nature of human beings. His doctrine of predestination made God the cause of evil, in agreement with Manicheans. In one of his earliest writings, soon after his conversion he asked, "From what cause do we do evil?"[30] This was to be a fascination to Augustine throughout his life. As a Manichee, Augustine would have recited; "I have known my soul and the body that lies upon it, they have been enemies since the creation of the worlds."[31] The Manicheans in Augustine's day had much in common with the Mystery religions, with their secret prayers and rites, a reliance on asceticism and disdain for the physical things of life. Their Scripture was a set of seven books, which are a kind of a

Persian fairytale.

Eventually, Augustine became disillusioned with Manichaeism. One problem for him was the bogus cosmology of Mani. According to this "inspired" writer the waxing and waning of the moon was not merely the distant image of a celestial event, it was literally caused by the influx of released fragments of "light" flowing upward from the earth. Augustine was told that only the greatest teacher of the Manicheans, Faustus of Milevis could answer his doubts about the literal nature of the dubious Manichean cosmology. Faustus arrived in Carthage in 383. Augustine eagerly anticipated receiving an answer from the great Faustus. What he got was a rebuke for his lack of faith. "I found at once that the man was not learned in any of the liberal studies save literature, and not especially learned in that either."[32] Augustine reasoned that if Mani claimed to be an inspired person, yet made "false statements" about the heavens, then his claims to be "a divine person" were a lie. Within a year, Augustine moved away from Manichaeism, back to the classics and to Neoplatonism. After his conversion to Christ, Augustine reflected on his Manichean past as follows: "Food in dreams is exactly like real food, yet it does not sustain us, for we are only dreaming."[33]

In 385, Augustine left Carthage for Rome to pursue his fortune, sneaking off at night, as we know, to avoid interrogation from Monica. He left behind his concubine and his son and traveled with friends to Rome to pursue his dream to be a great teacher of rhetoric. His mother left his father behind in order to pursue her son. In 386, Augustine moved again, this time to Milan where the imperial court sat. There he fell under the influence of Neoplatonism. For a while his greatest influence was Plotinus, along with his most important pupil, Porphyry. Augustine morphed from rhetorician to philosopher. "Swiftly I turned in on myself."[34]

In Milan, Augustine also fell under the spell of Ambrose, the bishop of the imperial city. Ambrose was the greatest orator in the Western church at that time. He also was perhaps the greatest advocate of combining Neoplatonist thinking into Christian theology. Surely this eased Augustine's passage into the Christian church. Influenced by Ambrose and his mother, Augustine moved toward Catholic Christianity. Augustine clearly could not become a Christian while having a concubine. Under the pretense of his becoming engaged to a well-connected Christian woman, Monica finally succeeded in convincing Augustine to put away his concubine in early 387. The arranged marriage never occurred and Augustine remained celibate for the rest of his life.

Augustine "retired" to Cassiciacum (at the foot of the Italian Alps) in September 386. He was thinking at the time that the ideal Christian is one who retires from the world to contemplate God. To his friend Nebridus he said their goal is "to grow god-like in their retirement."[35] Under the Neoplatonist spell, he was attracted to the idea of autonomous Christians who can "refine themselves on their own, in order to contemplate and remain in God."[36] "Is it then the walls of a church which makes a Christian?"[37] Augustine later swung the pendulum radically in the opposite direction, toward requiring that all Christians follow an established "wall" of tradition under an apostolic hierarchy. Like Basil and Gregory of Nyssa before him, Augustine was strongly influenced by Neoplatonist thinking, with its perfect forms and impassible God. Even near the end of his life, the Platonic ideal still strongly affected his view of Christianity. He understood Christianity to be a highest philosophy.

Many Christians at this time withheld from baptism because of the implied commitment and the potential of lapsing from this commitment at a later date. This would have described Augustine. His philosophical tendencies made it so that, to him, to be converted meant a radical turning away from all pleasures, etc. When he heard about "Saint" Anthony, he was convicted that he was playing games and not changing his life. "I tore my hair and hammered my forehead with my fists; I locked my fists and hugged my knees."[38] Augustine broke down in tears. He was converted at this point, but as was typical of the time, he waited until Easter, 387 to be baptized by Ambrose. According to tradition of the day, he was baptized in the nude, being dipped three times in the baptistery in Milan. We can only imagine how joyful Monica was to finally realize the conversion of her son at age 33.

In 388, Augustine headed back to Africa. His mother came along, but she died in Ostia waiting for passage to Carthage. Augustine returned to Thagaste. Here in Thagaste Augustine wrote his first ecclesiastical polemic *Against the Manichees*. Driven, perhaps by events, or perhaps by the twin deaths of his son Adeodatus and his lifetime friend Nebridus, Augustine moved inexorably toward a life of active involvement in church affairs. According to Augustine himself, he did not seek the office of bishop. In fact he told his friends that he feared the office so much, he purposefully avoided visiting any city that was without a bishop.[39] In 391 he visited the small coastal city of Hippo, feeling safe on that ground because they already had an acting bishop. Despite his plans, that year he was appointed a presbyter (priest) in Hippo. Soon after, he was made bishop.

The situation in Hippo strongly influenced the path of Augustine's career. Here the orthodox Catholic church was a minority, with a much larger Donatist congregation in the city. The Catholic bishop of Hippo, Valerius, broke with tradition by asking his subordinate priest to preach, with the aim of defeating the Manicheans and Donatists, winning people back to the Catholic

Church. Soon after his arrival, Augustine so thoroughly defeated the leader of the local Manicheans in a public debate that the man left the city for good. In this debate Augustine argued strongly for freedom of the human will against Manichaean determinism. There is irony in this fact, because the free will doctrine Augustine used to defeat the Manichees was to change dramatically at a later date.

Original Sin and Predestination

By the time he published his *Confessions*, Augustine had come around to a strong position of depravity of the human soul and of predestination. He was to reduce the freedom of the will in the non-Christian to a freedom to do evil. In a sense, he had accepted the Manichaean view. By the mid-390s Augustine, using simple but unbiblical logic, reached the conclusion that man is totally deprived in his nature—that we are completely dependent on God, even for our initial decision to believe in him—that our ability to choose plays no role in our salvation. This is the view known as monoergism.

Note that before the 390s the leading Christian teachers had placed relatively little emphasis on the theology of salvation. They had put the lion's share of their attention into the question of the nature of God and Christology, as well as rules for righteous living. With Augustine and Pelagius, as the fourth turned to the fifth century, the church began to put more attention on the question of how one is saved (soteriology). Does mankind choose to be saved or does God choose who is saved? Augustine concluded that the decision to believe is not in our hands at all. It is totally of God. He used a psychological argument about the nature of human desires and proof-text passages such as 1 Corinthians 4:7: "What do you have that you did not receive? And if you did receive it, why do you boast as though you did not?"

Augustine's two most important works are *Confessions* and *The City of God*. Both are significant in expressing his view on free will and the sovereignty of God. The latter also emphasized Augustine's ideas on the role of the state in supporting and sustaining the Church. *Confessions* was written considerably earlier, being completed by 397. This is an amazing book, revealing the true genius of Augustine as an original thinker. It is the first true autobiography that we know of. It is considered by most to be the first piece of psychological literature. In it, Augustine describes in excruciating detail the emotions that surrounded what he felt was his degradation and depravity, both before and, to a lesser extent, after his baptism. He strikes a strong blow for his theology of original sin and total depravity of mankind—and thus for predestination—

by revealing the psychology of his "sin," even as a small child. Rather than focus on the growth of his carnal nature in terms of sexual sin, he brilliantly chooses to show the "sin" of a baby or a small child. The most striking scene in the entire book is the breathtaking description of the sin when he and some comrades committed what most of us would see as a small act of youthful vandalism. Along with his friends, Augustine stole a number of pears from an owner's tree, not because they were hungry, but because of their depraved, uncontrolled desire to do evil. "For what could I not have done, seeing that I could enjoy even a gratuitous act of crime."[40] In a stroke of genius, Augustine defeats the idea of an age of accountability (which seems a necessity if we are to reject original sin), not by some sort of logical analysis of Scripture, but by appealing to our emotions. He makes what we would consider to be a minor, indeed a perfectly normal act of a youth into a compelling argument for an inborn sinful nature. If we can commit such a small act of depravity, seemingly for no reason at all, and without regret, then what heinous acts are we not capable of? *Confessions* is a fairly short work. Anyone who is interested in understanding how the idea of monoergism came into Christianity ought to read this book.

Do we have free will? According to Augustine in his *Confessions*, we are only free to "throw ourselves headlong"[41] into sin and depravity. In appealing to our emotions rather than our intellect, Augustine drives home what is, in reality, a strong intellectual argument. If, even as infants, we have "besetting sins"[42] and a "maimed will,"[43] then we do not have a real free will and the ability to choose to believe certainly cannot come from ourselves, but as a sovereign act of a gracious God. According to Augustine in his *Confessions*, our being "sinful at birth" (Psalm 51:5) is not a poetical metaphor. Instead, he makes a case that from the time we are conceived this is quite literally true.

When *Confessions* made its way to Rome, Pelagius was "deeply annoyed" by the direction in which Augustine was headed.[44] His annoyance was probably more because of Augustine's pessimistic view of the ability of a baptized person to put behind their sinful nature than over his view of free will of the unbaptized. Due to influence from Neoplatonism, and perhaps from an unbaptized Manichaeism, Augustine viewed the physical world as being somehow evil. In *Confessions*, he created a picture of a converted person in constant struggle against their fallen physical nature. Speaking of himself, already in a saved state, he said, "There is indeed some light in men, but let them walk fast, walk fast, lest the shadows come," because we live in "a limitless forest, full of unexpected dangers."[45] Our soul is subject to an incurable illness. Another important work by Augustine in this area is his *On Free Will*.

By 395, Augustine had been appointed as bishop in Hippo, a position he was to hold until his death. There he established and ran a monastery. Augustine lived a celibate life, although he never became a monk. The priests in his ministry, unlike many of the bishops and priests in the church at that time, also lived as celibates.

Augustine and Donatism

When Augustine took the role of bishop in Hippo, there were roughly 300 bishops each in Catholic and Donatist Christianity already in place in North Africa and Numidia. Augustine was thrust into the political and ecclesiastical war between these groups. There is no doubt that Augustine's view of the nature of the Church—views which became the accepted paradigm for Western Catholic Christianity throughout the Middle Ages—were shaped by his attempt to win North Africa and Numidia for the Catholic version of Christianity. He was driven to a hard-line view on the sacramental system and on the role of state in church affairs in part by his reaction to the Donatist sect.

What was the essential difference between the Catholic and the Donatist Church? Since 311, when this sect formed, the Donatists had taken the position that the church must remain a pure vessel—separate and different from the world. To them a baptism or communion performed by a priest who had been defiled by sin was also defiled. How committed must a church leader be? Can the church tolerate members who are rather blatantly not Christian in the orientation of their life? With the flood of the unrepentant into the ranks of the church after the Edict of Toleration, the Catholic Church moved rather sharply in the direction of watering down the standard of what it means to be a Christian. The Donatists continued to fight against this trend. They considered the church to be a true vine, which needed regular pruning. It is easy for us to side with the Donatists in this conflict. Even if we do not, the search for how best to do church today certainly includes finding a balance in enforcing high Christian standards of behavior of both members and leaders in the Christian church today. We must "admonish the idle," but also "help the weak" (1 Thessalonians 5:14). Where does the requirement for Christians to live a holy life end, and where does the need to give grace to the sinner begin? We can reflect on this question as we see Augustine battling his Donatist rivals.

To Augustine, the Church can absorb the world. The authority of the Church is not held in the righteous behavior of its priests and bishops, never mind its members, but in the Church universal as an abstract entity. Christianity is maintained, not by Christians living like Christ, but by proper maintenance of the sacraments. He conceived of the sacraments as having a power in and of themselves, apart from faith on the part of the participants. This fits well with Augustine's Neoplatonism. To him the Church's "sacraments" were similar to the Neoplatonic idea of a perfect form of which the earthly version is a dim reflection. This view of Augustine was absorbed by the Western Church. Therefore, the Roman view became that the church can absorb the world without losing its identity. This Catholic mindset can be seen even today by its willingness to "baptize" local pagan rituals.

Does the church have a right to use the weapons of the world to fight against the world? The Donatist response was definitely no. To them the church is composed of the "pure." It is "the Church of the righteous who are persecuted and do not persecute."[46] Augustine believed the opposite. The church must use the weapons of the state, including the police and the army, to enforce the priority of the Catholic Church. This position of Augustine led the Catholic Church to some of the most embarrassing behavior in the history of Christianity.

Augustine's vision was of a restored "City of God,"—a worldwide Christian government, which came to be known as Christendom. This theocracy had a right to use military power if necessary to enforce Christian unity, a unity based to a large extent on the sacraments. Tellingly, this unity was not necessarily based on a personal faith in Jesus Christ. Baptism, the Eucharist and, most importantly, ordination of the priesthood were like a mysterious spiritual tattoo that marked those who were under the authority of the universal Church.[47] Bestowal or withholding these sacraments became a tool of both political and religious power. Augustine developed (although he did not originate) the idea that righteousness does not relate to the spirituality of the individual priest who performs the rites, but that, through the Church, the words have power in and of themselves. Augustine said about the "sacraments" of the Eucharist, "The word is added to the element, and there results the Sacrament, as if itself also a kind of visible word."[48] On baptism he said, "Take away the word, and the water is neither more nor less than water."[49] The Sacrament is a visible word. Therefore the sacrament has power in and of itself.

The Donatists saw things much differently. They pictured the church as a sort of an ark—a separate holy people, composed of the few who are called out from the world. To them a sacrament was a thing empowered, not by the abstract Church or by ordination, but by the faith of the individual who takes part in the Christian rite. Surely this is much closer to the New Testament view of the Christian church.

By 397 Augustine began an unrelenting effort to destroy the Donatist movement. He outlawed "mixed" marriages with Donatists and forbade Catholic Christians (who were still a decided minority in Hippo) to leave property to their own children if they were outside the authority of the Catholic Church. In his actions, Augustine used his authority to divide rather than unite, even though it was over nonessential doctrines.

Was the Donatist movement motivated by political concerns? Was it a local attempt to throw off a distant Roman political authority, or was Augustine's move against the group an attempt to impose Catholic religious authority on a group that was no less patriotic to Rome than the Catholics? There is an element of truth to both descriptions, but the evidence favors the latter view. It was the attack against the Donatists from an outside imperial authority that eventually led to a militaristic response of the Donatists in order to protect their vision of Christianity.

The year 405 marked a turning point. Augustine definitely began to advocate the use of violence on the part of a Catholic Christian state against fellow Christian Donatists in order to suppress this "heresy." In June of that year an "Edict of Unity" was issued in Carthage which declared the Donatists heretics. What makes this move appear from the distance of history to be particularly outrageous is that the supposed "heresy" was not based on theology or any important Christian doctrine, but on church politics and the question of church hierarchical authority. Apparently it was heresy simply to not agree with the authority of the orthodox Catholic Church. Here we can see the opening of the full bloom of Christendom. Augustine called the edict an act of God's providence.[50]

The Donatists rightly replied that for one Christian to persecute another was a clear turning away from the traditional teaching of the Church. They affirmed the individual's ability to choose to do good or evil, making arguments that would be reflected in Pelagius in the following decade. Augustine responded in defense of his violent persecution that "God disciplines the one he loves," and to use the state as an arm of this discipline is part of God's sovereign will in history. God can use preordained disasters such as the repression of the Donatists to accomplish his will.[51] We see here again the strong correlation between Augustine's developing predestination and his attitude toward the role of the state in church affairs. It is not hard to detect here a foreshadowing of the justification for the Roman Inquisition or the Crusades.

A key event in the life and career of Augustine as well as in the history of Western Christianity was the sack of Rome in 410 by Alaric the Goth. This event shook both the pagans' and the Christians' confidence in their worldview. The British ascetic Pelagius, future opponent of Augustine, described the effect of the events as an eyewitness.

205

It happened only recently, and you heard it yourself. Rome, the mistress of the world, shivered, crushed with fear at the sound of the blaring trumpets, and the howling of the Goths. Where, then was the nobility? Where were the certain and distinct ranks of dignity? Everyone was mingled together and shaken with fear; every household had its grief and an all-pervading terror gripped us.[52]

Christians and pagans interpreted this historical tragedy very differently. On the one hand, to the Christians the pagan gods (with their capital at Rome) seemed defeated. On the other hand, this event, occurring after two generations in which Christianity appeared to be ascendant in Rome, caused others to question the good effect of Christianity on the course of Roman history. To quote Jerome: "If Rome can perish, what can be safe?"[53] As a response to Alaric's victory, and in order to inspire confidence in the people, the government in Carthage issued what was to be a temporary edict of toleration of the Donatists. As is typical with outbreaks of anarchy there was also a conservative backlash, supported by Augustine, which suppressed paganism and Donatism in North Africa more strongly than before. Augustine believed that strong measures by the state were required to enforce moral behavior on a church that contained many unrepentant pagans. "You, you spoilt son of the Lord: You want to be received but not beaten."[54]

One of the responses of Augustine to the crisis was to begin his monumental work *City of God* in 411. The first three books were published in 413. This great work, in twenty-two volumes, was completed in 426. Augustine's most important written work proposed a solution to a looming anarchy, to be achieved by enacting Christian-inspired laws, backed by divine authority. God's will should be enforced by a Christian state. More fundamentally, *City of God* was a thorough refutation of the pagan worldview and a praise of an already existing, but not yet fully revealed Christian empire of God. The book contrasted the metaphorical city Bablyon with the city of God: Jerusalem. In *City of God*, Augustine contrasted the static view of history found in Plotinus and Porphyry, with its distant and uninvolved god, to a Christian view of human history in which God moved over time to reveal in ever-increasing detail a more perfect City. The other city is called Babylon, but in reality, the opponent to the City of God is pagan Rome. Augustine describes the besetting sin of Rome as pride and a desire for praise. This was the sin of Cain and the sin of Romulus, who killed his brother Remus.

In late 410, with the temporary toleration of the Donatists in place, many Donatist bishops came out of hiding. Augustine was literally in fear for his life from Donatist extremists and deeply concerned about a revived movement in North Africa. As a solution, he and his allies called for a *collatio*, literally a comparison of Catholic and Donatist claims under the auspices of Marcellinus, a Catholic dignitary. When the collatio was called to order in June 411, an assembly of 284 Donatist bishops paraded before Marcellinus. Some of the transcripts of this dramatic inquisition have been preserved. The Catholic bishops, including Augustine, had the advantage of precedent based on the legal decision of Constantine against the Donatist movement nearly one hundred years earlier. The Donatists had the weight of the majority of public opinion in Africa and Numidia behind their claim to be the true church. Marcellinus chose the politically safe route, siding decisively against the Donatists based, not on the superiority of the claim of the Catholics to legitimacy, but on precedent.

From this point a persecution of the Donatist church proceeded that was even more brutal than that which preceded it. This decision had the hearty approval of Augustine. Donatist church property was seized. Unrepentant members could not inherit from their parents. Other harsh measures were used. The pressure became so great that many faithful supporters of the local Donatist churches committed suicide rather than betray their faith community and join with the Catholics. Augustine's doctrine of predestination allowed him to justify the sometimes violent repression of his fellow Christians. He said:

> Seeing that God, by a hidden, though just, disposition, has predestined some to the ultimate penalty [of hell], it is doubtless better that an overwhelming majority of the Donatists should have been collected and reabsorbed [into the Catholic Church], while a few perish in their own flames: better indeed than that all Donatists should burn in the flames of Hell for their sacrilegious dissension.[55]

Can anyone imagine Jesus making a statement like this? Here, Augustine, and the Catholic Church after him, fail to follow Jesus' life and teaching. In his zeal as a persecutor of other Christians, Augustine clearly lost sight of the admonition that we should love our enemies. Never mind that the Donatists, as legitimate Christians, with no essential difference in theology from the Catholics, should not have even been considered enemies of the Christian church.

The wholesale destruction of the Donatist Church that ensued was justified by Catholic bishops using Augustine's *City of God*. His belief in the legitimacy of using state persecution as an instrument of God's admonition of his people became standard usage in Christendom.

Pelagius and Pelagianism

Since perfection is possible for man, it is obligatory.

—Pellagius

Unlike Augustine, we know relatively little about the life of Pelagius. Much of what was written about Pelagius by his contemporaries comes from his bitter opponents. Naturally we expect that his adversaries made a caricature of him—exaggerating his views to make him look more heretical than he really was. Unfortunately this tendency to make a straw man of one's enemies is especially true of Augustine. Of the writings attributed to Pelagius, there is some controversy about which are genuine. Fortunately, there are at least a small number of documents that scholars are fairly sure are from Pelagius. From these we can get a feeling for what he actually taught publicly.

We know that Pelagius came from Britain. He was an ascetic—a monk. At some point he ended up in Rome, but at what age we can only guess. It is clear that he was shocked at the general condition of the church. Of course, this was also true of Augustine—and any sensitive Christian at the time, for that matter. The acceptance of the unrepentant into the church had completely changed the character of the orthodox Christian church by this time. Pelagius felt that the average Christian needed to take far more responsibility for personal holiness. One of his early works was *Expositions of the Letters of St. Paul.* In this essay he proposed the idea that when people are baptized they gain an even greater freedom of will than they had before becoming a Christian. Using our free will and with the help of God working in our lives we can, and indeed we must, become more and more holy.

This idea of spiritual glorification/sanctification had been a theme, especially in the Eastern Church, for many years, but Pelagius seems to have taken the idea a definite step further. He proposed in a letter to Demetrias in 413 that commended her decision to become a nun, that "since perfection is possible for man, it is obligatory."[56] On the surface, this is clearly a dangerous teaching. Quite possibly, it is heretical. Whether Pelagius believed literal perfection is actually possible is extremely doubtful, but we can say for sure that his reform movement really stressed the need for all Christians, not just monks and nuns, to live a Christian holy life. This call for a radical, called-out, holy life gained for Pelagius in Rome an enthusiastic following. It began to spread widely throughout the Roman Christian world.

Pelagius definitely rejected the doctrine of original sin. He felt, not without justification, that the Catholic Church's loose attitude toward accepting the blatant worldliness of the unrepentant former pagans then coming into the church en masse was destroying the Christian character of the church. Like the Donatists, but even more radical than they, he believed in a called-out, holy Church. In his work *On Nature* he expressed his impatience with Augustine's developing theology. He publicly preached that the doctrine of original sin was giving members of the church an excuse to not take seriously the responsibility to live a holy life.

It is particularly important to note that Augustine viewed the Church as an abstract organization that was being directed and changed by the action of God. He took a historical perspective, whereas Pelagius viewed the Church more as a collection of individuals with a personal relationship with their God and therefore personal responsibility to become holy. Augustine's developing sense of predestination is what led him to take a larger and more abstract view of the Church.

Pelagius was one of the refugees who fled Rome at the time of the troubles created by the campaign of Alaric and the sacking of the city. In 411 he appeared in Africa. Apparently he even ended up in Hippo for a short time, although the evidence points toward the conclusion that Augustine was in Carthage at the time. The two never met face-to-face. Pelagius soon moved on to Jerusalem, where he spent most of the rest of his life. His ideas received a warmer reception in the Eastern Church. While he was in North Africa, a disciple of his named Caelestius provoked a controversy in Carthage that caught the attention of Augustine, busy as he was with the Donatist controversy. According to Pelagius himself, Caelestius took an even more radical stance toward the requirement for personal holiness than he had. It is difficult for us to judge this, but we know that Pelagius later disowned Caelestius's views.

With typical clarity of thought, Augustine saw immediately the broader implications of the ideas of Caelestius and Pelagius. He recognized that rejecting original sin would undermine any reason for infant baptism. In arguing against Pelagius, he used as precedent the teaching of Cyprian of Carthage to settle the case. There is no doubt that Cyprian, unlike those before him, defended the baptism of infants.

With historical hindsight, we can see the irony here. Which came first in developing doctrine, original sin or infant baptism? In the early fifth century Augustine defended original sin because of the *fait accompli:* the accepted tradition of baptizing infants. Christian tradition was now a controlling factor in determining theology, rather than vice versa. Viewed chronologically, original sin as a theology postdated infant baptism as a practice, although one can argue that to some extent the two grew up together. Infant baptism led to original sin, and now the doctrine of original sin was being justified and explained by infant baptism.

In Augustine's publicly waged campaign against Pelagius and Pelagianism we hear a constant refrain: "See where it leads to…." If we reject original sin, what will be the implications? As already stated, in order to defend his theological and doctrinal position, Augustine used a common technique, which was to create a "straw man" version of Pelagius. The way Peter Brown, noted biographer of Augustine put it, "Indeed, Pelagianism as we know it, that consistent body of ideas of momentous consequences, had come into existence, but in the mind of Augustine, not Pelagius."[57] Augustine used a view of Pelagius at least partly made up in his mind as a foil to defend his view of salvation and of the sovereignty of God.

Who was right, or perhaps better to ask, who was closer to right in this debate? From where you are, along with the fellowship you are a part of, toward which of these extremes ought we to move? Perhaps we cannot fully settle this question because we are not privy to all that Pelagius taught. The thrust of Pelagius' teaching was that all Christians, not just a privileged clergy, ought to live a truly holy, set-apart life. He wanted to abolish the blatant worldliness in the church. Augustine was aware of this worldliness, but in his place as a bishop and with his confidence in the providence of God, he was grudgingly willing to tolerate it. Augustine was a bishop with a flock to protect, while Pelagius was a reformer. Augustine could not tolerate free thinkers in the church. Pelagius and his followers were emotional and passionate, while Augustine remained a philosopher by nature, and therefore rational. Pelagius urged each individual to "feel the pain of others as if it were his own and to be moved to tears by the grief of other men."[58] In the midst of a campaign to completely suppress Donatism, Augustine felt he could not afford to be led by such emotions.

Job was the biblical hero of the followers of this reform movement. Theirs was a strict moral reform, which was charged by Augustine with being too works-oriented. He accused them of forgetting the grace of God. Quite likely this criticism was deserved to some extent. The problem is that once this battle was engaged, the two tended to move away from each other to defend their position rather than doing what, in Christian love, they ought to have done, which is to engage in a Christian relationship and seek a wise consensus. The result of this distant engagement, in the end, was to impel Western Christianity in the direction of greater authoritarian control and the use of state force to suppress all dissent.

From Jerusalem, Pelagius defended his reform movement. Whether out of personal conviction or to protect his views from being suppressed we cannot know, but he disowned the teaching of his more radical compatriot Caelestius. A small council of bishops was convened in the East to examine Pelagius. At the synod he explained that Augustine was misrepresenting and exaggerating his teaching. He was heartily accepted as orthodox by this council. Remember, though, that the concept of Christian sanctification was a common feature of Eastern church thinking, especially for those influenced by Antioch. The West, with its rational emphasis on sacrament, did not agree. In fact, this remains an important distinction between Roman and Eastern Orthodox Christianity even today.

One quality Augustine had in abundance was a dogged determination. He had an uncanny sense of when to engage his opponents and when to let events proceed on their own. He bided his time, continuing to publish many works against the Pelagians, writing letters to influential clerics and lay Christians who were on the fence. Finally, he appealed to "pope" Innocent in Rome to adjudicate between himself and Pelagius. We can only wonder what might have happened if either Augustine or Pelagius had taken the biblical advice to "go and show him his fault, just between the two of you" (Matthew 18:15). Given the weight of the issue, and given the tendency of human nature to focus on the differences and not notice common ground, surely it would have been worth traveling to the ends of the earth to obey the admonition of Jesus. Probably they could have reached an understanding, even if they could not fully agree. Such was not to be the case.

Augustine was a wily character. Innocent almost certainly would have ruled in his favor. Unfortunately for him, before the audience could be arranged, Innocent died and was replaced by a new bishop in Rome, Zosimus. Caelestius and Pelagius were called to Rome to answer to charges. After Pelagius spoke, Zosimus pronounced him innocent of heresy. In fact he is said to have wept with joy at his teaching. He sent a letter to Augustine, admonishing him for his arrogance in opposing Pelagius.

True to his character, Augustine was undeterred. He continued to raise the charge that Pelagius denied the grace of God. Unfortunately for the cause of Pelagius, a riot broke out in Jerusalem, possibly instigated by his followers. At this time, the emperor of the West decided to intervene in the Pelagian controversy for reasons that are still not known. Probably by coincidence, a pro-Pelagian riot broke out in Rome at the worst possible time. The greatest enemy of all autocratic dictators is public disturbance. The die was cast. Both Caelestius and Pelagius were condemned and expelled from Rome. The decree was published on April 30, 418. In a sign of his own personal weakness, Zosimus reversed his own recent decision and renounced Pelagius as well.

Augustine followed up this shameful decision with a vigorous purge of all Pelagians in North Africa. He demanded all agree that "nobody in this flesh, nobody in this corruptible body, nobody on the face of the earth, in this malevolent existence, in this life of full temptation—nobody can live without sin."[59] Of course, we can agree with Augustine that no Christian can live without sin, but the tactics employed in the purge were not Christian.

The Pelagians did not disappear immediately. In fact, when Zosimus died in December of the same year, a new champion of the cause of reform appeared to take the place of Pelagius—Julian, bishop of Eclanum. We are not quite done with this story, as Augustine continued to do battle with Julian, but at this point it will be useful to sum up the issue and try to reach some conclusions.

With Augustine and his allies we are passing into the Medieval period for Western Christianity. Freedom of expression and thought are rapidly disappearing in the church, to be replaced by an authoritarian religious structure based on a tradition handed down from the church fathers, enforced by approved bishops, and eventually by a system of archbishops that, in the West, looked to a head bishop in Rome.

Pelagius felt that man had imitated Adam but had not inherited sin from him. Puritans were later to say, "In Adam's fall, we sinned all." Augustine would have agreed with the Puritans. Pelagius felt that we did not sin in Adam. Rather we sinned *like* Adam. Pelagius was right about original sin and infant baptism, but Augustine was at least partially right in his psychological analysis of human character. Pelagius was too optimistic. We are not capable of sinless perfection. Is this because we inherited sin? Is it because we inherited a sinful nature? Perhaps we are best leaving this question as a mystery, but a study of the two can help us reflect on our own biblical view of mankind after Adam. Augustine represents Medieval Christianity. He accepts corruption in individual church members as inevitable. He also accepts corruption of the church to a point—that unchristian behavior will be in the Christian church. He leaves the sovereign God to choose his elect from among the church; in the meantime, good and evil can dwell together in the church.

Julian of Eclanum

You think that your Lord is capable of committing a crime against justice such as is hardly conceivable even among the barbarians.

—Julian of Eclanum, about Augustine

Pelagius disappeared from the scene about 418. The inheritor of his mantle of reform and human responsibility was Julian of Eclanum. The African bishops exported their strong-arm tactics against theological dissent to Italy. They began to do more than merely use the threat of exile of dissenting bishops. Julian was thirty years younger than Augustine. He came from an aristocratic family, accustomed to the liberal arts of a gentleman. He engaged in an extended written debate with Augustine, defending the right of free discussion of theology and especially the freedom of will and conscience. The methods of the gentleman Julian were not particularly gentlemanly. Julian charged Augustine with being a closet Manichean. The charge is unfair, as surely Augustine was a sincere follower of Jesus, but the pessimistic view of Augustine can be seen as reflecting a remnant of the worldview he had accepted as a Manichean. He accused Augustine of "bellowing the doctrine of original sin in all its fantastic and disgusting ramifications," saying that, "[Augustine] was merely recalling from memory the teachings he had imbibed from Mani [the founder of Manichaeism]."[60]

We can perhaps understand Julian's bitterness toward Augustine here because by the time he wrote these words, he had been driven from his seat as bishop of Eclanum in Italy by Augustine's allies. In a familiar pattern, he fled to the East, to exile in Cilicia. Julian was a brilliant and original thinker. In many ways his ideas foreshadowed the gentle, humanistic Christianity of Thomas Aquinas and the Aristotelean scholasticism of the thirteenth century. It was his misfortune to live at a time when the Roman Empire was falling apart and open-minded inquiry was considered by many a dangerous thing.

> You ask me why I would not consent to the idea that there is a sin that is part of human nature? I answer it is improbable, it is untrue, it is unjust and impious; it makes it seem as if the Devil wore the maker of men. It violates and destroys the freedom of the will...by saying that men are so incapable of virtue, that in the very wombs of their mothers they are filled with bygone sins. You imagine so great a power to such a sin, that not only can it blot out the new-born innocence of nature, but, forever afterwards, will force a man throughout his life into every form of viciousness.... What is disgusting as it is blasphemous, this view of yours fastens, as its most conclusive proof, on the common decency by which we cover our genitals.[61]

Julian accused Augustine of making God the Creator of evil as well as good. He critiqued Augustine's "proof" of genetically inherited sin: our inborn shyness about our bodies was this proof.

The evidence is that Julian's criticism only hardened Augustine's view. In his last letter he said, "Tiny babies are not weighed down by their own sin, but they are being burdened with the sin of another."[62] Julian rightly replied that this would make God unjust. He used Ezekiel 18:20 as evidence that a just God would not hold any individual responsible for the sin of another: "The soul who sins is the one who will die. The son will not share the guilt of the father, nor will the father share the guilt of the son." He added, "You think that your Lord is capable of committing a crime against justice such as is hardly conceivable even among the barbarians."[63]

Augustine defended his doctrine of inherited sin using Exodus 34:6–7.

> The Lord, the Lord, the compassionate and gracious God, slow to anger, abounding in love and faithfulness.... Yet he does not leave the guilty unpunished; he punishes the children and their children for the sin of the fathers to the third and fourth generation.

Here Augustine made the common mistake of using one passage in the Bible to disprove another. In Ezekiel 18:20 God is talking about the eternal consequences to each individual for their sin. No one will be punished eternally for the sin of another. On the other hand, in Exodus 34:6–7 God is talking about the communal consequences of sin that are experienced here on earth. He is expressing the moral law that our sin brings "punishment" on us and our children and our children's children in this life. Israel experienced this temporal punishment many times during its history.

The Old Testament: Free Will and Predestination

We are going to take a brief side trip into the Old Testament to see what it might offer to the age-old debate in the Church over the balance between human free will and God's sovereign will. At the risk of over-simplifying, we can summarize the Old Testament story in this way: God created Adam and Eve, giving them the free choice to remain in righteous fellowship with him or to eat of the fruit of the tree of knowledge. They abused their freedom and sin came into the world. They lost their innocence, but did they lose their free will? Did they and their offspring become totally depraved—incapable of choosing to do good? The evidence says no to this question. The story line of the rest of the Old Testament is

God, in his sovereign will, working to restore the intimate fellowship that was lost in the Garden. His plan was to send a savior—a Messiah—to suffer and to die so that imperfect men and women could attain to the righteousness of God. God's intention and his sovereign will was "to be just, and the one who justifies those who have faith in Jesus" (Romans 3:26).

What was God's plan? From the Old Testament we can conclude that his plan was to choose a person of incomparable faith, and, through him, to create a people and a nation to whom and through whom to send the Savior. In this, God was imposing his sovereign will on his creatures. He did not force Abraham to put his faith in him. However, once Abraham put his faith in his Creator, God chose to do what he normally does not do, which is to intervene in the life of Abraham and his descendants. He gave him a promised son, even though his wife was well past the age of bearing children. This was God intervening and enforcing his will upon Abraham and Sarah. Why? The evidence in the Old Testament is that God only intervenes—suborning human free will—when it serves a greater purpose, which is to prepare the way to send the Messiah into the world.

God intervened, both to send Abraham and Isaac to Mt. Moriah and to place a ram in the thicket. Thus he created a wonderful picture of what he would do in the future. Like Abraham, he would offer his one and only son as a sacrifice on Mt. Moriah. Did God destroy the free will of Abraham here? Did he force Abraham to go? No he did not. He used the free will of Abraham, combined it with his sovereign will to prepare a people for his purpose, and the rest is history. God intervened again in the life of Isaac. He chose Jacob, not Esau. This was not Jacob's choice. "Jacob I loved, but Esau I hated" (Romans 9:13; Malachi 1:2–3). Clearly there is predestination here! Did God force Jacob to put his faith in Him? Did he steal Esau's personal free will in order to accomplish his divine will? We can see no evidence supporting this thesis. As with Abraham, God intervened just sufficiently in their lives to move forward his sovereign plan to send a Savior to the children of Jacob.

We can see the fingerprint of God's predestined will all over the life of Moses. There is no doubt about that. Even as a child, there was a king who was jealous of a seemingly powerless little Jewish baby. The parallel to Herod and Jesus is no accident here. In order to free his people and to create a wonderful foreshadowing of our own salvation from "slavery in Egypt," God hardened Pharaoh's heart. Did God steal Pharaoh's freedom of choice? The answer seems to be yes and no. In order to bring about the foreshadowing of his plan of redemption from sin, God overrode Pharaoh's free will, at least temporarily. It seems that when God's sovereign will to send the Messiah is involved, God is willing to supersede our own personal will for that purpose, but for that purpose only. Pharaoh could have relented after sending his troops to destroy God's people. He could have put his faith in God. In fact, few in history have been given more reason for putting their faith in the God of Israel than Pharaoh. There is no evidence that Pharaoh's ultimate fate was predetermined by God. In any case, God imposed his sovereign will when he sent Israel to the shores of the Red Sea. They had to be baptized into Moses as a prefigurement of our own escape from bondage to sin (1 Corinthians 10:1–2).

The story can be continued with numerous examples. God's sovereign will sent the people to Mt. Sinai. Moses definitely did not choose that destination! God gave them a law and a covenant as a sort of stepparent, preparing them for the new and greater covenant he sent through Jesus. God's providence is written large all over Mt. Sinai. Yet, did he force his people to believe, or not to believe for that matter? There is no evidence that he did so. In fact, through Moses he pleaded with his people:

> This day I call heaven and earth as witnesses against you that I have set before you life and death, blessings and curses. Now choose life, so that you and your children may live, and that you may love the Lord your God, listen to his voice, and hold fast to him. (Deuteronomy 30:19–20)

This seems to be clear evidence that God gave the choice to be saved or not to be saved into the hands of his people. This is no cosmic puppet master. His sovereign will is to give them and us a choice. His predestined plan is to offer us the opportunity to choose life. Again, anything God had to do to complete his plan, even to the point of overriding our own freedom, at least temporarily, he was willing to do. The question remains: Is there any evidence of God predestining the eternal fate of any individual in the Bible?

To these examples we could add what God did through Joshua, Samuel, David, Solomon, Elijah, Jonah, Daniel and many more. God did not force any of these men to believe in him. There are plenty of examples in the history of Israel of men and women who rejected God's plea for them to "choose life." Yet, God's plan moved forward. From

God's perspective, the Lamb of God was slain "from the creation of the world" (Revelation 13:8). Come what may, God was going to send his Son to die in Jerusalem. He foretold this to his people in Daniel 9:24–25. Is predestination biblical? The Old Testament certainly says yes to this question. God's will is always done. However, it is apparent from the biblical evidence that God's will is that we have our own local will over our own lives. Love gives a choice. This is what God did.

The first reading of Romans 9 may strike one as a declaration that God chooses who will be saved and who will be lost—God has mercy on whom he wants to have mercy, and he hardens whom he wants to harden. However, as with any biblical teaching we must put such stark statements in their full biblical context. In Romans 9, God is responding to a challenge from the Jews. They ask God why he offers salvation to the Gentiles. Are we not the chosen people? God's response is uncompromising: Yes, you are my chosen people. You are the Jacob whom I loved. The examples he chooses are ones in which God, in his sovereign will, chose to bless the Jewish people. However, God says to his people: If I choose to offer salvation to the Gentiles, "Who are you, O [Jewish] man, to talk back to God?" (Romans 9:20).

God's Church is composed of those who use the freedom afforded to them by God, out of his love for them, to choose to accept the gospel message, repent of their sins and be baptized for the forgiveness of their sins.

Augustine's predestination gave too much power to the Devil. Was this a reflection of his Manichee past or evidence of overreacting to Pelagius and Julian? "Now this Devil will cast his shadow over mankind: The human race is the Devil's fruit tree, his own property, from which he may pick his fruit.[64] He proposed a kind of double predestination in which God created the mass of humanity and predestined the majority of them to hell fire. "Men's evil wills are prepared by God and predestination. God, in his timeless wisdom had decided to prepare only the will of a few."[65] This is truly a harsh view of God.

Augustine's life was coming to an end. With Julian out of the way and with an imperial decree threatening deposition to any bishop charged with Pelagianism, his theology was "safe" in the churches. However, he faced continuing dissent in the monasteries, especially in Gaul. The ascetic movement was a natural place for the role of individual choice to be honored. The monasteries were populated by male and female penitents who came of their own free will to submit themselves to a spiritual discipline. If their decision was not their own, but was instead a matter of a predestined sovereign decision of God, that would reduce the impulse to take up the ascetic life. Augustine was an ascetic, but he had less influence in the monastic communities that ringed the Mediterranean. Teachers from the East such as John Chrysostom and John Cassian had moral influence in the monastic islands even in Gaul and at Hadrumetum in Africa.

John Cassian (360–435) was one of the most influential leaders in bringing monasticism to the West in the early fifth century. It is not surprising that his commitment to the monastic life included a sense of the importance of a personal commitment to holiness and to salvation as well. He challenged Augustine and his allies on double predestination. "How can we imagine without grievous blasphemy that He does not generally will all men but only some instead of all to be saved."[66] He believed, with Augustine, in the essential nature of God's grace, but he also believed that human beings can move toward God and his grace of their own volition.

In the period immediately after Augustine's death, his defenders opposed John Cassian. Caesarius, a bishop from Arles (France) agreed with Augustine and double predestination. If God willed all to be saved and only some were in fact saved, this would make God weak. Surely his will is always done (never mind the fact that even Jesus prayed that God's will be done). He reasoned from this that God only offers his grace to some. He declared at the Council of Orange in 529, "The grace of God is not granted in response to prayer, but itself causes prayer to be offered for it…. Undeserved grace precedes meritorious works."[67] We see here a foreshadowing of Reformation theology. We will see in the next volume that, more for practical than theological reasons, the church moved away from this position in the Middle Ages.

Now, after 427, Augustine faced a "revolt of the monasteries" against his views. He said of monks, "They place the initiative in their salvation on a wrong footing by placing it in themselves."[68] The monks complained that if Augustine was right—that men were only moved to repent by God, and that God only moved a very few, that would be too pessimistic a view of God. The new converts appearing at the monasteries in the upheavals resulting from the depredations of the Vandals were making themselves slaves of God. This obedience lost some of its attraction if the decision came from God, not from the penitents. The last step in his developing predestination came in 429 when Augustine published his *On the Predestination of the Saints* and *On the Gift of Perseverance*. With this last letter we have completed the fifth and final leg in what would eventually come to be known as the TULIP doctrine, to be discussed later in this series.

As Augustine penned these words, the Roman world he had come to accept as a support to his City of God was falling apart around him. In 429 an army of Vandals, Goths and Alans, led by the Vandal king Alaric, crossed the Straight of Gibraltar, passed through Mauritania and Numidia, sacking the great Roman cities and bringing near anarchy to the countryside. Alaric and his Vandals were Arians. Heretics were destroying the churches across North Africa. Augustine commanded the bishops to stay with their flocks. He had taught that perseverance of the soul was the greatest gift of God. Unfortunately, in the face of torture and death most of the bishops did not persevere. Many fled toward Hippo and Carthage. Augustine admonished them, "Let no one dream of holding our ship so cheaply, that the sailors, let alone the captain, should desert her in time of peril."[69] The Vandal army surrounded Hippo and blockaded her harbor. In the midst of this tragedy, Augustine died of a fever on August 28, 430. Within months, Hippo was overrun.

We are nearing the Council of Ephesus (431), but before we ponder the implications of the third ecumenical council, let us pause for just a moment to notice the careers of two other Western Christians, both of which had an affect on that of Augustine.

Ambrose of Milan (339–397)

> For that sacrament which you receive is made what it is by the word of Christ.
> —Ambrose of Milan

Ambrose is a towering figure in Christianity in the second half of the fourth century, but not principally for his theological or literary contributions, as important as they were. True to our pattern, as a Western church leader he earned his place in the history of Christianity because of his practical work as a church leader in Milan, the administrative capital of the western Roman Empire. He is the Cyprian of his generation—one who moved the organization of the Christian church and the relationship between the Church and the State. We can detect both good and bad in the direction he moved the church, but we cannot miss the fact that his role was decisive.

Ambrose's rise to prominence took a path somewhat like that of Cyprian. He was raised to the role of bishop as a mature man who was a highly respected civic leader, but who was a very young Christian. The year was 374. There was great foment in the city of Milan between the Arian and Nicene factions at a time when a new bishop was to be appointed upon the death of Auxentius, an Arian. The infighting threatened to split the church in Milan and to lead to violence. Such a situation was sure to bring in the government, with a likely bad result for the Nicene position. The situation called for a strong, mature, trusted leader who could find common ground and bring the warring parties together. Into the fight walked Ambrose, seeking to find a peaceful solution. At 35 years of age, he was an accomplished civil administrator and mayor; a man of strong opinions, well respected in the community, yet one who was known to be able to bring people together. Because of his reputation for fairness, he was one of the few orthodox believers the Arians felt they could

Ambrose of Milan

trust. According to the accounts we have, when Ambrose took the pulpit to appeal for calm, a child's voice cried out in the assembly, "Ambrose for bishop." The crowd wanted to accept him by acclamation. There was one problem, though: He was not yet a Christian. He had not been baptized. The little qualification issue was taken care of within a week (never mind the admonition in 1 Timothy 3:6 that the elder/bishop must not be a recent convert). Ambrose was baptized and appointed bishop of this very important imperial city.

The course of events proved the choice to be a wise one. Although not a man of great intellectual depth, Ambrose had a number of gifts useful to a man of action. He had great political skills. He was a very persuasive public speaker who seemed to have the ability to know when to fight his battles and when to hold back. When the time for battle came, he was a courageous and resolute leader.

One of those battles came in 385. Justina, the mother of Emperor Valentinian II, was an Arian, as were most in the imperial faction. She requested that her son the emperor force Ambrose to hand over the main basilica in Milan to be used by the Arian Gothic troops. Ambrose organized a sit-in of the orthodox believers in the grounds of the basilica, prepared for a long siege. He led songs of encouragement that he wrote for the occasion. In the face of such strong but peaceful resistance the dowager empress withdrew her request. The implications of this confrontation were far more than the possession of a single building. Who has authority over whom? Does the temporal power, in this case the Emperor of Rome, answer to spiritual authority? Ambrose's actions in Milan were to set an important precedent for Christianity in the West.

Several similar episodes where Ambrose took a principled stand against a supposedly Christian political leader can be mentioned. Perhaps the most striking example was in 390. By this time, proto-orthodox Theodosius II (not Theodosius I who replaced Valens in 378) was emperor. In this incident Ambrose took a public stand on a moral principle against an emperor from his own religious camp. The occasion was that Theodosius II, in his role as emperor, had ordered the massacre of over six thousand souls after a riot in Thessalonica at which a number of imperial officials including the mayor had been killed. When Theodosius II came to worship at the basilica in Milan, Ambrose refused to allow him to participate in the communion service until he made public penance for his violent act against innocent civilians. Ambrose showed great moral courage in this tense standoff. Theodosius II was already a baptized believer. Therefore, in principle he was subject to the spiritual discipline of his bishop. Nevertheless, he was the emperor! In the event, Theodosius II submitted to a period of public penance. This set a very powerful precedent that church leaders had spiritual/ecclesiastical authority even over the most powerful political leader in the world.

Ambrose of Milan was known as a conciliator and as one who was respectful to his enemies. Unfortunately, this did not seem to apply to his relationship with the Jews. In 388 the bishop of the church in Callinicum, a city in Mesopotamia, led a "Christian" riot that resulted in the destruction of the synagogue in that city. A number of monks joined in the mob guilty of this atrocity. Theodosius demanded that the synagogue in Callinicum be rebuilt at the expense of those responsible for the riot. The onus of this expense fell to the bishop of the local church. Ambrose vehemently opposed the order of Theodosius, not by reason of justice but because the glory of God was at stake.

> Shall the bishop be compelled to reerect a synagogue? Can he religiously do this thing? If he obey the emperor, he will become a traitor to his faith; If he disobey him, a martyr. What real wrong is there, after all, in destroying a synagogue, a 'home of perfidy, a home of impiety,' in which Christ is daily blasphemed? Indeed, he must consider himself no less guilty than this poor bishop; at least to the extent that he made no concealment of his wish that all synagogues should be destroyed, that no such places of blasphemy be further allowed to exist.[70]

In this instance, the emperor acceded to the request of Ambrose, setting a dangerous precedent that Christian mobs could destroy synagogues and pagan temples with impunity, with predictable results.

Ambrose's theory of the relationship between church and state was not that of Augustine. He did not envision the bishop using the power of the state to exercise military authority over church affairs. Neither did he believe that the state would enforce church decisions—that the two would be joined at the hip—but that the Church would have spiritual authority over state decisions in purely spiritual matters. Of course, in the incident with Justina and the basilica in Milan, the distinction between a church issue and a civic issue was not clearly separated.

There is irony in the fact that Augustine went considerably farther than Ambrose in the joining of church and state. Ambrose played the second most significant part in the conversion of Augustine after his mother Monica. It was his brilliant exegetical preaching, combined with his intellectual clarity and his bringing together of Christian and Neoplatonist thinking that drew Augustine back to the Christian church.

Ambrose's chief skills were not necessarily as a philosopher and intellectual, but his work in these areas is still impressive. He wrote *On the Duty of the Clergy*. This was an important work on the role of priests as prophet and moral guide for the church. He also wrote *De Fide* (*On the Faith*), which helped to develop the Latin ideas and vocabulary with regard to the doctrine of the Trinity. Also important are his *On the Mysteries* and *On the Sacraments*. Here we find him taking a role in the developing idea of sacrament that was to be completed by Augustine. Also his is one of the first, if not the first, argument for the idea that through the priestly rites performed by the bishop at communion, the bread and wine are literally changed into the body and blood of Christ.

> But if the blessing of a man [here Ambrose is using the role of Elisha in 2 Kings 6:5–7 as a proof text] had such power as to change nature, what are we to say of that divine consecration where the very words of the Lord and Savior operate? For that sacrament which you receive is made what it is by the word of Christ.[71]

This is not a full-blown Medieval transubstantiation, but it is a significant foreshadowing of that later doctrine.

Ambrose had a decisive influence in the development of the Western liturgy. In this he is a Western equivalent of Basil and John Chrysostom. He brought Greek antiphonal singing to the West. This involved two semi-independent choirs singing in response to one another. It was later developed by Gregory (or more likely those influenced by Gregory) into what is known as Gregorian chant. Ambrose wrote many hymns. Unfortunately, he also gave impetus to the cult of relics of martyrs and "saints." He was one of the first to introduce the placing of relics below the altar in a basilica.

Due to his accomplishments Ambrose was eventually recognized in 1298 as one of the four "doctors" of the Roman Catholic Church. In this he was joined by Augustine, Jerome and (pope) Gregory I. In 1568 the Eastern Orthodox Church officially recognized its four "doctors" as Basil, John Chrysostom, Gregory of Nazianzus and Athanasius of Alexandria.

Jerome (347–420)

Ignorance of the Scriptures is ignorance of Christ.

—Jerome

Jerome was born in the city of Stridon, in Dalmatia in modern-day Slovenia. His was a Christian upbringing, with a strong classical education. He put his education in Latin and Greek to good use. Jerome was baptized during his student days. Very early and throughout his life he was attracted to the ascetic lifestyle. By the late fourth century it was commonplace that strongly committed Christians felt the need to separate themselves, not only from the world, but from the church. He was Western in his thinking and upbringing but spent the majority of his career in the East.

Jerome spent a number of years studying in Rome, followed by time in Gaul studying theology. Out of interest in pursuing the ascetic life, he traveled to the Holy Land. Jerome described a dream he had in 373 or 374 during an illness in Antioch in which he was rebuked as a "Ciceronian and not a Christian." At this point he abandoned his studies of the classics and pursued a long and distinguished career as the leading scholar of the Bible in his time. He spent a number of years living as a hermit. He also studied for a time under Apollinaris in Antioch, whose teaching had not yet been labeled heretical. He began a systematic study of Hebrew at Antioch. In 382 he was ordained as a priest there, apparently against his will.

From there he traveled back to Rome where he was commissioned by the bishop Damasus to begin what was to be his life's greatest work: translating the Greek New Testament and later the Hebrew Old Testament into Latin. This translation became known as the Latin Vulgate (the common person's Latin Bible), which was the standard Bible of Western Christianity for well over one thousand years. He befriended a number of wealthy, devoted Christian women whom he challenged to abandon luxury and to lead an ascetic lifestyle. He was successful in these attempts, but in the process he angered many influential clerics in Rome. One gets the sense that Jerome had a personality that led him to be intolerant of those who held views different from

his own. Jerome made at least as many enemies as friends in his many travels.

Jerome was no longer welcomed in
Rome. In 385 he traveled with a female disciple, Paula, to Palestine, where they established dual male/female monasteries. After
time in Jerusalem, Bethlehem and Galilee,
he passed on to Egypt where he made pil-
grimages to remote places—homes of his
monastic heroes. From there he finished his
eclectic studies at the Catechetical School
of Alexandria. After a considerable time
in Egypt he finally settled to a hermit's life
near Bethlehem, where he spent the final
thirty-two years of his productive life. Here

St. Jerome in his study by Domenico
Ghirlandiao.

in seclusion he completed most of his scholarly works.

He was the Cicero of Christianity—applying Christian thinking to philosophy and to culture. He has been described as "bitter, vindictive, vain and
inconsistent."[72] Clearly, these are not Christian qualities! Evidence of his acer-
bic personality is the fact that a large portion of his massive literary output was
devoted to polemical works.

1. *Against Helvidius* (supporting the perpetual virginity of Mary)
2. *Against Jovinian* (claiming that monasticism was the superior Christian
   lifestyle)
3. *Against Vigilantius* (supporting the cult of the martyrs)
4. *Against Rufinus* (his former good friend, an Origenist; attacking the
   orthodoxy of Origen)
5. *Against Pelagius*

In each of these polemics, the view of Jerome eventually became that of
the orthodox Church. Although a great scholar of the Bible, the biblical validity of the position he took in these polemics is questionable.

Jerome's Vulgate translation was vastly superior to the other Latin
versions available at the time. His decision to produce an Old Testament from
the Hebrew rather than from the Greek Septuagint was very controversial.
Both the East and the West had come to accept the Septuagint as an inspired
translation—a situation not unlike the way some groups view the King James
Version today. Jerome did not necessarily win the debate during his lifetime,
but the quality of his translation won out in the long run. Of the Hebrew

he said, "We have the obligation to expound the Scripture as it is read in the church, and yet we must not, on the other hand, abandon the truth of the Hebrew."[73]

Jerome's independent mindset and his scholarship of the Hebrew Bible led him to another controversial conclusion. He believed that the Old Testament Apocrypha did not belong in the canon of inspired Scripture. Here he was going against virtually the entire church in his time. Since as early as the second century, books such as the Wisdom of Sirach, 1 and 2 Maccabees, Tobit and Judith had been used with equal or nearly equal authority to the rest of the Old Testament by the Christian church. Perhaps Jerome noticed the lower quality of some of these books. Possibly the more recent date of their writing influenced him as well, but chief of his concerns is that these Jewish writings were originally in Greek, not Hebrew. In his commentary on the Samuels he said:

> This preface to the Scriptures may serve as a helmeted introduction to all the books which we turn from Hebrew into Latin, so that we may be assured that what is outside of them [the works originally in Hebrew] must be placed aside among the Apocryphal writings.[74]

Add to this the fact that the Jews did not include the Apocrypha in their Hebrew canon. The Church had been using a Greek Old Testament for over three hundred years at this point, and Hebrew scholarship was extremely rare in the Church, which helps explain the fact that other Christian scholars had not focused on the original language issue. In spite of his convictions, under pressure from friends, he conceded to translate a number of the Greek Apocryphal works into Latin. We can assume that he would cringe to know that these noncanonical books ended up in his Vulgate Translation and as part of the Roman Canon. It is a common misconception that Jerome decided to include the Apocrypha in the Vulgate, resulting in Catholicism accepting these books. The opposite is true. The Old Testament Apocrypha was already considered canonical by the Church as a whole and Jerome tried unsuccessfully to remove it.

His work as a translator was definitely not the only influence Jerome had. Because he held himself aloof from the Christian fellowship, Jerome limited his influence as an administrator of the local church. He was no Basil. However, because he was seen as somewhat independent of Rome, of Alexandria and of Antioch (he spent many years studying in all three cities), Jerome's views were seen as independent. This gave him special influence on some church issues.

His literary work was vast. After Augustine, his contemporary, Jerome was the most voluminous writer of ancient Christianity. He translated a great number of Greek Christian authors into Latin, especially Origen. He published a great number of commentaries on both Old and New Testament books. Of special note is his commentary on Daniel, which was a response to the skeptical criticism of that book by the Neoplatonist philosopher Porphyry. In order to discount the fantastic accuracy of the prophetic predictions in Daniel, Porphyry had claimed the book was written by a pious Jew in the mid-second century, after the time of Antiochus Epiphanes. In order to prove Porphyry's criticism invalid, Jerome identified the legs of iron in Daniel 2 and the fourth beast in Daniel seven as Rome. In the commentary Jerome ably defended the historical validity of the person Daniel and the inspiration of his prophecies.

Although he was not completely above allegorizing, Jerome was of the Antiochian persuasion in his hermeneutics. He left behind hundreds of letters on virtually every important topic in Christianity. He wrote a number of "lives" of monks such as Hilarion, Malchus and Paul. His most famous historical work is *Lives of Illustrious Men*, which is a compilation and study of Christian writings up to his time. Jerome produced a number of wonderful quotes. Two examples are: "Be ever engaged, so that whenever the devil calls he may find you occupied"[75] and "Ignorance of the Scriptures is ignorance of Christ."[76]

Events Leading to the Council of Ephesus: Nestorius

God was not born of a woman.

—Nestorius

We now return to the story of the Christological controversies and to the Antiochian and Alexandrian schools. In doing so, we must introduce a new and important word, which began to be used in various ways by the Christian church. It is the Greek word *theotokos*. The word literally means God-bearer. For a number of years it had been applied by the church to the Virgin Mary, the mother of Jesus. In fact, in many Christian songs Mary was referred to as *theotokos* as a symbolic title, similar to the way we might refer to the Lamb of God in a song today. All of us know merely by hearing the words that "the lamb" is a reference to Jesus. In the early fifth century, the word *theotokos* was used of Mary, not in order to glorify her in any way, but to express the theological idea that Jesus, from the very beginning, even as an infant, was fully God.

Only considerably later was the word *theotokos* used as a means to magnify and glorify Mary. The use of the word *theotokos* was particularly amenable to the Alexandrine school who wanted to emphasize the transcendent deity of Jesus over and above any kind of humanity he may also have possessed.

The background to the events about to be described is the continued disagreement between the Antiochene and Alexandrine schools of thought. With the reign of Theodosius the balance of power shifted. The emperor in Constantinople supported the theology of Antioch.[77] The Alexandrine point of view, with its one-nature theology, was led by Cyril, archbishop of Alexandria from 412–444. Matters came to a head when Theodosius appointed Nestorius to the decisive position of archbishop of Constantinople.

The early life of Nestorius is obscure. It is probable but not completely certain that he studied directly under Theodore of Mopsuestia. In any case, after being appointed archbishop, Nestorius took the cryptically dualistic Christology of Theodore to its logical conclusion. To him, if Jesus had a human nature (*physis*), then, logically, he must also have had a human person (*proposon*) to have that nature. It is this person who was born of Mary. In 428, soon after being raised to the bishop's chair in the Eastern capital, Nestorius ordered that the church there no longer use the term *theotokos* for Mary. Instead, he proposed that the church use the word *christotokos*, or Christ-bearer. This was no mere semantic issue for Nestorius.

Unfortunately for Nestorius, Cyril, bishop of Alexandria, had sent a number of spies to Constantinople with direction to watch for any "dirt" in the form of heretical theology coming from the mouth of Nestorius or his Antiochene allies. He was looking for fuel to add to his contention that Nestorius was pushing the theology of the already-condemned Paul of Samosata—adoptionism. Nestorius gave him what he was looking for. Soon, placards appeared in Constantinople outside church buildings, drawing direct parallel between the sayings of Nestorius and Paul. It was a kind of negative political advertising so familiar to us today. The negative advertising had the desired effect of polarizing the situation. In 429 Nestorius published a letter officially making Constantinople a *theotokos*-free zone, and those who used this word were threatened with excommunication. This was too much for Theodosius who, as all emperors, feared divisive theological debates. Playing right into the hand of Cyril and his allies, he called for an ecumenical council to be held in Ephesus in 431.

We can see right away that neither Cyril nor Nestorius behaved in an ideal Christian way. Their entire conflict can be seen as two opposing parties using semantics as a means to gain the upper hand politically. Cyril's actions appear more outrageous than those of Nestorius, with his spies and his anonymous placards and his cynical use of Theodosius, but both men played political games. Nestorius was a divisive person as well.

However, it is not accurate to view this conflict as mere politics. It was also not simply semantics. Both men can be accused of playing unchristian political games, but the evidence is that both were sincere in their pursuit of correct theology. Let us look at the distinction a bit more carefully. Nestorius preferred the descriptor *christotokos* for Mary because he wanted to stress the undiminished human nature of Jesus. How far Nestorius went in this thinking is not clear. Indeed, it is not even clear if Nestorius was a Nestorian, as the word came to be defined. The only work we have that is almost certainly from his own hand is *The Book of Heraclides*. This was published after he was deposed at Ephesus and probably represents a softening of his position in the hope of being restored to his post. What we can say for sure is that Nestorius believed that Jesus being fully human was essential to his being able to save human beings. We can make a good case that he let human reason rather than biblical theology swing him too far in one direction. Nestorius concluded that Jesus began as a human and acquired his deity over time. He said that "God was not born of a woman." Therefore he rejected *theotokos* as a descriptor for Mary. Contrary to the accusations of Cyril of Alexandria, Nestorius did not go all the way to adoptionism and the theology of Paul of Samosata.

It is difficult to judge Nestorius from the distance of almost 1600 years, especially because we have so little of what he said or wrote directly from his hand. However, he appears to have fallen prey to the very human desire to make his theology logical. He concluded quite reasonably, at least from a human perspective, that a single being cannot be both fully human and fully divine. He did not leave sufficient room for mystery. Nestorius did not deny the deity of Jesus—he was no Arian. He fully accepted Nicene theology. However, he felt that use of the title *theotokos* for Mary amounted to a form of Apollinarianism. In other words, he felt that use of this title was a cryptic way to insert one-nature Christology (*monophysitism*) into the faith, denying the full human nature of Jesus. His solution was to propose a two person (*prosopon*), two nature (*physis*) Christology. In this he went beyond his mentor Theodore of Mopsuestia. He proposed that in Jesus there was a conjunction (Greek: *synapheia*, Latin: *conjunctio*) of a person with a divine nature and another person with a human nature.

Cyril of Alexandria saw the support of Theodosius for the theology of Nestorius as a threat, both to Alexandrine theology and to the ecclesiastical influence of his partriarchate. The traditional bond between Rome and

Alexandria held, as local synods in both cities condemned Nestorius in 430. Celestine, bishop of Rome, had the great Western teacher, John Cassian, write a letter against Nestorius called *On the Incarnation*. In response to this controversy, which threatened to escalate into violence, Emperors Theodosius II and Valentinian III called for the general council that met in Ephesus in AD 431.

The Council of Ephesus (431)

The third general church council began on June 22, 431 in Ephesus. That the synod of bishops should be considered among the great church councils is debatable. It produced no new creed and even relatively few new canons. We can see it as principally a prelude to the great Council at Chalcedon. In any case, it is listed by both East and West as one of the authoritative gatherings of the church.

Rome sent a delegation of bishops, as did many of the churches of the East. A total of 153 bishops attended the gathering. When the meeting began, the Roman bishops and those from Syria, sympathetic to Nestorius, were delayed. Cyril of Alexandria was the only patriarch present. He chose to force the meeting forward. With only a minority present, Cyril pushed through a formula from his letter against Nestorius. "One and the same is the eternal Son of the Father and the Son of the Virgin Mary, born in time after the flesh; therefore she may rightly be called Mother of God (*theotokos*)."[78] Clearly, no bishop influenced by Nestorianism would accept this statement. The council also anathematized Nestorius. He was labeled "the new Judas" for insisting on a separate, human nature for Jesus. When John, the bishop of Antioch, and his allies arrived in Ephesus on June 26, they withdrew from the assembly and began a rival synod there, condemning Cyril, his allies and their decisions. The Roman delegation arrived still later and were convinced by Cyril to accede to his decisions, in part by his agreeing to also condemn the teaching of Pelagius.

Emperor Theodosius stepped in to resolve the conflict. He confirmed the condemnations of both Cyril and Nestorius, but was convinced by lavish gifts from Alexandria and its allies to relent in his condemnation of Cyril. Soon after the council ended, John of Antioch sent a representative to Alexandria, seeking a compromise creed acceptable to both Antioch and Alexandria. The attempt was successful, and in 433 a statement with close parallels to the future two-nature Chalcedonian creed was produced. This compromise was later to produce problems for Cyril among his allies in Alexandria. They had strong monophysite leanings, which was impossible to justify with the 433

"Formula of Reunion." In order to reach the compromise, John of Antioch agreed to accept the condemnation of its favorite son: Nestorius. The bishop of Constantinople was deposed and went into exile.

However, the ideas of Nestorius lived on. As was already stated, the Church of the East continued to teach a semi-dualist theology similar to that of Nestorius. In fact, the theology of the Church of the East came to be known as Nestorianism. This group of churches continued in the Persian realms, Central Asia and India for hundreds of years. Even today, one can find small groups that can be identified as Nestorian.

In the end, the compromise achieved in 433 was not successful. By seeking to please nearly everyone, it pleased almost no one. How the Son could have a human mind and a divine mind, yet still be one person remained unclear by this formulation. It only led to more bitter disputes between the two Eastern patriarchates of Antioch and Alexandria, requiring the final successful compromise at the Council of Chalcedon.

Events Before Chalcedon

Two natures before the union; but after the union only one.

—Eutyches

The events between Ephesus (431) and Chalcedon (451) get even muddier and the actions of the parties become even more ungodly. The reader will be pleased to learn that the story in this volume will end in a relatively amicable and successful synod in 451! Although Cyril appeared to accept the two-nature terminology in 433, churches influenced by Alexandria definitely did not. As with what happened after Nicaea, the attempt at compromise had the effect of causing the two camps to harden their positions and move away from the compromise. Perhaps there are lessons for us today here, although our issues are different. In many church matters, compromise between different views is often advisable in order to create unity. However, achieving compromise without consensus can, paradoxically, cause more division than existed in the first place.

Alexandria moved decidedly in the direction of what we now call monophysite Christianity. The schism has not been healed to this day, despite Chalcedon. Coptic monophysite Christianity in Egypt and Ethiopia remain separated from the Greek and Roman churches even today. Cyril and his allies felt strongly that God cannot suffer or change, so continued to minimize as far as possible any kind of human nature for the Son. When Cyril of Alexandria died in 444, he was succeeded by Dioscorus. The new patriarch of Alexandria had all the negative aspects of Cyril and few of his positive traits. He worked in league with an obscure monk named Eutyches. The two, working together, decided that compromise with two-nature theology could no longer be tolerated. Dioscorus turned to cynical politics, militancy and even violence to achieve his ends.

Eutyches was an elderly monastic leader in Constantinople before the conflict between Antioch and Alexandria brought him to the forefront. His theology embraced the phrase, "two natures before the union; but after it one." He was a strong opponent of Nestorius when the former was bishop of Constantinople. His monophysite view made the humanity of Jesus a mere abstraction. The Christ was for all practical purposes divine and not human. He did not completely reject the humanity of Jesus, but to him his humanity was a "drop of wine in the ocean of his deity." His ideas were reminiscent of Apollinaris and Docetism. His opponents asked, if Christ was not fully human, how can he save us who are fully human? Eutyches was excommunicated by a local synod in Constantinople in 448. This gave Dioscorus the political opportunity he appears to have been waiting for. Some have proposed that he actually helped bring about the condemnation of Eutyches in order to give himself an excuse for action. He called for a council in Ephesus in 449.

In the meantime, Leo "the Great," bishop of Rome, published a response to the controversy. His *Tome* was to become the basis for the Chalcedonian creed. He agreed with the condemnation of the firebrand Eutyches and supported the two-nature terminology. His timely and wise intervention was to greatly increase the reputation and authority of the position of bishop of Rome.

Dioscorus was not intimidated by Leo or anyone else for that matter. A group of 135 bishops assembled in Ephesus. All those who were suspected of supporting the two-nature Christology were excluded from the assembly by club-wielding Egyptian monks. Among those excluded was Theodoret, the most respected theologian of the Antiochene school. This group of thugs set upon Flavian, the representative of Constantinople, with their clubs. Their attack was so vicious that he died from the beating. Some at the synod called for the supporters of the two-nature Christology to be burned. Dioscorus and his allies had lowered themselves to murder to defend their view. At the assembly the condemnation of Eutyches was rejected. However, Dioscorus overplayed his hand by his actions at Ephesus. His scheming, double-dealing action lost for him many of his allies. Leo condemned his actions, labeling the council at Ephesus the "Robber Synod." The turn of events was to have permanent implications. For the first time, and from this time forward, the church in Rome no longer supported the Alexandrine school in its battles with Antioch. Not only this, but when Theodosian died in a horse-riding accident in 450, Dioscorus lost his imperial support as well. Pulcheria, the sister of Theodosius and her consort, Marcian, took the throne in the East. The heretical decision at Ephesus II was overturned and the immoral acts of Dioscorus were repudiated. Flavian was given an honorable funeral at Hagia Sophia, the great cathedral in Constantinople. The tide had definitely turned. The new emperor called for what became known as the fourth great ecumenical Council at Chalcedon.

The Council of Chalcedon (451)

If the most important figure in the period in question is Augustine, the most important single event between the Council of Nicaea and the Middle Ages is the Council of Chalcedon. Whatever one thinks of the outcome, it was surely the grandest gathering of bishops in the early church. On October 8, 451 nearly 500 bishops assembled at Chalcedon, not far from Constantinople. The great majority of these were from the East, with a small contingent from North Africa and delegates from Leo in Rome. Also present were eighteen high Roman officials, including the empress Pulcheria and Emperor Marcian. The assembly had much in common with a politicized parliament or congress. The pro-Antiochenes and the allies of Pope Leo sat on one side, while the Alexandrines, headed by Dioscorus, sat on the other. If it were not for the calming influence of the emperor, the two sides probably would not have sat in the same room together. In the ensuing conflicts they definitely would not have stayed to the end or produced a compromise statement of faith without his commanding presence.

The assembled bishops got right down to business. Theodoret of Cyrus entered the assembly. He was the one who had been condemned and nearly burned to death at the Robber Synod. In the ensuing pandemonium, the empress restored order and Theodoret was seated in a place of honor. Dioscorus was livid at this result. Next, the proceedings of the "Robber" Synod at Ephesus were read. The murder of Flavian and the blatantly unchristian behavior exhibited at this meeting were on the minds of all. The great majority, even including the allies of Alexandria, were sufficiently horrified at the events of Ephesus in 449 to discredit its findings. Dioscorus was the only important church figure to stand up to the opposition. He defiantly defended the decision to depose Theodoret and to support the theology of Eutyches. At the end of the first day the direction of the meeting was set. Dioscorus was deposed as patriarch of Alexandria, and his leading henchmen at Ephesus were sent with him into exile in the desert.

It was clear to those who remained at the council that a new statement of the faith was required—one which would bring together as wide a range of the theologies represented within the Orthodox Church as possible, while protecting the mystery of the incarnation of Jesus. The bishops settled down to this task. *The Tome* of Leo was read to the bishops. The letter of Leo became the template for the creed that was produced at the Synod. This document was used as a source, along with the letters of Cyril of Alexandria to Nestorius and to John of Antioch. It seems that in this case, calm and wise heads prevailed. After much discussion and several days, a final statement was published. It is the greatest statement on Christology produced by the early church. The decision of the council eventually became known as the Definition of Chalcedon or the Chalcedonian Definition of Faith. It was not titled a creed at the time, as those present considered it an elaboration and explanation of the Nicene Creed, not as a replacement for it. Here it is:

> In agreement, therefore, with the holy fathers we all unanimously teach that we should confess that our Lord Jesus Christ is one and the same Son; the same perfect in Godhead and the same perfect in manhood, truly God and truly man, the same of a rational soul and body; consubstantial [*homoousios*] with the Father in Godhead, and the same consubstantial with us in manhood; like us in all things except sin; begotten of the Father before all ages as regards his Godhead and in the last days the same, for us and for our salvation, begotten of the Virgin Mary the *Theotokos* as regards his manhood; one and the same Christ, Son, Lord, only-begotten, made known in two natures without confusion, without change, without division, without separation; the difference of the natures being by no means removed because of the union but the properties of each nature being preserved and coalescing in one person (*prosopon*) and one substance (*hypostasis*), not parted or divided into two persons but one and the same Son, only-begotten, divine Word, the Lord Jesus Christ; as the prophets of old and Jesus Christ himself have taught us about him, and the creed of our fathers has handed down.[79]

The Definition was given the blessing of the emperor, with Empress Pulcheria presiding over the assembly. The key to this Definition is that Jesus Christ is one person but has two natures. Coptic monophysitism was definitely ruled out by this statement, as was Nestorian two-person theology. That the bishops of Chalcedon were set on their being just one person in Jesus is very strongly emphasized if we consider a literal translation of the key phrase.

"...the properties of each nature being preserved and coalescing in one person (*prosopon*) and one substance (*hypostasis*).

Important phrases in the Definition include "without confusion, without change." This protected against monophysitism, which teaches that Jesus' nature changed when he took on human form. Also there is "without division, without separation," which protected against Nestorianism, which would make a distinction between the divine and the human nature of Jesus—separating Jesus into two persons. The joining of two substances into one person is a mystery. It defies rational human comprehension. This mystery is called the "hypostatic union" or the "mystical union."

As with the other general ecumenical councils, additional decisions were reached at the synod beyond the statement of faith. The bishops specifically identified Nicaea, Constantinople and Ephesus I as the only other general, authoritative councils. A number of canons were published (remember that canon were decisions and were identified by "we decide" rather than "we believe). The most historically significant of these is known as the twenty-eighth canon. This established the authority of Rome based, not on its connection to Peter, but on its location and political importance. Using this standard, the bishop of Constantinople was seen by the council to have equal authority to his counterpart in Rome. The leadership in Rome, of course, did not agree with this decision. Leo continued to insist on his preeminent position of authority based on apostolic succession. This political debate between East and West over ecclesiastical authority and the twenty-eighth canon raged for over one thousand years and has not completely subsided even today.

The council specifically recognized the five great spheres of influence in the church to be Rome, Constantinople, Alexandria, Antioch and Jerusalem. This designation led to the patriarchal system in the Middle Ages. It is worth noting, at the same time, that the Church of the East was conspicuously left out of this protopatriarchal system.

One other decision of note at Chalcedon involved the role of the rapidly growing ranks of ascetics. There was fear among the bishops over the balance of power with the monks. The piety of the ascetics gave them much personal influence over the members of the churches, especially in North Africa, but also to an increasing extent all over the now-divided empire. We have already seen that Augustine had to contend with monks who did not accept his view of free will. He had the power of the pulpit, but no defined ecclesiastical authority over those with whom he disagreed. The independence of the monks from a defined authority under the bishops made them "loose cannons," at least from the point of view of the bishops. Of course, the voice of the bishops was the only important one at the ecumenical councils. The decision at Chalcedon was to legislate that monks must be under the authority of the bishop in whose territory their monastery was located. There would be no more Alexandrian monks intimidating crowds at the great councils, as had happened at the "Robber Synod" in Ephesus. However one feels about the wisdom and biblical basis for this decision to suppress the independence of the ascetics, it is clear that a strong independent voice within the church was silenced or at least greatly diminished by this decision. A strong case can be made that the spirituality of the individual members of the churches in both Greek and Latin-speaking areas was weakened as well.

Chalcedon is the last of the Ecumenical Councils that is recognized both by the Roman West and by those Protestants who recognize the authority of Councils. This makes Chalcedon of particular importance for our Church history, even though Eastern Orthodox and Monophysite churches do not accept it as authoritative. It is appropriate at this point to step back and evaluate the place of the great ecumenical councils both in the history of the church and in the practice of believers today.

How are we to view Chalcedon, and most especially the Chalcedonian Definition of Faith? There are three traditional views of the place of the great ecumenical councils:

1. They are authoritative for the church as a whole and on at least an equal footing with the Scriptures. This is the view of the Roman Catholic, Eastern Orthodox and Coptic Churches.

2. The Creeds are accepted as a positive development in the history of Christianity and are to be accepted, but they are definitely of lesser authority than the Scriptures themselves. This is the position of most of what are traditionally known as Protestant Churches. Note: Those in this group generally only accept the first four general Councils: Nicaea, Constantinople, Ephesus and Chalcedon, whereas the Roman, Orthodox and Coptic churches recognize the authority of other councils after Chalcedon.

3. Creeds in general are nonbiblical, and the decisions of councils carry absolutely no authority whatsoever. This is the view of most independent churches, including many Pentecostals, Restoration Movement churches (Church of Christ, Christian Church) and Anabaptists (Mennonites, Amish, etc.)

Worship and Life in the Church Up To 450

We have been focusing on ecclesiastical matters, politics, and doctrinal and theological developments in the church in the last half of the fourth and the first half of the fifth century. Many other developments in worship and spiritual life deserve mentioning before we close our first volume on the history of Christianity.

Worship and Church Organization

As already noted, the hierarchical structure of the church continued to increase throughout the late fourth and early fifth centuries, both in the number of levels of authority and in the degree of control over churches and monasteries as well as in the range of acceptable belief and practice. By the Council of Chalcedon, the forerunner of the patriarchate had arisen, with chief centers of ecclesiastical control in Rome, Constantinople, Alexandria, Antioch and Jerusalem. Beneath the bishops of these "sees" were the metropolitans. Carthage, Ephesus and other cities had metropolitan authority over the churches and bishops in their regions. The organization of the churches into metropolitans mirrored, up to a point, the provincial structure of the former Roman Empire. This was not merely an accident, as in some provinces the bishop took temporal (i.e. political and governmental) as well as religious duties. Synesius took the role of bishop in Ptolemais (Egypt) in 410. Among his duties was helping to lead the defense of the city against raiding nomads. It is likely he was offered the position of bishop primarily because of his ability as a civic leader and as a soldier. A decision at Nicaea required metropolitans to hold local synods of their bishops. This increased their authority over the bishops in their provinces. At the local level, the "parish" system was put into place, with a bishop over each local parish. Bishops became mainly administrators (and sometimes well paid at that), while the presbyters/priests were over spiritual affairs in individual churches. In smaller towns where there was no bishop, the local priest took on many of the functions of a bishop.

It is a mistake to take too cynical a view of the bishops in the fifth century. Many if not most of them were deeply spiritual, even if they became overly caught up in the politics of the church. As the spirituality of the average member plummeted with the mass "conversions" of pagans, the bishops, as a rule, were sincere, devoted followers of Christ. After the time of Augustine, most of the bishops were taken from monasteries. Celibacy, though not legislated, became the rule for bishops throughout the former empire.

By the end of the fourth century, clergy were wearing special clothing for the liturgy and eventually for daily activities. This was the result, largely, of falling behind the changing styles of the times. As the church gradually began to represent that which was stable and conservative, it lost touch with the common people in its mode of dress. Officials in the church wore clothing from a bygone era. The change toward using special clothing for bishops and priests is one relatively minor symptom of the problem of the church representing the conservative establishment in the culture. There is no evidence that wearing ecclesiastical clothing developed for theological reasons. Instead it was more the result of an accident of history.

The trend in the church toward ritualized, prescribed forms of worship strengthened considerably during this period. Involvement by the common believer in congregational worship nearly disappeared. At the Council of Laodicea in 367 congregational singing was banned entirely. Singing in church was reserved to a choir (some interpret the decision at Laodicea to prescribe that only clergy could lead the choir rather than that laypersons could not sing). Hymns had become a powerful tool of heretical or unorthodox believers. Remember that Arius spread his ideas largely through popular hymns. The bishops sought to more carefully control beliefs in the church by limiting singing to those songs and singers authorized by the bishop. Congregational singing did not cease through all the churches immediately after 367, but the trend was set.

As a set liturgy developed with the work of the Cappadocian fathers and others, prayer in Christian worship became nearly completely ritualized. It is difficult to know what the prayer life of the average member was like at this time, but in the church services prayer as many of us think of it today—a person speaking personally to his or her God or speaking spontaneously to God to represent the thoughts and needs of the entire group—was replaced by ritualized reciting of standardized "prayers." The spontaneous and heartfelt prayers we see exemplified in the Old Testament (for example Daniel 9:4–19), by Jesus (for example John 17:1–26) or in the church (for example Acts 4:24–30) appear to have, for the most part, disappeared in the church. This was a tragic loss for the church as it headed into the Middle Ages.

A parallel development in the church was in its music. Ambrose of Milan wrote many liturgical chants, which were prayers in a very simplified musical form. Later, Pope Gregory and those who took on his tradition created the famous Gregorian chants. As mentioned above, these chants were performed by specialized choirs or by the presiding bishop or priest, effectively ending any real participation in the worship by the congregants.

Sacramentalism

Augustine formalized a direction in which the church was already moving. He provided a theological argument for the idea of sacraments. As practiced,

Christianity evolved from belief in salvation based on faith of the individual in the grace of God through the blood of Jesus to the belief that salvation is based on participation in Christian sacrament within the confines of the established church. The word sacrament derives from the Latin *sacramentum*, which meant oath. In its present usage by the Orthodox and Roman churches, a sacrament is the application of a material substance (holy water, wine, bread, oil) or an outward ceremony as a channel for an inner spiritual grace. The Greek equivalent was *musterion*, or mystery. Christian ceremonies took on much of the trappings of the Greek "mysteries," which were secret ceremonies that imparted mystical grace upon the participant. The sacrament functioned *ex opere operato* (from the work done). In other words, the action itself, under the auspices of "the Church," was the means of receiving the grace of God, apart from the faith or the righteousness of the one giving or the one receiving the sacrament. The sacrament was a ritual performed by an ordained bishop or priest. The church became an institution with the power to grant salvation, even in the absence of real faith. No longer was the church thought of as an unseen mystical union of those saved by the blood of Jesus.

By the late fourth century, three sacraments were recognized in both the East and the West. These were baptism, the Eucharist and chrism (oil of anointing). Acts suggestive of later official sacraments, such as ordination of priests and confession, were also being developed by the fourth and fifth centuries. We are familiar with baptism and the Eucharist (the Lord's Supper or communion to most of us) from their biblical connections. Chrism is less familiar to those who use the Bible as their principle source of Christian teaching. Initially, the oil of anointing was associated with baptism. As we have already seen, the inclusion of anointing with oil in baptismal ceremonies dates to at least the second century. In Syria, the application of oil was before baptism, whereas it was done afterward elsewhere. Eventually, baptism came to be associated with forgiveness of sins, freedom from demonic possession and reception of grace, but the laying on of hands by the priest/bishop and the anointing with oil were associated with receiving the Holy Spirit. This became the sacrament of chrism. Biblically, of course, all of these are connected with baptism (with the exception of exorcising of demons). The laying on of hands and the anointing with oil are not prescribed in the Bible.

Over time, as infant baptism became more common, chrism, or anointing with oil, was withheld to later in life. Eventually, this evolved into the modern Confirmation. In the East, priests were allowed to perform the anointing, but in the West, the sacrament now known as Confirmation was reserved to the bishop. Doctrinally, forgiveness of sins and reception of the

Holy Spirit were separated in time. This thought is insupportable biblically.

The Lord's Supper underwent a gradual transformation in both East and West. Over time, the Eucharist was associated more with the idea of epiphany (Greek *epipheneia*, manifestation) in the East. It was an appearance of the Holy Spirit among the communicants. The development in the West was significantly different. True to the Roman spirit, thinking on the communion focused on the words spoken by the priest. The Eucharist became a sacrifice, performed by a priest on an altar. The ideas of epiphany and sacrifice were found in both East and West, but the emphasis was somewhat different.

The idea of the real presence of Jesus Christ among his people as they share the Lord's Supper, as well as the symbolic association of the bread and wine with his body and blood, go back to the earliest church. Paul speaks of a "participation" in the blood and body of Christ (1 Corinthians 10:16). These ideas evolved over time. By the third century, authors sometimes associated the bread and blood with Jesus in a realistic way, and sometimes they were spoken of as symbols. In the fourth century we see a further development. Cyril of Jerusalem (315–386) said in his *catachesis*:

> Moreover, the things which are hung up at idol festivals, either meat or bread, or other such things polluted by the invocation of the unclean spirits, are reckoned in the pomp of the devil. For as the bread and wine of the Eucharist before the invocation of the holy and adorable trinity were simple bread and wine, while after the invocation the bread becomes the body of Christ, and the wine the blood of Christ, so in like manner such meats belonging to the pomp of Satan, though in their own nature simple, become profane by the invocation of the evil spirit.[80]

Notice the use of the word invocation here. The implication is that the words spoken by the one officiating over the Lord's Supper have a sort of mystical power to actually transform the elements. This idea is not found in the Bible or in the earlier church fathers' writings. This is not quite the later theory of transubstantiation, but it is something close to it. Cyril asked the Christians to ignore the fact that the bread and wine still tasted like regular bread and wine. He asked them to apply faith and to "Judge not the matter from the taste."[81] Cyril's view was in the minority in the fourth century, but this changed over time. In the late fourth century, Gregory of Nyssa expressed a similar thought: "…by the power of the benediction through which he transelements the natural quality of these visible things to that immortal thing."[82] He coined the verb "transelements" (Greek: *metastoicheiosas,* change of substance; in other words, transubstantiation) to express the idea of a transformation of the elements in the communion. Gregory's statement leaves more room for a symbolic understanding of the transformation, but it definitely implies some sort of mystical change by the reciting of the benediction by the priest—in other words a sacrament.

The language associating the Lord's Supper with an actual sacrifice was present as early as the second century. In the third century Cyprian said that the bishop "offers a true and full sacrifice." The explicit nature of this sacrifice was strengthened with Ambrose of Milan and even more so with Cyril of Jerusalem. Ambrose was a bit closer to a biblical view when he said that "the holy bread and cup of eternal life…" are an "unbloody offering." Cyril said in his *Mystagogical Catechesis* that, "We offer up the Christ who was sacrificed for our sins, propitiating…the merciful God." Here we see a late-fourth-century author beginning to make the connection between the real, physical presence of Jesus and the idea of re-sacrificing Jesus. It is difficult to justify this with biblical statements such as Hebrews 9:27–28, which tells us that "just as man is destined to die once, and after that to face judgment, so Christ was sacrificed once to take away the sins of many people." The idea that developed after Cyril is that in the Eucharist, a "priest" offers us a literal sacrifice of the literal body and blood of Jesus to give grace to those who participate in the ceremony by taking the bread and wine.

Other practices developed in the late fourth and early fifth centuries that eventually became accepted by both Roman and Orthodox churches as sacraments. We have already seen that the idea of penance was begun by the end of the second century. Canons handed down at the councils in the fourth century legislated prescribed actions and periods of penance for particular offenses. However, the theological development of penance into a sacrament did not occur for several centuries.

One of the most important developments in sacramentalism in the late fourth and early fifth centuries was in the ordination of priests. We have already seen that in his confrontation with the Donatists, Augustine began to argue that the ordination of priests transformed them in a mystical way. They were indelibly changed. When the bishops laid their hands on the one to be consecrated, a permanent transformation occurred. By this "consecration" a priest became able to perform sacraments. The power of the sacrament lay, not in the righteous behavior of the priest, but in the power imparted to him by the Church.

The Cults of Martyrs

Throughout the period in question, the inexorable trend toward veneration of the martyrs continued. This inclination was not to reach its peak for several hundred years. In 386 Ambrose discovered the bodies of two long-forgotten martyrs under the church in Milan. The publication of this discovery was the impetus for a new burst of interest in relics of the martyrs, especially in the West, and even more particularly in Gaul. The church in Gaul, influenced in part by the popular piety of Martin of Tours, became more superstitious over time. Belief in the Christian message was spread more and more by spectacular claims of the miraculous, rather than by appeal to the rational or moral truth of the gospel. We know that Augustine's mother Monica was an enthusiastic participant in meals celebrated at the tombs of the martyrs. In the first half of the 400s a bishop with the wonderful name of Vigilantius publicly denounced the cult of martyrs and especially the veneration of relics as mere pagan superstition. He argued that those in the grave are asleep (1 Corinthians 15:51).[83] They certainly do not intervene on behalf of the living. Jerome opposed Vigilantius in his efforts at reforming the practice of revering the saints. Vigilant voices such as that of Vigilantius were heard less and less over time.

We have a general idea what the practices of the cults of the martyrs were. Each "saint" had an annual commemoration of his death. The celebration involved a procession (marching together to the holy site) and a feast. The burial site of the martyr became a place of prayer. Eventually, shrines (Latin: *martyria*) were erected at the site of the grave, with the burial site at the center. Also in the late fourth century, the practice of removing relics (actual physical objects from the bodies or objects directly associated with the saints) and bringing them into churches for veneration and prayer began. Eventually, as memories of actual burial sites faded, "relics" were discovered as the result of a claimed vision or dream rather than a historically verifiable burial site. Not that it would really matter, but over time the probability that newly discovered relics of the saints were genuine remains decreased to near zero. As early as the fourth century, calendars of days to commemorate specific saints were compiled. At this early date, there was no great effort to standardize such calendars from region to region.

No less a leader than Ambrose taught that the martyrs were a kind of spiritual neighbor. Those taking part in veneration of the saints could relate more easily to the weaknesses of the martyrs, combined with their holy lives, than they could to a more distant and less relatable Son of God. The influence of Greek philosophy on Christian thinking exaggerated this gulf.

What was the motivation for the increasing reliance on cultic activity and the veneration of relics? The answer is complicated. The sincere faith of believers is part of the explanation. It is certainly tempting to inspire support of the masses by appeal to what the masses naturally look for. This obviously includes the attraction of all people, but especially the less educated, to magic, to the occult, to mysterious forces of good and evil. The church leaders rightly reasoned that the masses needed something concrete such as a physical object, an icon or a holy person who has set foot on the earth as a starting point for worship. With Augustine, God became more remote, more an intellectual idea, more distant. The church realized that the average worshipper, illiterate and uneducated, needed something tangible as a center of worship. This will help to explain the great reliance on art in the churches in the Middle Ages. With hindsight we can only regret the reliance of the church on such worldly reasoning, but we can understand the difficult position the church was in as we approach the end of the Roman period. Theirs was a church not principally for dedicated and repentant followers of Jesus. It had become a church for the wheat and the chaff. The pagan world was swallowed by the church. In defense of the church at this time, given the presupposition of Augustine's City of God, they had little choice but to appeal to what was popular to the unspiritual masses.

To represent this thinking we can take a quote from the great Pope Gregory I. This comes from over one hundred years after the period in question, but it represents where the thinking of the church was going, even in the fifth century.

> The temples of the idols...should not be destroyed, but...altars constructed, and relics deposited.... And, since they are wont to kill many oxen in sacrifice to demons, they should have also some solemnity of this kind in a changed form...on the anniversaries of the holy martyrs whose relics are deposited there.... For it is undoubtedly impossible to cut away everything at once from hard hearts, since one who strives to ascend to the highest place must needs rise by steps or paces, and not by leaps.[84]

On the one hand, we can recognize the practical sense and the wisdom of Gregory here. However, on the other hand we can only cringe at the worldly wisdom of the one who stood in the place of the "Vicar of Christ" in Rome.

After the Edict of Milan (313), there were very few new martyrs to venerate. (This was to change somewhat in later centuries as monks carried the gospel into vehemently pagan areas at the fringe of the former Roman Empire). Yet the human need to make the distant God of Augustine more relatable did not disappear. The first non-martyr to be proposed for the early version of sainthood at the time was Martin of Tours. He died a natural death in 397. The argument of his biographer for his acceptance as a martyr/saint is interesting: "Although the character of our times could not ensure him the honor of martyrdom, he will not remain destitute of the glory of a martyr, because both by vow and virtues he was alike able and willing to be a martyr.[85] Apparently, this convoluted logic was not accepted by all at the time. Martin was not "canonized," and it was only several centuries later that the first non-martyr was officially canonized by the Western Church based on claims of a "confirmed" miracle as a result of praying through one not killed for his faith. This remains the practice of the Roman Church to this day.

A new trend made its appearance in the time period in question. Believers began to think in terms of holiness as an abstract thing with a reality of its own, rather than as the quality of one's life and one's relationship with God. The idea of a holy place began to be found in Christianity. The practice of pilgrimage to holy sites developed at this time. Pious Christians made a practice of visiting pilgrimage sites such as Jerusalem and the Church of St. John in Ephesus. We have records, as well, of believers going to visit holy men, especially in the deserts in North Africa. Churches were built at sites near these "holy" men, such as the one in Abu Mena in Egypt and Qal'at Sim'an in the Syrian desert.

The cult of Mary was not well developed during this time. When Nestorius argued with Cyril over whether she was the mother of God or mother of Christ, the focus was not on Mary, but on Jesus. Although there was some movement toward venerating Mary before Chalcedon, this was so greatly magnified in the sixth century and later that we will hold off on discussing the place of Mary in Christianity for the second volume of this series.

Asceticism

We have already seen the story of the genesis of asceticism within the Christian church. The tendency to leave the world and seek a relationship with God through renouncing physical pleasure and passions increased in the late fourth and the fifth centuries. Impetus for this movement came from the Greek philosophical idea that the physical creation is essentially evil. The movement reached its greatest strength in the Middle Ages. The period from 350 to 450 marked a transition from disorganized and spontaneous individual ascetics leaving the world and even the organized church, to a more well-organized form of monasticism, with orders of monks and nuns under the authority of a bishop. This became the predominant form of ascetic practice, which continues to the present day. Most of the important trends in both Western and Eastern monasticism were begun during this time.

The words used by the early church to describe their ascetics are instructive. For example the word "hermit" derives from the Greek word for desert. The word "monk" is Greek for the word alone. Another common early word for those who left the world to seek God in the desert was "anchorite," which means one who withdraws.

These three words would apply very well to our first great ascetic, Anthony of Egypt (251–356). Of all the Christian ascetics, he is perhaps best known of those who withdrew alone into the desert. Most of what we know of Anthony we learn from Athanasius' *Life of Anthony*. Having grown up in wealth, he chose to renounce all worldly pursuits at the age of 34 in 285. He fled into the desert west of Alexandria. He certainly was not the first follower of Jesus to renounce physical comfort in this way, but Anthony considerably raised the bar for self-denial in the Christian community. Over the course of the next thirty years he moved from place to place—always seeking greater solitude. He lived in the open desert in the alkaline region of Nitria, west of the Nile, for about thirteen years. After this, he closed himself in a tomb, receiving food from pious villagers in the area. Next, according to Athanasius, he resided alone in an abandoned Roman fort in the desert east of the Nile. Wishing to become a martyr, he left the fort briefly for Alexandria in 311 where he confronted the civic officials. He publicly confessed himself a Christian and visited those arrested in the persecutions under Diocletian. He did not get his wish to be killed in the name of Christ. After only a short time in civilized Alexandria, Anthony returned to the fort in the desert. Pilgrims began to seek the advice of the now-famous monk at this fort. He only spoke to visitors through a crack in the wall, choosing complete physical isolation for himself.

Anthony became so popular that he found himself unable to devote sufficient time to private worship. He decided to withdraw even farther into the Egyptian desert, to an isolated place that eventually became the site of the famous monastery of Saint Anthony the Great. Athanasius tells us a number of fantastic stories of miraculous temptations that overcame Anthony. Mythical stories about Anthony's defeat of demons became a common theme of religious art in the Middle Ages. It is difficult to judge the veracity of some of the stories that come to us through Athanasius. According to one, Anthony fled to a cave to escape the demons that were tormenting him. While there, he was beaten nearly to death by a number of demons who were tempting him. Thinking him dead, his disciples carried off his body. When he recovered, he demanded to be taken back to the cave, where he defeated the demons. The motif of the spiritual soldier fighting against seen or unseen demons became a dominant one for these early ascetics. This did much to support the popularity of their movement. This focus on a mystical fight against demons became a key component of Medieval Christianity.

On a more believable level is his account of the personal relationship between Anthony and Athanasius. The bishop of Alexandria had a tremendous respect for Anthony, raising him up as an archetypal example of the Christian life. Athanasius brought Anthony from the desert in 338 to publicly refute the teachings of Arius. This he did with some success. Anthony returned to his private monastery where he lived until his death at the incredible age of 105 years in 356.

Inspired in part by Anthony, hermits began what could be described as one-upmanship in terms of radical denial of selfish desires. This is exemplified by the parallel ascetic movement in the Syrian desert. Symeon Stylites (390–459) lived on a small platform on

Anthony of Egypt

top of a pillar. The "Stylites," as they were known, lived for ever-longer periods on ever-higher pillars with ever-smaller platforms. Whether we should honor this as a sincere expression of faith or be skeptical of what appears to be self-promotion is debatable. Probably for most it was a sincere if misguided attempt to give glory to Jesus.

Anthony did not ever establish an order for the anchorites attracted to his ascetic lifestyle, although a colony of hermits devoted to his example grew up in the area of his monastery. His was an individual spirituality. The first we know of who attempted to organize the rather chaotic ascetic movement was Pachomius (290–346). Not all were as enthusiastic about the excesses of the hermits as Athanasius. Some saw the attraction of the common Christians to the pious but independent monks as a threat to their ecclesiastical authority. They sought to bring the monks under some sort of rule. Pachomius organized the monks in local regions. The monks who agreed to work together were known as "cenobites." Cenobite means "life in common." Ultimately the terms hermit and anchorite applied to those eremitic (hermitlike) ascetics who separated themselves, while the word monk was applied to the cenobites who were gathered into communities. Pachomius provided these semi-communal groups with a loose set of rules. The monks lived is isolated huts and did not speak to one another, but gathered together to share meals. Rather than live off charity from local Christians, the cenobites were ordered by Pachomius to raise their own food.

By the fourth century, as we have already seen, many of the leading bishops were chosen from among the ascetic groups. Often, they were chosen for this work against their will, as these monks preferred to work apart from society in order to escape the temptations of worldly pleasures. On the positive side, it was these same monks-turned-bishops who vigorously resisted the rising tide of worldliness in the leadership of the church. These ascetic bishops were willing to publicly shame bishops who sought worldly wealth, honor and position. They were a counterbalance to the paganization of the church and in many ways were the saving grace for the church, at least in the late Roman period. Basil, the greatest organizer of asceticism in the East, is an example of this tendency. The great bishop of Caesarea is most responsible for defining the direction that asceticism took in the Greek-speaking church. Basil was always concerned with organizing, institutionalizing and protecting the church. His vision was that the monks should be organized in communal groups dedicated to serving the benevolent needs of the society in which they found themselves. It is hard to find fault with this vision. He systematically sought to establish parallel cenobitic communities of both monks and nuns. These dual monasteries served in one location under a single male head, but the women were organized separately, with their own leadership. This system is still in place in both Orthodox and Roman monastic orders. Many credit Basil's older sister Macrina with being the real creator of the monastic system commonly associated with Basil. Macrina was a powerful and influential leader of women in her own right. We should assume her influence on Basil was significant as well. She can represent for us what became an important element of Christianity in the Middle Ages. By the fourth century, women were completely cut off from influence in the church. However, the missionary and leadership role of Macrina, working at the side of her brother, represents the only remaining place where women found the ability to express their spiritual fervor through public work. The female monasteries were a place where spiritual women were able to lead, to study and to serve their communities in the late Roman period as well as in the Middle Ages.

A few others who influenced the direction of monasticism bear mention at this point. Jerome was not one to work well with others, but his was a very public voice in support of the ascetic life. He himself spent almost his entire career living as an ascetic in the vicinity of Jerusalem. Western by birth and temperament, he gave monasticism a public face in Rome, bringing many prominent women into the monastic life before moving to the East. Martin of Tours is another who brought monastic ideals to the West. As we have already seen, he was perhaps the most important missionary in Northern Gaul and Germany. He was not part of any of the monastic movements in the East. However, he lived according to ascetic ideals, choosing to stay at the outskirts of the cities he evangelized. Even when he settled into the role of bishop of Tours, he continued to observe an ascetic lifestyle. He represents for us an important future trend in the spread of Christianity. Ultimately, most of the missionary work of spreading the gospel was done by itinerant monks.

Although he is much more known to us as a theologian and bishop, the career of Augustine had a dramatic impact on the acceptance of the ascetic lifestyle for those committed to the Christian ideal. Even after reluctantly taking the position of bishop, Augustine continued to live the life of an ascetic. All of those he brought into his inner circle were ascetics as well. His influence, perhaps more than any other, led to the acceptance of the ideal of celibacy for all bishops and priests—even those who did not formally enter into the cloistered monastic lifestyle.

Important Figures in the Development of Asceticism Before AD 500

Name	Dates	Location	Importance
Anthony	251–356	Egypt	Greatest example of individual ascetic/hermit lifestyle
Pachomius	292–346	Egypt	First to organize hermits into cenobitic communal groups
Basil and Macrina	330–379 (Basil)	Cappadocia	Greek monasticism, orders of both monks and nuns dedicated to benevolent work
Martin of Tours	316–397	Gaul	Created the ideal of the itinerant missionary monk
Symeon Stylites	390–459	Syria	Syrian monasticism, represents the tendency toward extreme denial of pleasure
Augustine	354–430	Hippo (Africa)	The ideal of the ascetic bishop and celibacy of priests and bishops
John Cassian	c. 360–433	Gaul	The grandfather of Western monasticism

John Cassian (c. 360–433)

I will speak first about control of the stomach...and about how to fast and what and how much to eat.

—John Cassian

The work of John Cassian (c. 360–433) was also influential on the rise of organized, ascetic Christianity. Whereas Jerome moved from the West to the East, Cassian moved from East to West, bringing the Egyptian form of monastic community to the south of Gaul. His writings, which include *Conferences* and *Institutes*, were very influential in explaining and promoting Eastern monastic ideals in the West. His influence on the monastic movement was both intellectual and practical. It is difficult to know where to place John in this history. Is he an important theologian in his own right? Is he the first to bring organized monasticism to the West and the "grandfather of

John Cassian

Western monasticism?[86] Is he the most influential voice for Eastern theological thinking in the West and a counterbalance to the theology of Augustine during this important transitional period? In fact, he is all three. He is also the last major figure we will be describing in this volume.

John Cassian was born in present-day Romania, in the region of the Danube delta. He entered a monastery in Jerusalem at a young age in 382, living the life of a monk from this point forward. Not long afterward, he asked for permission to make pilgrimage to the desert monks in Egypt. Here he appears to have formed a lifelong enthusiasm for the Egyptian form of asceticism. He remained in Egypt until 399. From Egypt he traveled to Constantinople where he was ordained a deacon by John Chrysostom. He was forced to leave Constantinople when Chrysostom was exiled in 404, eventually ending up in Masillia (modern-day Marseille) in southern Gaul. It is here that he founded dual monasteries for men and women in what eventually became known as the Abbey of St. Victor. Cassian remained a strong advocate of the semi-isolated hermit lifestyle. In the end, under the influence of Benedict of Nursia, this more individualistic form of asceticism was mostly abandoned in the West.

John's *Conferences* are a series of discussions of the ascetic life. Their purpose was for "training the inner man and the perfection of the heart." The

Institutes (*De Institutis Coenobiorum*) are a practical discussion of what a monk should wear, how he should organize his prayer life, how an ascetic can overcome the eight vices (gluttony, lust, greed, arrogance, anger, envy, spiritual laziness and boasting) and other practical wisdom gained from the Egyptian cenobitic monks. These had a great influence on Benedict's monastic rules and the Benedictine order of monks.

John brought an Eastern theological mindset to the West. He is perhaps best known for his opposition to Augustine's monoergism. Eventually, he was labeled a semi-Pelagian in the West. In book 13 of *Conferences* John made it clear that he believed that salvation was a matter of grace on God's part, working synergistically with our own move toward faith, using personal free will. "He affirmed the paradox that everything is the work of God's grace, yet everything can be ascribed to free will."[87] It has been said of John that in his thinking, "Grace and human freedom are manifested simultaneously and cannot be conceived apart from one another."[88] His soteriology was a healthy medium between Augustine's predestination and Pelagius' overly optimistic belief in the ability of humans to change themselves. He believed that external grace from God works together with internal grace to bring about sanctification.

In addition, Cassian wrote *On the Incarnation* (430) upon request of the archdeacon of Rome who eventually became Pope Leo I. This was a defense of Western theology, written to oppose Nestorius. With this work, John Cassian helped to shape decisions at the Council of Ephesus and the Chalcedonian creed.

Cassian also brought a version of Origen's hermeneutics to the West. This included his belief in a four-level meaning to the biblical text. These four levels are the historical/literal, the allegorical, the anagogical and the tropological. We have already seen the historical/literal interpretation of the Cappadocian fathers (and of most conservative schools today) and the allegorical methods of the Alexandrian school. The anagogical interpretation (Greek: *anagogikos*, that which leads up to) refers to the implication of the passage to one's future eternal life. The tropological interpretation (Greek: *trepein*, to turn, repent) is the moral sense of the scripture. This fourth sense of the scripture can be roughly equated with modern homiletics, or the application of the scripture to the life of the individual Christian. Cassian's hermeneutical approach became standard in the West in the Middle Ages. Although we may not want to return to a free allegorical hermeneutics, a comprehension of the four-level interpretational scheme is useful for understanding much of Medieval thought. We will do well to not completely reject this tradition of biblical interpretation.

This is a good time for us to reflect on what the modern Christian can learn from the early ascetic movements. Several possible lessons come to mind. It is possible to take an entirely negative view of the over-the-top, unbiblical separation of disciples of Jesus from the world. One might point out that it is hard to be the light of the world when one is completely hidden from the world. Paul gave a clear warning against teaching a thorough rejection of all physical pleasure. In 1 Timothy 4:1–5 he warns us against those who, in later times, will "forbid people to marry and order them to abstain from certain foods, which God created to be received with thanksgiving by those who believe and who know the truth." Paul was familiar with suffering. He practiced fasting and other spiritual disciplines. However, contrary to the Greek idea that the physical creation is evil, Paul reminded those who would be tempted to preach abstention from all pleasure that "everything God created is good, and nothing is to be rejected if it is received with thanksgiving, because it is consecrated by the word of God and prayer" (1 Timothy 4:4–5).

Certainly, there is a negative side to the excesses of these early hermits. However, one of our lessons of church history is that we can overreact to one extreme and retreat to another. We should not fall victim to a pendulum-swing mentality. We can learn much about spiritual discipline from these pioneers. If we are humble, we can learn from Anthony, Pachomius, Basil and friends. Surely we can learn from sincere Christian men and women who fled the world, even if we choose to remain in the world. We can also understand their predicament, which was an increasingly worldly and paganized church in which personal spiritual expression was minimized or even discouraged. Where could a committed believer in Christ go to live the genuine Christian life? They did not have other "denominations" to choose from.

There is one aspect of the Christian life in which we can learn a lot from the ascetic strand in church history, even if we do not fully embrace the lifestyle. This is the area of spiritual disciplines. Our monastic friends can teach us about fasting, about meditation, contemplation, and about the need, at times, to withdraw from the mind-numbing pace of everyday life. We do not need to reinvent the wheel when it comes to personal spiritual disciplines. We have many volumes on the subject written by those who have chosen the monastic lifestyle, dedicated to this important aspect of our relationship with God. Although we may not embrace celibacy as the ideal for all those in the public ministry, perhaps we can recognize that more have the gift of staying unmarried than we think and we can honor those who use this as a means of Christian service and dedication. Perhaps we can develop ministries for those who choose not to marry, rather than feel sorry for them.

Summary

As we close our first volume in the history of Christianity, let us look back on the first four hundred twenty years of the Christian faith. That is a long time—consider our world four hundred and twenty years ago. In the last decade of the 1500s, Galileo had not yet begun his career and the scientific revolution was in its infancy. Jamestown had not been settled and the Pilgrims had not landed. Europe had just begun to explore Africa and Asia. The East and the West were barely aware of one another. A lot can happen in this much time.

In fact, a lot did happen from the death of Jesus to the Council of Chalcedon. The Christian movement had been transformed from a group of about one hundred frightened, persecuted, uneducated men and women with no financial means in a backwater part of the Roman Empire to become the most influential institution in the world. Surely this is the greatest revolution in all human history. In fact, by this time there was no close second to the church in its influence in every aspect of life in Europe, Northern Africa and Western Asia. The Jesus movement conquered the Greek and Roman worlds and was beginning to spread beyond. Knowledge of Jesus had spread from Jerusalem to Judea, to Samaria and to the ends of the world. Who would have believed this possible on the day Jesus was crucified? But Jesus was raised from the dead, the apostles and the women who had followed Jesus were emboldened to preach the word, Jewish prejudice was overcome, Greek pagan philosophy was confronted and defeated by Christian theology, Roman military might was defeated by the love and sacrifice of the followers of Jesus and the rest, as they say, is history. "Never in human history have ancient religions so deeply entrenched in the culture of a civilized people been eradicated so completely over so large an area."[89]

However, as we have seen, the seed of defeat was found in this victory. The church made a tragic turn to swallow the world rather than overcome it. Gradually but inexorably, the church emulated much of the world it was supposed to replace. As Roman power collapsed in the West, Christian bishops embraced temporal power, and the era of Christendom ensued. What happened during the next one thousand years of the supposedly "Dark" Ages? Did the Christian ideal disappear completely? What about the Church of the East? How did the rise of militant Islam influence the course of Christian history? What were the theological and historical roots of the Reformation? These questions will remain for the second volume of this series.

CHAPTER NOTES: _____

1. Samuel Hugh Moffet, *A History of Christianity in Asia*, Volume I: Beginnings to 1500 (Maryknoll, NY: Orbis Books, 1998), p. 144.

2. Zosomen, *Ecclesiastical History*, II.9–15.

3. Kenneth Scott LaTourette, *A History of the Expansion of Christianity*, Volume I: The First Five Centuries (Grand Rapids, MI: Zondervan, 1970), p. 231.

4. Costas Indicopleustes, *Christian Topography*, III.

5. A summary and explanation of this material, with additional references, is found in Kenneth Scott LaTourette, *A History of the Expansion of Christianity*, Volume I: The First Five Centuries (Grand Rapids, MI, 1970), pp 224–232.

6. Philostratus, *Ecclesiastical History*, III.4–5.

7. Details of Patrick's life until his forty-fifth year come from Patrick's autobiography, *Confessions*, translated by N. J. D. White, *A Translation of the Latin Writings of St. Patrick* (London: Society for Promoting Christian Knowledge, 1918).

8. Athanasius, *The Incarnation of the Word of God*, VIII.54.

9. Theodosian, *Codes Theodosianus*, XVI.10.5.

10. These smaller, non-Catholic councils include the following: Antioch in 341; which took a moderate position; Sardica (Bulgaria) in 343, which affirmed Nicaea but condemned Athanasius; Antioch in 344 which was semi-Arian and supported the use of the word *homoios*; Sirmium (Pannonia, Hungary) in 347, 351, 357, 358 and 359 (The synod in 357 resulted in a creed sometimes known as the "Blasphemy of Sirmium" because of its strong Arian stance. At this meeting the words *homoousios* and *homoiousios* were condemned.); Arles (Gaul, France) in 353, at which Western bishops were forced to renounce Athanasius, and Ariminum/Seleucia in 359, which was also in support of the position that the Son is like the Father (*homoios*).

11. Jerome, *Dialogus Adversus Luciferianos*, XIX.

12. Julian, Epistle 49, p. 90, from Charles Schmidt, *Social Results of Early Christianity* (London: Butler and Tanner, 1889), p. 328.

13. Julian, *A Letter to a Priest*, from Gaetano Baluffi, *The Charity of the Church, a Proof of Her Divinity* (Dublin: M.H. Gill and Son, 1885), 16.

14. Gregory of Nyssa, *On the Deity of the Son and the Holy Spirit*, from Harold O. J. Brown, *Heresies: The Image of Christ in the Mirror of Heresy and Orthodoxy from the Apostles to the Present* (Garden City, NY: Doubleday, 1984), p. 104.

15. Basil, *Epistles*, 223.2.

16. Basil, Hexameron, IX.1 from Philip Schaff, *Nicene and Post-Nicene Fathers*, 2nd Series (Edinburgh: T & T Clark, 1895).

17. Taken from J. P. Migne, *Patrologiae Graecae*, 37.1053.

18. Gregory of Nazianzus, *Epistles*, 131.

19. Ibid. 37.1059.

20. Ibid. 37.1157–1159 from Gregory's poem "De Vita Sua."

21. Gregory of Nazianzus, *Five Theological Orations, V.*

22. *Theophilus* is Greek for lover of God.

23. From Robert Wilkin, "John Chrysostom" in *Encyclopedia of Early Christianity,* ed. Everett Ferguson (New York: Garland Publishing, 1997), p. 30.

24. Theodoret, *Ecclesiastical History*, V.9, from *The Nicene* and *Post-Nicene Fathers of the Christian Church*, (Buffalo, NY: Christian Literature Publishing Co., 1886), III.138.

25. Gregory of Nazianzus, *Epistles*, 101.

26. Theodore of Mopsuestia, *Commentary of Theodore of Mopsuestia on the Nicene Creed*, edited by A. Mingana (Cambridge: Heffer, 1932), p. 82.

27. Augustine, *Confessions*, VI.2.2. Quotes from *Confessions* are taken from Rex Warner, *The Confessions of Augustine*, (New York: Penguin, 1963).

28. Ibid., I.6.9.

29. Ibid., I.7.11.

30. Augustine, *De Libero Arbitrio*, I.2.4.

31. Allbury, *Manichaean Psalmbook*, p. 56, taken from Peter Brown, *Augustine of Hippo* (Berkeley: University of California Press, 2000), p. 38.

32. Ibid., V.6.2.

33. Augustine, *Confessions*, III.6.10.

34. Augustine, *Contra Academicos* II.2.5.

35. Augustine, *Epistles*, IX.1.

36. Augustine, *On the Trinity*, IV.15.20.

37. Augustine, *Confessions*, VIII.2.4; here Augustine is not describing how he felt when he wrote *Confessions*, but reflecting on his thoughts in 386.

38. Augustine, *Confessions*, VIII.8.20.

39. Augustine, *Sermons*, CCCLV.2.

40. Augustine, *Confessions*, II.7.15.

41. Ibid. IV.1.1.

42. Ibid. VI.8.13.

43. Ibid. VIII.8.19.

44. A. D. Nock, *Conversion: The Old and the New in Religion from Alexander the Great to Augustine of Hippo* (Lanham, Maryland: University Press of America, 1988), pp. 179–180.

45. Augustine, *Confessions*, X.25.33, X.35.56.

46. Here Augustine is quoting the Donatists on this question: Augustine, *Collatio Carthage* III.258.

47. For example, Augustine, *On Baptism*, I.4.5, III.19.25.

48. Augustine, *Homilies on the Gospel of John*, LXXX.3 NPNF 1st edition, VII.344.

49. Ibid. LXXX.3.

50. Augustine, *Epistles*, 80.3.

51. Augustine, *Epistles*, 173.3.

52. Pelagius, *Epistle to Demetriadem*, 30.

53. Jerome, *Epistles*, 123.16.

54. Augustine, *Sermons*, 296.10.

55. Augustine, *Epistles*, 152.3, 154.1.

56. E. Portalié, *A Guide to the Thought of St. Augustine*, translated by R. J. Bastian (Chicago: H. Regnery Co., 1960), p. 188.

57. Peter Brown, *Augustine of Hippo*, (Berkeley: University of California Press, 2000).

58. Pelagius, *On the Christian Life*, I.4.

59. Augustine, *Sermons*, 181.1, 3.

60. Augustine, *Contra Secundum Juliani Responionem Opus Imperfectum*, III.170.

61. Ibid. III.67ff.

62. Ibid. I.48ff.

63. Ibid. I.48.

64. Augustine, *DeNuptiis et concupiscentia*, I.23.26.

65. Augustine, *Epistles*, 194.2.3–4.

66. John Cassian, *Conferences*, 13.7, translation from Edgar C. S. Gibson, *A Select Library of the Nicene and Post-Nicene Fathers*, 2nd Series, Vol 11 (Buffalo, NY: Christian Literature Publishing Co., 1894), p. 425.

67. These quotes come from canons 3 and 18 published at the Synod of Orange in 529. The translation is taken from William C. Placher, *A History of Christian Theology*, (Philadelphia: The Westminster Press, 1983).

68. Augustine, *Epistles*, 225.7.

69. Augustine, *Epistles*, 228.11.

70. Ambrose of Milan, *Epistles*, XL.16.1101.

71. Ambrose, *On the Mysteries*, IX.52, taken from *The Nicene and Post Nicene Fathers of the Christian Church*, 2nd edition. (Buffalo, NY: Christian Literature Publishing Co., 1890), X.324.

72. Everett Ferguson, *Church History, Volume One, From Christ to Pre-Reformation* (Grand Rapids, MI: Zondervan, 2005).

73. Jerome, *Commentary on Micah*, I.16.

74. Jerome, *Commentary on Samuel*, taken from W. H. Fremantle, *A Select Library of the Nicene and Post-Nicene Fathers of the Christian Church*, second series, vol. 6, *St. Jerome; Letters and Select Works* (Buffalo, NY: Christian Literature Publishing Co., 1893).

75. Jerome, *Epistles*, 125.

76. Jerome, from the prologue to *Commentary on Isaiah*.

77. By this time, the split between the Eastern and Western Roman Empire was permanent. There were two emperors. Theodosius ruled the East from Constantinople. The Western emperors were consistent in support of Alexandria in the fourth and early fifth centuries, perhaps partially for theological reasons, but also for political reasons, as a counterbalance to the East.

78. Aloys Grilmeier, *Christ in the Christian Tradition*, Vol. 1, *From the Apostolic Age to Chalcedon*, translated by John Bowden (Atlanta, GA.: John Knox Press, 1975), p. 462.

79. Translation from Gerald Bray, *Creeds, Councils and Christ* (Downer's Grove, IL: Intervarsity Press, 1984), p. 162.

80. Cyril of Jerusalem, *Catechetical Lectures*, 19.7, translation by Edwin Hamilton Gifford, *Nicene and Post-Nicene Fathers*, Second Series, Vol. 7 (Buffalo, NY: Christian Literature Publishing Co., 1894).

81. Cyril of Jerusalem, *Catechetical Lectures*, 22.6.

82. Gregory of Nyssa, *Dogmatic Treatises*, XXXVII.

83. Use of this passage is not necessarily intended by the author to prove the doctrine of soul sleep. The question of what happens when we die is a controversial issue and beyond the scope of this book. For a thorough treatment of this question, the author suggests a CD series by Douglas Jacoby, *What Happens When We Die*, available at www.ipibooks.com.

84. Gregory I, *Letter 76*, to Mellitus, translation taken from James Barmby, *A Select Library of the Nicene and Post-Nicene Fathers*, 2nd Series, Vol. 13 (Buffalo, NY: Christian Literature Publishing Co., 1898), p. 85.

85. Sulpicius Severus, *Letter 2*, excerpt from William C. Placher, *A History of Christian Theology*, (Philadelphia: The Westminster Press), p. 130.

86. John Cassian is known as the grandfather of Western Monasticism because of his influence on Benedict of Nursia. Benedict is considered by most scholars to be the most important figure in creating the Western form of monasticism. His story will be told in Volume 2 of this series.

87. Taken from Everett Ferguson, *Church History, Vol. One: From Christ to Pre-reformation*, (Grand Rapids, MI: Zondervan, 2005), p. 283.

88. Vladimir Lossky, *The Mystical Theology of the Eastern Church* (Yonkers, NY: St. Vladimir's Seminary Press, 1976), p. 198.

89. Kenneth Scott Latourette, *A History of The Expansion of Christianity*, Volume 1, (Grand Rapids, MI: Zondervan, 1970).

IΠDEX

On Baptism: 86, 111, 253.

On the Holy Spirit: 184.

On the Incarnation: 177, 229, 249.

On the Unity of the Church: 124, 164.

Origen: 29, 40, 57, 63, 78, 81, 95, 97, 106-108, 110, 113-121, 128, 132, 140, 147, 154, 159, 154, 159, 164, 183, 185-187, 224, 226, 249.

Patrick: 171, 173, 174, 252.

Pelagius/Pelagianism: 12, 120, 194, 196, 201, 202, 205, 208, 209, 210, 211, 212, 217, 224, 229, 249, 254.

Philip the Arabian: 98

Philo: 113, 114.

Plea Regarding Christians: 94, 92.

Plotinus: 104, 114, 137, 138, 139, 197, 199, 206.

Polycarp: 31, 32, 35, 43-44, 46, 51-56, 61, 64, 71, 75, 80, 85, 88, 91-92.

Pothinus: 75, 89.

Predestination: 15, 197, 198, 201, 205, 207, 209, 214, 215, 217, 218, 249.

Prescription Against Heretics: 108, 163.

Prisca: 73, 74, 92.

Sabellianism: 129, 130, 147, 175, 181-183, 191, 192, 196.

Sacramentalism: 124, 237, 240.

Sapor II: 168-170.

Sassanid Empire: 97, 104, 163, 167, 168, 170, 181.

Second Apology of Justin: 62, 93.

Severus: 97, 117, 128, 149, 150.

Shepherd of Hermas: 42, 43, 78, 92.

Sozomen: 168.

Stoics: 57, 58, 60, 62, 64, 64, 65, 99, 115, 133, 138.

Tertullian of Carthage: 24, 106-115, 121-123, 128, 130, 134, 140, 163, 164.

Theodore of Mopsuestia: 194, 195, 196, 227, 228, 231, 253.

Theodosius I: 189, 191, 229.

Theotokos: 226-229, 233.

Trajan: 35, 44, 74, 87, 88.

Ulfilas: 171-173, 179.

Valentinus: 52, 66, 70, 71, 75, 77, 114, 117, 121.

Valerian: 94, 103, 104, 108, 124, 128, 141.

Worship: 26, 27, 32, 38, 40, 48, 51, 58, 59, 64, 67, 82-84, 93, 96, 98, 100, 107, 132, 134-137, 184, 185, 190, 221, 236, 237, 242, 244.

Illumination Publishers International

For the best in Christian writing and audio instruction, go to the Illumination Publishers website. We're committed to producing in-depth teaching that will inform, inspire and encourage Christians to a deeper and more committed walk with God. You can email us at our website below.

www.ipibooks.com

-